The Fundamentals of International Human Rights Treaty Law

International Studies in Human Rights

Volume 106

The titles in this series are listed at the end of this volume.

The Fundamentals of International Human Rights Treaty Law

By

Dr. Bertrand G. Ramcharan LI.M (LSE), Ph.D. (LSE)

Barrister-at-Law (Lincoln's Inn)
Distinguished Fellow, Human Rights Law Centre,
University of Nottingham

Previously: First Swiss Chair of Human Rights,
Geneva Graduate Institute of International and Development Studies;
Chancellor of the University of Guyana
UN High Commissioner for Human Rights
(A · I, 2003-2004)

MARTINUS NIJHOFF PUBLISHERS

LEIDEN • BOSTON
2011

This book is printed on acid-free paper.

Library of Congress Cataloging-in-Publication Data

Ramcharan, B. G.
The fundamentals of international human rights treaty law / By Bertrand G. Ramcharan.
p. cm. — (International Studies in Human rights ; 106)
Includes bibliographical references and index.
ISBN 978-90-04-17608-9 (hardback : alk. paper)
1. Human rights. 2. Treaties. I. Title.

K3240.R3556 2011
341.4'8026—dc22

2010050173

ISSN 0924-4751
ISBN 978 90 04 17608 9

"The Convention is a living instrument which...must be interpreted in light of present-day conditions"

The European Court of Human Rights[1]

"...(I)ts function is to determine whether the requirements of a given Convention are being met, whatever the economic and social conditions existing in a given country. Subject only to any derogations which are expressly permitted by the Convention itself, these requirements remain constant and uniform for all countries. In carrying out this work, the Committee is guided by the standards laid down in the Convention alone, mindful, however, of the fact that the modes of their implementation may be different in different States. These are international standards, and the manner in which their implementation is evaluated must be uniform and must not be affected by concepts derived from any particular social or economic system."

ILO Committee of Experts on the Application of Conventions and Recommendations[2]

"Treaty-based human rights petitions procedures take the State down from the pedestal of sovereignty to the level of the individual. One of their great merits is the principle of equality of arms."

Judge Jakob Th. Möller[3]
2 August, 2009

"The production, testing, possession, deployment and use of nuclear weapons should be prohibited and recognized as crimes against humanity."

Human Rights Committee[4]

---

1 Tryer v. the United Kingdom, Judgment of 25 April, 1978, Series A No. 26, pp. 15-16, para. 31; the Soering judgment, p. 40. para. 102; Lozidou v. Turkey, judgment of 23 March, 1995, Series A. No. 310, pp. 27-27, para. 71.

2 International Labour Conference, 63rd Session, 1977, Report III, Part 4A, Report of the Committee of Experts on the Application of Conventions and Recommendations, ILO, Geneva, 1977, pp. 10-11, para. 31.

3 Author (with A. de Zayas), United Nations Human Rights Committee Case Law 1977-2008. N.P. Engel, 2009.

4 General Comment No. 14: Article 6 (Right to Life), Adopted at the twenty-third session (1984).

Table of Contents

Foreword

The implementation of human rights is in crisis world-wide. The annual reports of Amnesty International, Human Rights Watch and other human rights organizations continue to reveal widespread gross violations of human rights in numerous countries the world over. Democracy is non-existent or a sham in many countries. National resources are squandered by despotic rulers instead of being used to satisfy the basic economic and social needs of their people. Corruption is rife. The judiciary lacks the strength, the means, or the will to protect human rights in many places. National human rights institutions are non-existent or non-performing in a number of cases. Countries ratify human rights treaties without making the slightest attempt to give effect to them. Self-righteous representatives gather in the halls of the United Nations and use their majorities to insist that countries grossly violating human rights be treated with kid gloves through dialogue and cooperation, instead of through forthright condemnation of atrocities. The UN Human Rights Council does little for the actual protection of human rights, and its Universal Periodic Reporting Process, for the time being, lacks teeth. The situation is dire.

And yet, we have to persist in efforts for the faithful application of international human rights law in every country. Without this all will be lost. International and regional human rights treaties will be called upon to shoulder a heavy burden in the quest for the universal realization of human rights – alongside the UN special procedures that investigate, document and denounce gross violations of human rights and alongside the human rights non-governmental organizations (NGOs). International human rights treaty law has a vital strategic role to play in the future vindication of human rights world-wide.

International treaties for the protection of human beings started with the International Committee of the Red Cross (ICRC) which has rendered great service by producing a volume on customary international humanitarian law.[5] Monitoring the implementation of international humanitarian law is led by the ICRC and there is, so far, no reporting or pe-

5 ICRC, Customary Humanitarian Law (2005).

titions system. The jurisprudence of the international criminal tribunals for the former Yugoslavia and Rwanda has contributed a great deal to the clarification and elucidation of international humanitarian law.

A pioneering role in the development of labour conventions and standards has been played by the ILO, which has a solid body of jurisprudence and doctrine on how states are to be judged on their compliance or non-compliance with international labour norms. The ILO Committee of Experts on the Application of Conventions and Recommendations has led the way in insisting that a State comply with its international obligations above all else.

The European Court of Human Rights, the Inter-American Court and the African Commission on Human and People's Rights (the African Court has not so far had any practice or jurisprudence) have contributed a solid body of jurisprudence and practice that helps reinforce the principle of the rule of law internationally and regionally.

The treaty-based human rights bodies operating under the main international human rights treaties serviced by the United Nations have, in their consideration of States' reports and their examination of individual petitions, contributed greatly in clarifying the content of the national responsibility to protect human rights and the duty of cooperation in good faith incumbent upon every government.

There is thus much to draw upon if a Government wishes to do so in good faith and to work for the emplacement of an adequate and effective national protection system within its country. But we must assist those leaders and officials within countries who wish to do so by giving them the gist of what the treaty monitoring bodies have recommended when it comes to the national and local application of international human rights treaties.

This is the merit of the present work, which draws upon the extensive practice of human rights treaty monitoring bodies internationally and regionally and seeks to present in simple terms what a government should strive for when it comes to: the supremacy of international human rights law; the concept of a national protection system; the meaning of democracy and the rule of law; the primacy of human rights in times of crises and emergencies; the need for effective preventive strategies; the duty to respect, to protect, and to ensure the application of human rights; the duty to provide redress for violations of human rights; the essence of supervision in reporting systems; the essence of petitions and fact-finding procedures; and the centrality of universality, equality and justice.

The African Commission on Human and Peoples' Rights, which has had to overcome many difficulties and still faces many challenges, struck the right note in its reporting guidelines for States. The purpose of the reporting exercise, it stated in its Guidelines for National Periodic Reports, is not only to show achievements made on the statute books, but also to reveal the extent of implementation in terms of how far the rights and freedoms of the Charter are being fulfilled and how far the duties are successfully carried out. The 'aim of the exercise is to show the degree of actual satisfaction of the rights, duties, and freedoms of the Charter; the reporting obligation therefore extends to the practice of the courts and administrative organs of the State Party, and other relevant facts.'[6]

For having distilled the essence of international human rights treaty law from such a deep well of jurisprudence and practice, we owe a debt of gratitude to the author, Dr Bertie Ramcharan, who, with unsurpassed passion, dedication, knowledge and wisdom, has given so many years to the promotion and protection of human rights.

Jakob Th. Möller
Visiting Professor of International Human Rights Law, University of Akureyri, Iceland.
Previously Judge on the Human Rights Chamber for Bosnia and Herzegovina
Previously Director of the Petitions Branch of the Office of the High Commissioner for Human Rights and Secretary of the UN Human Rights Commission[7]
15 December, 2009.

6 Guidelines for National Periodic Reports, Documents of the African Commission, p. 49. See, also, M. Evans, T. Ige, and R. Murray, The Reporting Mechanism of the African Charter on Human and Peoples' Rights, in M. Evans and R. Murray (Eds.), The African Charter on Human and Peoples' Rights. Cambridge University Press, 2002, pp. 36-60, at p. 40.

7 Author (with A. de Zayas), United Nations Human Rights Committee Case Law 1977 – 2008. N.P. Engel, 2009.

Introduction

This book has a simple objective: to present the fundamentals of international human rights treaty law in a way that can be helpful to the national leader, official, or legal adviser whose duty it is to help put a human rights treaty regime into the law and practice in his or her country. It is a book of international law, as provided for in the principal international and regional human rights treaties and draws upon the jurisprudence and practice of their monitoring organs.

The fundamentals of international human rights treaty law, as presented in this book, may be stated simply in the following legal guide list for national officials and national monitoring bodies:

1. Following ratification, a human rights treaty must be inserted into national law whereupon it takes precedence over any conflicting national law or practice.
2. In compliance with the treaty obligation, a country must put into place a national protecting system to ensure compliance with its provisions.
3. Human rights treaty obligations are best implemented under democracy and the rule of law.
4. Only derogations expressly provided for in the treaty may be made – when absolutely necessary – but they must be proportionate to the threat being dealt with, which must have been publicly declared.
5. Governments have an obligation to take preventive measures against violations of human rights treaty obligations.
6. The duty to respect means that a good faith effort must be made to comply with the provisions of a human rights treaty in law and in practice. The duty to protect means that the State and its agents must act for the prevention of violations of human rights and, if violations do take place, must act to bring them to a stop speedily and provide an appropriate remedy to the victim(s). The duty to ensure refers to 'the duty of the States Parties to organize the governmental apparatus and, in general, all structures through which public power

is exercised, so that they are capable of juridically ensuring the free and full enjoyment of human rights.'[8]

7. A Government has a duty to provide appropriate and adequate redress for violations of human rights.
8. In supervising Government reports under a human rights treaty the aim of the exercise is to show the degree of actual satisfaction of the rights and freedoms in the convention.[9] Wilfred Jenks, former Director of the ILO, brought out the pith and substance of reporting systems when he referred to:

> "... a general spirit imbuing the ILO supervisory bodies, to some unwritten wisdom guiding their action based on certain fundamental principles: firm adherence to accepted international obligations and standards; a scrupulous thoroughness; the strictest objectivity; recognition of the need for a sympathetic understanding of what lies beyond the letter of the law, of problems of timing, and of practical difficulties; and acceptance of the duty to observe the highest standards of tact and courtesy in the valuation of complex and delicate problems." [10]

9. In considering petitions under a human rights treaty the aim of the exercise is to render justice to the petitioner.
10. In undertaking fact-finding under a human rights treaty the aim of the exercise is to shed light on the degree of satisfaction of the rights and freedoms in the convention.
11. The principle of equality is fundamental in the implementation of human rights treaty obligations. Equality must be assured in law and in practice.
12. The principle of justice is the key yardstick in the implementation of human rights treaty obligations. Justice is served by commencing on the side of the petitioner but by being scrupulously fair to all sides.

---

8 Inter-American Court of Human Rights, The Velasquez Rodriguez case, 4 Inter-Am. Ct. H.R. (ser C), para. 165.

9 Guidelines for National Periodic Reports, Documents of the African Commission, p. 49.

10 Wilfred Jenks, Human rights, social justice and peace – The broader significance of the ILO experience', Norwegian Nobel Institute, Symposium on the international protection of human rights, 1967, p. 37.

In the course of this work we shall examine these twelve legal propositions in the content of the major international and regional human rights treaties and in the jurisprudence and practice of their monitoring bodies:

- The ILO Committee of Experts on the Application of Conventions and Recommendations , the Committee on Freedom of Association, and other ILO monitoring bodies (ILO Conventions and Recommendations)
- The International Committee of the Red Cross (ICRC)
- The European Court of Human Rights (European Convention on Human Rights)
- The Inter-American Court of Human Rights (American Convention on Human Rights)
- The African Commission on Human and Peoples' Rights (African Charter on Human and Peoples' Rights)
- The Human Rights Committee (Covenant on Civil and Political Rights)
- The Committee on Economic, Social and Cultural Rights (Covenant on Economic, Social and Cultural Rights)
- The Committee on the Rights of the Child (Convention on the Rights of the Child)
- The Committee against Torture (Convention Against Torture)
- The Committee on the Elimination of Racial Discrimination (Convention on the Elimination of All forms of Racial Discrimination)
- The Committee on the Elimination of Discrimination against Women (Convention on the Elimination of Discrimination Against Women)
- The Committee on the Human Rights of Migrant Workers (Convention on the Human Rights of Migrant Workers and their Families)
- The International Court of Justice
- The *Ad Hoc* International Criminal Tribunals established by the UN Security Council (The International Criminal Court has so far only had limited jurisprudence).

The twelve legal propositions presented above are drawn from international human rights treaty law as elucidated and developed by human rights treaty organs for a century now. It is the ILO that pioneered the supervision of international human rights treaties, and its monitoring organs have contributed immeasurably to their interpretation and application. Two ILO bodies have played a particularly important role: The Committee of Experts on the Application of Conventions and Recommendations, and the Committee on Freedom of Association of the Governing Body of the ILO. The rich practice of the Committee on Freedom of Association has been distilled in a Digest of decisions, now in its fifth edition. The following excerpts from the digest bring out rather well the fundamentals of international human rights treaty law.

The ILO Committee on Freedom of Association has consistently held that the purpose of the procedure of the Committee is to promote respect for trade union rights in law and in fact.[11] The object of the special procedure on freedom of association is not to blame or punish anyone, but rather to engage in a constructive tripartite dialogue to promote respect for trade union rights in law and in practice.[12]

The Committee always takes account of national circumstances, such as the history of labour relations and the social and economic context, but *the freedom of association principles apply uniformly and consistently among countries.*[13] Where national laws, including those interpreted by the high courts, violate the principles of freedom of association, the Committee has always considered it within its mandate to examine the laws, provide guidelines and offer the ILO's technical assistance to bring the laws into compliance with the principles of freedom of association, as set out in the Constitution of the ILO and the applicable conventions.[14]

The Committee considers that when a State decides to become a Member of the ILO, it accepts the fundamental principles embodied in the Constitution and the Declaration of Philadelphia, including the principles of freedom of association. The membership of a State in the International Labour Organization carries with it the obligation to respect in national legislation freedom of association principles and the Conventions which the State has freely ratified.[15]

The ultimate responsibility for ensuring respect for the principles of freedom of association lies with the Government. It is the responsibility of the Government to ensure the application of international labour conventions concerning freedom of association which have been freely ratified and which must be respected by all state authorities, including the judicial authorities.[16]

---

11 ILO, Freedom of Association. Digest of decisions and principles of the Freedom of Association Committee of the Governing Body of the ILO, Fifth (revised) edition. International Labour Office, Geneva, 2006, p. 7.

12 Ibid, p. 8.

13 Ibid, p. 8.

14 Ibid, p. 8.

15 Ibid, p. 9.

16 Ibid, pp. 9-10.

Trade union rights, like other basic human rights, should be respected no matter what the level of development of the country concerned. The level of protection for exercising trade union rights which results from the provisions and principles of Conventions Nos. 87 and 98 constitutes a minimum standard which may be complemented and it is desirable that other supplementary guarantees should be added resulting from the constitutional and legal system of any given country, its traditions as regards labour relations, trade union action or bargaining between the parties.[17]

The fundamental objective of the trade union movement should be to ensure the development of the social and economic well being of all workers.[18] Governments should recognize the importance for their own reputation of formulating detailed replies to the allegations brought by complainant organizations, so as to allow the Committee to undertake an objective examination.[19]

The Committee has emphasized the importance to be attached to the basic principles set out in the Universal Declaration of Human Rights, considering that their infringement can adversely affect the free exercise of trade union rights.[20] The rights conferred upon workers' and employers' organizations must be based on respect for those civil liberties which have been enunciated, in particular, in the Universal Declaration of Human Rights and in the International Covenant on Civil and Political Rights. The absence of these civil liberties removes all meaning from the concept of trade union rights.[21]

The Committee has considered that a system of democracy is fundamental for the free exercise of trade union rights.[22] A genuinely free and independent trade union movement can only develop where fundamental rights are respected.[23] The Government has the duty to defend a social climate where respect for the law reigns as the only way of guaranteeing respect for and protection of individuals.[24] All appropriate measures should be taken to guarantee that, irrespective of trade union affiliation, trade union rights can be exercised in normal conditions with respect for

17 Ibid, p. 10.
18 Ibid, p. 11.
19 Ibid, p. 11.
20 Ibid, p. 13.
21 Ibid, p. 13.
22 Ibid, p. 13.
23 Ibid, p. 13.
24 Ibid, p. 14.

basic human rights and in a climate free of violence, pressure, fear and threats of any kind.[25]

A free trade union movement can develop only under a regime which guarantees fundamental rights, including the right of trade unionists to hold meetings in trade union premises, freedom of opinion expressed through speech and the press and the right of detained trade unionists to enjoy the guarantees of normal judicial procedure at the earliest possible moment.[26]

It should be the policy of governments to ensure observance of human rights. The right to life is a fundamental prerequisite for the exercise of the rights contained in Convention No. 87. Freedom of association can only be exercised in conditions in which fundamental rights, and in particular those relating to human life and personal safety, are fully respected and guaranteed. The rights of workers' and employers' organizations can only be exercised in a climate that is free from violence, pressure or threats of any kind against the leaders and members of these organizations, and it is for governments to ensure that this principle is respected. A genuinely independent trade union movement cannot develop in a climate of violence and uncertainty.[27]

Facts imputable to individuals bring into play the State's responsibility owing to *the State's obligation to prevent violations of human rights.* Consequently, governments should endeavour to meet their obligations regarding the respect for individual rights and freedoms as well as their obligation to guarantee the right to life of trade unionists.[28]

We have set out the jurisprudence of the Committee at some length because it represents a model when it comes to international supervision of the national implementation of human rights treaties. In the chapters that follow we shall look at similar standards of supervision of other human rights supervisory bodies. Chapter I discusses the nature and characteristics of international human rights law. Chapter II discusses the concept of a national protection system which must be in place if a human rights treaty is to be adequately implemented. Chapter III discusses the jurisprudence and practice of treaty bodies on the foundation issues of democracy and the rule of law. Chapter IV discusses human rights in times of crises and emergencies. Chapter V discusses preventive strate-

25 Ibid, p. 14.

26 Ibid, p. 14.

27 Ibid, pp. 13-14.

28 Ibid, p. 16.

gies. Chapter VI discusses the duty of Governments to respect, to protect and to ensure human rights. Chapter VII discusses the duty of Governments to provide redress for violations that might take place. Chapter VIII discusses the essence of supervision in reporting systems. Chapter IX discusses the essence of petitions and fact-finding procedures. Chapter X concludes with a discussion of the bedrock principles of universality, equality and justice as they emerge from the jurisprudence and practice of human rights treaty bodies.

Chapter One

The Nature and Characteristics of International Human Rights Treaty Law

Introduction

We open this book with a discussion of the nature and characteristics of international human rights treaty law. International human rights treaty law situates itself within the broader corpus of international treaty law, notably the Vienna Convention on the Law of Treaties (1969) and applicable international customary law. However, international treaty law in general has received widespread treatment and, in this chapter, we shall focus on the views of the International Court of Justice and international judicial tribunals on the nature of international human rights treaty law, the primacy of international human rights treaty law, the nature of treaty obligations, treaties and international customary law, treaties and general principles of international law, *jus cogens* rights and rights that may never be suspended or abrogated, and the progressive development of international human rights treaty law.

I. International Judicial Organs and the Nature of International Human Rights Treaty Obligations

In its Advisory Opinion Concerning Reservations to the Convention on the Prevention and Punishment of Genocide, the International Court of Justice (ICJ) provided important insights into the nature of international human rights treaty obligations that would be applicable to most of the human rights treaties in existence today. The ICJ, advancing the doctrine of the common interest of all humanity in the observance of international human rights treaty provisions, affirmed:

> "The origins of the Convention show that it was the intention of the United Nations to condemn and punish genocide as a 'crime under international law' involving a denial of the right of existence of entire human groups, a denial which shocks the conscience of mankind and results in great losses to humanity, and which is contrary to moral law and to the spirit and aims of the United Nations. The first consequence arising from this concep-

> tion is that the principles underlying the Convention are principles which are recognized by civilized nations as binding on States, even without any conventional obligation. A second consequence is the universal character both of the condemnation of genocide and of the cooperation required 'in order to liberate mankind from such an odious scourge' (Preamble of the Convention). The Genocide convention was therefore intended by the General Assembly and by the Contracting Parties to be definitely universal in scope. It was in fact approved on December 9th, 1948 by a resolution which was unanimously adopted by fifty-six States. The objects of such a Convention must also be considered. The Convention was manifestly adopted for a purely humanitarian and civilizing purpose. It is indeed difficult to imagine a Convention that might have this dual character to a greater degree, since its object on the one hand is to safeguard the very existence of certain human groups, and on the other to confirm and endorse the most elementary principles of morality. In such a Convention the contracting States do not have any interests of their own; they merely have, one and all, a common interest, namely the accomplishment of those high purposes which are the *raison d'etre* of the Convention. Consequently, in a convention of this type, one cannot speak of individual advantages or disadvantages to States, or of the maintenance of a perfect contractual balance between rights and duties. The high ideals which inspired the Convention provide, by virtue of the common will of the parties, the foundation and measure of all its provisions."[29]

The International Criminal Tribunal for the Former Yugoslavia (ICTY) in the case of *Kupreskic* and others expressed similar views:

> "The absolute nature of most obligations imposed by rules of international humanitarian law reflects the progressive trend towards the so-called 'humanisation' of international legal obligations, which refers to the general erosion of the role of reciprocity in the application of international humanitarian law over the last century. After the First World War, the application of the laws of war moved away from a reliance on reciprocity between belligerents, with the consequence that, in general, rules came to be increasingly applied by each belligerent despite their possible disregard by the enemy. The underpinning of this shift was that it became clear to States that norms of international humanitarian law were not intended to protect State interests; they were primarily designed to benefit individuals *qua* hu-

29 ICJ, Reservations to the Convention on Genocide, Advisory Opinion, 28 May, 1951, ICJ Reports (1951), p. 15.

> man beings. Unlike other international norms, such as those of commercial treaties which can legitimately be based on the protection of reciprocal interests of States, compliance with humanitarian rules could not be made dependent on a reciprocal or corresponding performance of these obligations by other States. This trend marks the translation into legal norms of the 'categorical imperative' formulated by Kant in the field of morals: one ought to fulfil an obligation regardless of whether others comply with it or disregard it."[30]

The Inter-American Court of Human Rights, in the case of Villagran Morales and others, of 19 November, 1999, declared in respect of the right to life:

> "The right to life is a fundamental human right, and the exercise of this right is essential for the exercise of all other human rights. If it is not respected, all rights lack meaning. Owing to the fundamental nature of the right to life, restrictive approaches to it are inadmissible. In essence, the fundamental right to life includes not only the right of every human being not to be deprived of his life arbitrarily, but also the right that he will not be prevented from having access to the conditions that guarantee a dignified existence. States have the obligation to guarantee the creation of the conditions required in order that violations of this basic right do not occur and, in particular, the duty to prevent its agents from violating it."[31]

The foregoing examples give an indication of the exalted nature of international human rights treaty obligations. They help to explain, in part, the primacy of international human rights treaty law over national laws that do not meet the treaty standards of protection.

II. The Primacy of International Human Rights Law

The principle of the supremacy of international law over municipal law has been included in the following provisions either drafted or subsequently accepted by the International Law Commission: Articles 13 and

30 International Tribunal for the Prosecution of Persons Responsible for Serious Violations of International Humanitarian Law Committed in the Territory of the former Yugoslavia since 1991, Kupreskic et al. Case No. IT-95-16-T of 14 January, 2000, p. 201.

31 Inter-American Court of Human Rights, Villagran Morales et al. Case (the 'Street Children' case, Judgment, 19 November, 1999.

14 of the Draft declaration on Rights and Duties of States; Articles 27, 46, 53, 64 of the Vienna Convention on the Law of Treaties (1969), and its draft Article 3 on State Responsibility.

The Preamble of the Draft Declaration on the Rights and Duties of States proclaimed that "the States of the world form a community governed by international law." According to Article 13 of the Draft Declaration, "Every State has the duty to carry out in good faith its obligations arising from treaties and other sources of international law, and it may not invoke provisions in its constitution or its laws as an excuse for failure to perform this duty." According to Article 14, "Every State has the duty to conduct its relations with other States in accordance with international law and with the principle that the sovereignty of each State is subject to the supremacy of international law." This principle was based on postulate 4 of the "International Law of the Future", published by the Carnegie Endowment for International Peace in 1944.

The Commission approved these articles without any debate on their substance. The principles contained in them were taken as self-evident by the Commission. Commissioner Alfaro, in the draft he prepared, which was used as the basis of discussion in the Commission, commented on these provisions as follows: Article 14 "deals with the authority of international law including everything agreed upon in the Charter of the United Nations and in the Statute of the World Court, which are international treaty law." Article 14 "proclaims that international law is obligatory for all States."[32] In the written comments of governments, the principle was accepted and, on the whole, taken as self-evident.[33]

Sir Gerald Fitzmaurice, in his course of lectures at the Hague Academy of International Law on "The General Principles of International Law Considered from the Standpoint of the Rule of Law", took as his starting point Article 14 of the International Law Commission's draft on Rights and Duties of States, which he commented upon as follows:

> "This provision enunciates the important principle of the subordination of the sovereignty of each State to the supremacy of international law – in short, of the sovereignty of the rule of law in the international field which might indeed be called the first and greatest principle of international law.

32 *Preparatory Study Concerning a Draft Declaration on the Rights and Duties of States*, A/CN.4/2, (15 December, 1948), p. 43.

33 Ibid. See the written comments of Mexico, p. 86, the United Kingdom, p. 86, Venezuela, p. 88.

From it all the rest follows: without it there may be customs, practices, habits, courtesies ... but there is no law."[34]

Sir Gerald proceeded to demonstrate that this principle applied automatically, and that at the back of the principle, the ultimate source or basis of legal obligation in international law rested in the explanation of law as a social necessity.

Professor Hans Kelsen, while making some criticism of the actual formulation of this principle by the International Law Commission, accepted it as part of general international law. The duty laid down in Article 14, he felt, "is implied in the concept of international law. ... The concept of international law implies the duty of every State to behave in all its relations in accordance with international law."[35]

He explained this more fully elsewhere:

> "There is, above the commonwealth described as the State, a legal order which defines the respective scopes of power of individual States by forbidding the encroachment of one into the sphere of another ... a legal order which regulates the relations of States by means of rules equally applicable to all. International law does this – but only when its supremacy over the legal systems of individual States is recognized, when ... it is contemplated as a legal system standing above the States, i.e. when the legal systems of individual States are regarded as component parts of a universal legal order."[36]

Principle I of the Principles of International law Recognized in the Charter of the Nuremberg Tribunal and in the Judgment of the Tribunal, as consolidated by the International Law Commission, stated that any person who committed an act which constituted a crime under international law was responsible for it and liable to punishment. In the commentary to Principle 1, the Commission stated that the general rule underlying it was that international law may impose duties on individuals directly without any interposition of internal law. Principle II stated that the fact that in-

34 Sir Gerald Fitzmaurice, Q.C., "The General Principles of International Law Considered from the Standpoint of the Rule of Law", 92 RCADI (1957, II), p. 6.

35 H. Kelsen, "The Draft Declaration of Rights and Duties of States", 44 American Journal of International Law (1950), pp. 259-276.

36 *Der Begriff der Souveranitat und die Theorie des Volkerrechts* (1920), cited in H. Lauterpacht, *Private Law Sources and Analogies of International Law* (1933), p. 55.

ternal law does not impose a penalty for an act which constitutes a crime under international law does not relieve the persons who committed the act from responsibility under international law. In its commentary on this principle the Commission observed that "The principle that a person who has committed an international crime is responsible therefor and liable to punishment under international law, independently of the provisions of internal law, implies what is commonly called the 'supremacy of international law over national law.'"[37]

The International Law Commission's draft on *jus cogens*, which became Articles 53 and 64 of the Vienna Convention on the Law of Treaties, was also clearly based on the assumption that international law overrides municipal law in matters of international public policy.

III. The Relationship between International Legal Obligations and Domestic Law: From Dualism, Monism, and Coordination, to Responsibility

Dualist doctrine, as summarised by Professor Ian Brownlie,

> "points to the essential differences of international law and municipal law, consisting primarily in the fact that the two systems regulate different subject-matter. International law is a law between sovereign states; municipal law applies within a state and regulates the relations of its citizens with each other and with the executive. On this view, neither legal order has the power to create or alter rules of the other. When municipal law provides that international law applies in whole or in part within the jurisdiction, this is merely the exercise of the authority of municipal law, an adoption or transformation of the rules of international law. In case of a conflict between international law and municipal law the dualist would assume that a municipal court would apply municipal law."[38]

Monism, as advocated by the great Sir Hersch Lauterpacht, asserts the supremacy of international law even within the municipal sphere. International law, "is seen as the best available moderator of human affairs, and also as a logical condition of the *legal* existence of states and there-

---

37 I.L.C. Report 1950, para. 102 of commentary to Principle II, YBILC 1950, Vol. II, p. 375.

38 I. Brownlie, Principles of Pubic International Law. Second Edition (1973), pp. 33-34.

fore of the municipal systems of law within the sphere of the legal competence of states."[39]

The theory of coordination was put forward, among others, by Sir Gerald Fitzmaurice, a former judge of the International Court of Justice. His view was that international law and municipal law did not come into conflict as systems since they worked in different spheres. Each was supreme in its own field. However, there may be a conflict of *obligations*, an inability of the State on the domestic plane to act in the manner required by international law; the consequence of this will not be the invalidity of the internal law but the responsibility of the state on the international plane.[40]

It is our submission that while the two systems of law are essentially interdependent, the theory of coordination does not suffice in the circumstances of our contemporary world, especially after the universal affirmation of the responsibility to protect by the UN General Assembly in 2005. There are areas involving, for example, planetary security, global threats such as terrorism, norms of *jus cogens*, the prevention of genocide, and fundamental guarantees of human rights that require norms of municipal law which correspond to international law as a matter of fundamental obligation of the State within the international legal system. This is the doctrine of responsibility: the responsibility to prevent and to protect.[41]

The African Commission on Human and Peoples' Rights has taken a firm position on the primacy of international human rights law over national law. In a case involving restrictions on freedom of freedom of expression under national law, the Commission underlined that Governments should avoid restricting rights, and have special care with regard to those rights protected by constitutional or international human rights law. No situation justified the wholesale violation of human rights. According to Article 9(2) of the African Charter on Human and Peoples' Rights, dissemination of opinions may be restricted by law. This did not mean, the Commission held, that national law could set aside the right to express and disseminate one's opinions:

> "To allow national law to have precedence over the international law of the Charter would defeat the purpose of the rights and freedoms enshrined in

39 Ibid, p. 34.

40 Ibid, p. 36.

41 See, generally, J.L. Brierly, *The Basis of Obligation in International Law and Other Papers*, Oxford: Oxford: Clarendon Press (1958).

the Charter. International human rights standards must always prevail over contradictory national law. Any limitation on the rights of the Charter must be in conformity with the provisions of the Charter."[42]

IV. The Nature of Treaty Obligations[43]

The Bloemfontein Statement adopted by leading African and Commonwealth lawyers and judges in 1995 set the nature of treaty obligations in terms of the rule of law and human rights as follows:

> "In democratic societies fundamental human rights and freedoms are more than paper aspirations. They form part of the law. And it is the special province of judges to ensure that the law's undertakings are realised in the daily life of the people. In a society ruled by law, all public institutions and officials must act in accordance with the law. The judges bear particular responsibility for ensuring that all branches of government – the legislature and the executive, as well as the judiciary itself, conform to the legal principles of a free society. Judicial review and effective access to courts are indispensable, not only in normal times, but also during periods of public emergency threatening the life of the nation. It is at such times that fundamental human rights are most at risk and when courts must be especially vigilant in their protection."

General Comment No. 31 adopted by the Human Rights Committee on 26 May 2004 is a superb statement of the nature of human rights treaty obligations. A State Party, the Committee declared, must respect and ensure the rights in the Covenant to anyone within its power or effective control. The obligations in the Covenant in general and under Article 2

42 Communications 105793, 128/94 and 152/96, Media Rights Agenda and Constitutional Rights Project v. Nigeria. Activity Report 1998-1999, Annex V. See also M. Evans and R. Murray, The African Charter on Human and Peoples' Rights. The System in Practice, 1986-2000, Cambridge, Cambridge University Press, p. 7. See generally, V. Leary, C. Thomas, M. Oelz, S.Beaudonnet, The use of international labour law in domestic courts: Theory, jurisprudence and practical implications, in ILO, Les normes internationales du travail: un patrimoine pour l'lavenir, ILO, Geneva, 2004, pp. 249-286.

43 Professor John Humphrey, one of the drafters of the Universal Declaration of Human Rights, had proposed that "The provisions of the International Bill of Rights shall be deemed fundamental principles of international law and of the national law of every member state of the United Nations".

in particular are binding on every State Party as a whole. All branches of government (executive, legislative and judicial), and other public or governmental authorities, at whatever level – national, regional or local – are in a position to engage the responsibility of the State Party.

States Parties must adopt legislative, judicial, administrative, educative and other appropriate measures in order to fulfil their legal obligations. It is important to raise levels of awareness about the Covenant not only among public officials and state agents but also among the population at large.

The positive obligations on States Parties to ensure Covenant rights will only be discharged if individuals are protected by the state not just against violations of Covenant rights by its agents, but also against acts committed by private persons or entities that would impair the enjoyment of Covenant rights in so far as they are amenable to application between private persons or entities. There may be circumstances in which a failure to ensure Covenant rights as required by article 2 would give rise to violations by States Parties of those rights as a result of States Parties' permitting or failing to take appropriate measures or to exercise due diligence to prevent, punish, investigate or redress the harm caused by such acts by private persons or entities. States parties have a duty to address the activities of private persons or entities such as the duty to ensure that private persons or entities do not inflict torture.

States parties are required to respect and to ensure the Covenant rights to all persons who may be within their territory and to all persons subject to their jurisdiction. This means that a State Party must respect and ensure the rights laid down in the Covenant to anyone within the power or effective control of that State Party, even if not situated within the territory of the State Party. The enjoyment of Covenant rights is not limited to citizens of States Parties, but must also be available to all individuals, regardless of nationality or statelessness, such as asylum seekers, refugees, migrant workers and other persons who may find themselves in the territory or subject to the jurisdiction of the State Party. This principle also applies to those within the power or effective control of the forces of a State Party acting outside its territory, regardless of the circumstances in which such power or effective control was obtained, such as forces constituting a national contingent of a State Party assigned to an international peace-keeping or peace-enforcement operation.

The Covenant applies also in situations of armed conflict to which the rules of international humanitarian law are applicable. While, in respect of certain Covenant rights, more specific rules of international humanitarian law may be specially relevant for the purposes of the interpretation of Covenant rights, both spheres of law are complementary, not mutually exclusive.

Article 2, paragraph 2 of the Covenant requires that States Parties take the necessary steps to give effect to the Covenant rights in the domestic order. It follows that, unless the Covenant's rights are already protected by their domestic law or practices, States Parties are required on ratification to make such changes to domestic laws and practices as are necessary to ensure their conformity with the Covenant. Where there are inconsistencies between domestic law and the Covenant, article 2 requires that the domestic law or practice be changed to meet the standards required by the Covenant's substantive guarantees.

Article 2 allows a State Party to pursue this in accordance with its own domestic constitutional structure and accordingly does not require that the Covenant be directly applicable in the courts by incorporation of the Covenant into national laws. The Committee takes the view, however, that Covenant guarantees may receive enhanced protection in those states where the Covenant is automatically or through specific incorporation part of the domestic legal order. The Committee invited those States Parties in which the Covenant did not form part of the domestic legal order to consider incorporation of the Covenant to render it part of domestic law to facilitate full realization of Covenant rights as required by article 2.

The requirement under Article 2, paragraph 2, to take steps to give effect to the Covenant rights is unqualified and of immediate effect. A failure to comply with this obligation cannot be justified by reference to political, social, cultural or economic considerations within the state.

Article 2, paragraph 3, requires that in addition to effective protection of Covenant rights States Parties must ensure that individuals also have accessible and effective remedies to vindicate those rights. Such remedies should be appropriately adapted so as to take account of the special vulnerability of certain categories of person, including in particular children. The Committee attaches importance to States Parties establishing appropriate judicial and administrative mechanisms for addressing claims of rights violations under domestic law.

Article 2, paragraph 3 of the Covenant requires that States Parties make reparation to individuals whose Covenant rights have been violated. Without reparation to individuals whose Covenant rights have been violated, the obligation to provide an effective remedy, which is central to the efficacy of Article 2, paragraph 3, is not discharged. In addition to the explicit reparation required by articles 9, paragraph 5, and Article 14, paragraph 6, the Committee considers that the Covenant generally, entails appropriate compensation. The Committee noted that, where appropriate, reparation can involve restitution, rehabilitation and measures of satisfaction, such as public apologies, public memorials, guarantees of non-repetition and changes in relevant laws and practices, as well as bringing to justice the perpetrators of human rights violations.

In general, the purposes of the Covenant would be defeated without an obligation integral to article 2 to take measures to prevent the recurrence of a violation of the Covenant. Accordingly, it has been a frequent practice of the Committee, in its consideration of individual petitions under the Optional Protocol, to include in its Views the need for measures, beyond a victim-specific remedy, to be taken to avoid recurrence of the type of violation in question. Such measures may require changes in the State Party's laws or practices.

Where investigations reveal violations of certain Covenant rights, States Parties must ensure that those responsible are brought to justice. As with failure to investigate, failure to bring to justice perpetrators of such violations could in and of itself give rise to a separate breach of the Covenant. These obligations arise notably in respect of those violations recognized as criminal under either domestic or international law, such as torture and similar cruel, inhuman and degrading treatment (article 7), summary and arbitrary killing (article 6) and enforced disappearance (articles 7 and 9 and frequently 6). Indeed, the problem of impunity for these violations, a matter of sustained concern by the Committee, might well be an important contributing element in the recurrence of the violations. When committed as part of a widespread or systematic attack on a civilian population, these violations of the Covenant are crimes against humanity (Rome Statute of the ICC, Article 7).

Accordingly, where public officials or state agents have committed violations of the Covenant rights, the States Parties concerned may not relieve perpetrators from personal responsibility. Furthermore, no official status justifies persons who may be accused of responsibility for such violations being held immune from legal responsibility. Other impediments to the establishment of legal responsibility should also be removed, such as the defence of obedience to superior orders or unreasonably short periods of statutory limitation in cases where such limitations are applicable. States Parties should also assist each other to bring to justice persons suspected of having committed acts in violation of the Covenant that are punishable under domestic or international law.

The Committee further took the view that the right to an effective remedy may in certain circumstances require States Parties to provide for and implement provisional or interim measures to avoid continuing violations and to endeavour to repair at the earliest possible opportunity any harm that may have been caused by such violations.

General Comment 31 is a solid reflection of the legal obligations of States under the Covenant and under international human rights treaties generally. Superimposed on all of this is the United Nations Charter, which has concrete legal obligations on every Member State to uphold universal human rights.

V. Obligations under the United Nations Charter

According to the very first article of the United Nations Charter, the Purposes of the United Nations are, among others, to achieve international cooperation in solving international problems of an economic, social cultural or humanitarian character and in promoting and encouraging respect for human rights and for fundamental freedoms for all without distinction as to race, language, sex, or religion and to be a centre for harmonizing the action of nations in the attainment of these common ends. Article 55 of the Charter gives the United Nations a mandate to promote universal respect for and observance of human rights and fundamental freedoms for all. In Article 56, all members pledged themselves to take joint and separate action in cooperation with the Organization for the achievement of the purposes set forth in Article 55.

In Resolution 2625 (XXV) of 24 October 1970, the UN General Assembly adopted the Declaration on Principles of International Law Concerning Friendly Relations and Cooperation Among States in accordance with the Charter of the United Nations, which is considered a codification of the legal principles of the United Nations Charter. In that declaration the General Assembly proclaimed that States have the duty to cooperate with one another, irrespective of the differences in their political, economic and social systems, in the various spheres of international relations in order to maintain international peace and security and to promote international stability and progress, the general welfare of nations and international cooperation free from discrimination based on such differences.

To this end: States shall co-operate with other states in the maintenance of international peace and security; States shall co-operate in the promotion of universal respect for, and observance of, human rights and fundamental freedoms for all, and in the elimination of all forms of racial discrimination and all forms of religious intolerance; States shall conduct their international relations in the economic, social, cultural, technical and trade fields in accordance with the principles of sovereign equality and non-intervention; States members of the United Nations have the duty to take joint and separate action in cooperation with the United Nations in accordance with the relevant provisions of the Charter.

Furthermore, States should co-operate in the economic, social and cultural fields as well as in the field of science and technology and for the promotion of international cultural and educational progress. States should co-operate in the promotion of economic growth throughout the world, especially that of the developing countries.[44]

Goodrich, Hambro and Simons, in their historic commentary on the Charter, noted that the United Nations was not intended to have the powers of a government; rather, its function was conceived as that of serving as a means of promoting cooperation between States in finding solutions to common problems and of achieving maximum support from members for the work of the Organization.[45]

On the legal thrust of Article 56 of the Charter, Goodrich, Hambro and Simons pointed out, as regards the phrase "in cooperation with the Organization", that while it did not mean that recommendations of UN organs become binding, it did mean "that members are obligated to refrain from obstructionist tactics and to cooperate in good faith to achieve the goals specified in Article 55."[46]

The more recent commentary on the Charter of the United Nations, edited by Bruno Simma (now a judge on the International Court of Justice), noted that as far as the protection of human rights is concerned Article 1(3) had been invoked with respect to the improvement generally within the United Nations system of the effective enjoyment of human rights and fundamental freedoms and with respect to particular human rights issues and situations.[47]

The same commentary concluded that Article 56 represented a specification of the obligations of member states set forth in Article 2(2) and Article 55. This specification dealt with the three elements of Article 56: joint action, separate action, and cooperation with the organization

---

44 GA Resolution 2625 (XXV), (24 October 1970).

45 L. Goodrich, E. Hambro and A. Simons, *Charter of the United Nations: Commentary and Documents*, (New York, London: Columbia University Press, 1969), p. 35.

46 L. Goodrich, E. Hambro and A. Simons, *Charter of the United Nations: Commentary and Documents*, Third Ed. (New York, London: Columbia University Press, 1969), p. 381.

47 B. Simma (Ed.), *The Charter of the United Nations. A Commentary* (Oxford: Oxford University Press, 1985), pp. 55-56.

and with the obligations assumed under Article 55. Wolfrum, the author of the Commentary on Article 56 in this volume agreed with Goodrich, Hambro and Simons, that Article 56 did "require that member states co-operate with the UN in a constructive way; obstructive policies are thus excluded".[48]

Article 103 of the Charter lays down that in the event of a conflict between the obligations of the Members of the United Nations under the Charter and their obligations under any other international agreement, their obligations under the Charter shall prevail. Mandatory decisions of the UN Security Council are a case in point.

VI. Mandatory Decisions of the United Nations Security Council

Under Article 24, paragraph 1 of the United Nations Charter Members of the United Nations, in order to ensure prompt and effective action by the United Nations, confer on the Security Council primary responsibility for the maintenance of international peace and security and agree that in carrying out its duties under this responsibility the Security Council acts on their behalf.

The International Court of Justice, in the Expenses Case and the 'Wall Case', has taken the view that since, under Article 24 of the United Nations Charter, the Security Council has the primary responsibility for the maintenance of international peace and security, it can, in that regard impose on States 'an explicit obligation of compliance if for example it issues an order or command ... under Chapter VII' of the Charter. The Council can, to that end, 'require enforcement by coercive action'.[49] Professor Ian Brownlie has pointed out that 'When competent organs of the United Nations make a binding determination that a situation is illegal, the states which are the addressees of the resolution or resolutions concerned are under an obligation to bring that situation to an end."[50]

According to Article 43 of the Charter, all Members of the United Nations, in order to contribute to the maintenance of international peace and security, undertake to make available to the Security Council, on its call and in accordance with a special agreement or agreements, armed

48 Ibid, p. 794.

49 *Certain Expenses of the United Nations* (Article 17, paragraph 2 of the Charter), Advisory Opinion of 20 July 1962, I.C.J. Reports 1962, p. 163. *Legal Consequences of the Construction of a Wall in the Occupied Palestinian Territory*, Advisory Opinion, ICJ Reports 2004, para. 26.

50 Brownlie, op. cit. Second Edition, p. 504.

forces, assistance and facilities, including rights of passage, necessary for the purpose of maintaining international peace and security.

The mandatory decisions of the Security Council on anti-terrorism measures, adopted under Chapter VII of the Charter, provide solid examples of actions required by Member States within their national legal orders.

VII. Treaties and International Customary Law

In the draft articles on State responsibility which it adopted recently, the International Law Commission included the following provision in article 3:

> "The characterization of an act of State as internationally wrongful is governed by international law. Such characterization is not affected by the characterization of the same act as lawful by internal law."

This article was first proposed by the Commission's then Special Rapporteur, Roberto Ago and discussed in the Commission in 1973.[51] When the article was discussed in the Commission at its 1209th and 1210th meetings in 1973 the principle contained in it received support from every member of the Commission who took part in the debate: Commissioners Ramangasoavina, Tsuruoka, Yasseen, Kearney, Sette Camara, Hambro, Ushakov, Elias, Vallat, Bartos, Ustor, Castaneda, Tammes, Bilge and Reuter.

In drafting the article the Commission followed its own draft on rights and duties of States discussed above, as well as Article 27 of the Vienna Convention on the Law of Treaties, which provides that "A party may not invoke the provisions of its internal law as justification for its failure to perform a treaty."

In a recent case, R. v. Hape,[52] the Supreme Court of Canada provided important guidance on the place of international customary law in the domestic law of States, in this particular instance, Canada. The Supreme Court stated that international custom, as the law of nations, was also the law of Canada unless, in a valid exercise of its sovereignty, Canada declared that its law was to the contrary."[53] In the assessment of Glen Linder:

51 The article was discussed at the 1209th and 1210th meetings of the Commission in 1973.

52 (2007) SCC 26.

53 Ibid, paras. 37-39.

> "The majority also appears to endorse the view that if the rule of customary international law changes, so too will domestic law. Apparently endorsing the relevant passage from Lord Denning's landmark judgment in *Trendtex*[54] our highest court has now clarified that even where a common law precedent exists that is contrary to a newer customary international law rule, courts must follow the customary international law rule, and not the inconsistent common law precedent."[55]

If the legislature wishes to enact legislation that is inconsistent with international law, the majority held, there must be 'unequivocal legislative intent to default on an international obligation.'

There is also respectable Commonwealth precedent for the proposition that where there is uncertainty international law may be used in ascertaining the meaning of national legislation, for example in the interpretation of human rights and fundamental freedoms.[56]

In 2005, the International Committee of the Red Cross, fulfilling a mandate entrusted to it by the International Red Cross and Red Crescent Conference, published Customary International Humanitarian Law, a codification of the main rules of international humanitarian law. It contained 161 succinct rules of the binding norms applicable in all armed conflicts, international and non-international. In a Foreword to the publication, the President of the ICRC, Dr Jakob Kellenberger, expressed the view that it had served to emphasize the universality of humanitarian law. All traditions and civilizations had contributed in the development of the this law, which was today part of the common heritage of mankind.[57]

The 161 rules summarised in the volume are cast in the form of numerous instances of prohibited conduct in warfare, the duty to take particular care, to take all possible measures, to undertake special efforts to respect and protect those at risk, and in a few instances, to take measures to prevent particular harm. The rules deal with the principle of distinction, specifically protected persons and objects, specific methods of war-

54 *Trendtex Trading Corp v. Central Bank of Nigeria*, (1977) 1 Q.B., p. 529.

55 Glen Linder, Canadian Council of International Law, Case Comment, R.v. Hape – The International Law Aspects.

56 See e.g. The Bangalore Principles on the Domestic Application of International Human Rights Norms. On this, also see e.g. a speech by Justice Michael Kirby, "The First Ten Years of the Bangalore Principles on the Domestic Application of International Human Rights Norms" (available online).

57 ICRC, Customary Humanitarian Law (2005),p. xi.

fare, weapons, treatment of civilians, and implementation. The chapter on implementation deals with compliance with international humanitarian law, enforcement of international humanitarian law, responsibility and reparation, individual responsibility, and war crimes.

The year of publication of the volume, 2005, was the year in which the United Nations General Assembly, endorsed the Responsibility to Protect concept, with its three dimensions: the responsibility to prevent, the responsibility to react, and the responsibility to rebuild. The Independent Commission on Intervention and State Sovereignty, which advocated the concept, considered the responsibility to prevent to be the nub of the responsibility to prevent. A question that immediately arises for reflection is how the responsibility to protect, and in particular the responsibility to prevent, is pertinent to international humanitarian law.

It is instructive that, with a few specialized exceptions, there are no general rules in the ICRC publication on the duty of states to act for the prevention of violations of humanitarian law, whether in respect to the substance of international humanitarian law or its implementation. It is particularly striking that the rules on implementation and enforcement make no mention whatsoever of the responsibility to prevent. The chapter on compliance with international humanitarian law opens with Rule 139: Each party to the conflict must respect and ensure respect for international humanitarian law by its armed forces and other persons or groups acting in fact on its instructions, or under its direction or control. One could argue that the duty to ensure respect for international humanitarian law encompasses the duty to prevent violations, but it would have been useful to spell this out for emphasis.

Rule 142 does provide that States parties to the conflict must provide instruction in international humanitarian law to their armed forces and this does have a preventive rationale. So does Rule 149: A state is responsible for violations of international humanitarian law attributable to it. Likewise, Rule 151: Individuals are criminally responsible for war crimes they commit, and Rule 154: Every combatant has a duty to disobey a manifestly unlawful order. Rule 156 clarifies that serious violations of international humanitarian law constitute war crimes. Likewise, Rule 157: States have the right to vest universal jurisdiction in their national courts over war crimes. Rule 161 clarifies that statutes of limitation may not apply to war crimes, while Rule 161 adds that States must make every effort to cooperate, to the extent possible, with each other in order to facilitate the investigation of war crimes and the prosecution of the suspects.

From the point of view of the substantive content of international humanitarian law it would seem that following the General Assembly and the Security Council endorsement of the responsibility to protect concept, the following preventive rules of international humanitarian law could be supported:

- States have the duty to do everything possible to prevent wars;
- States have the duty to act for the prevention of violations of international humanitarian law;
- The Security Council has the duty to act for the prevention of violations of international humanitarian law;
- Competent International Organizations have the duty to do everything possible to help;
- Competent International Organizations have the duty to act for the prevention of violations of international humanitarian law;
- The International Committee of the Red Cross has a duty to act for the prevention of violations of international humanitarian law.

The rule concerning the ICRC requires some discussion. In a Foreword to the ICRC volume on customary humanitarian law Yves Sandoz notes that the international community has given the ICRC the onerous mandate to work for the faithful application of international humanitarian law. This imposed a duty of constant vigilance. For the ICRC, impartiality meant not only avoiding discrimination between the different victims of a given conflict, but also constantly striving to ensure that all the victims of all the conflicts on the planet are treated equitably, without regional or ethnic preference and independently of the emotions sparked by media-selected images. The concern to avoid discrimination and to ensure impartiality on a global scale guides the ICRC in choosing its activities. When the time comes to make these choices, meeting the victims's urgent need for food and medical care logically remained the priority and claimed far and away the largest part of the organization's budget.

The ICRC's long experience, Sandoz continued, had convinced it that in order to be effective it had to engage in a wide range of activities that had to be viewed in relation to one another. Humanitarian action in the field might reveal new problems that, in turn, prompted discussion that led to standard-setting. Then there was work towards universal acceptance of the new rules by convincing States through their governments, their parliaments, their senior officials of the importance of respecting such rules. Finally, individual states must be encouraged to adopt national laws incorporating the new rules into domestic legislation to ensure that the public knows and understands basic humanitarian principles, to ensure that international humanitarian law is adequately taught in schools and universities, and to integrate the subject into military training. The ultimate goal of all this work is to benefit the victims of war and facilitate the task of those seeking.

This is statement of the IRCR methods, penned by someone who was for a long time its legal adviser, and essentially provides a humanitarian rationale for the efforts of the IRCR that has always been uppermost in its work. One must approach the IRCR methods with a great deal of respect. The humanitarian principle gives emphasis to helping those in need. But where does the prevention principle fit into this picture? The prevention principle might require forms of action that could complicate humanitarian activities. One should certainly leave the IRCR free to engage in its humanitarian activities and perhaps not seek to saddle it with the responsibility to prevent. It is possible that ICRC partners might carry out the prevention role. This is more or less what is taking place at the present time, with organizations such as the International Crisis Group and Human Rights Watch exposing gross violations of human rights and humanitarian law while leaving the ICRC free to engage in its assistance activities.

Sandoz indirectly addressed this issue when he noted that the ICRC had in recent years devoted significant resources to considering the state of the law and to spreading knowledge of it. But those resources were limited and choices needed to be made between various options within the legal domain: should priority be given to developing new law, promoting national legislation, clarifying certain aspects of practical implementation, consulting experts on sensitive questions, training the military 'or mobilising public opinion as a means of bringing about greater compliance'?[58]

In practice, the ICRC rarely does much of the last kind of actions, mobilising public opinion as a means of bringing about greater compliance. The humanitarian impulse militates against this kind of approach. Yet, one is on the horns of another dilemma. Violations of international humanitarian law are rampant and Judge Abdul Koroma, in his Foreword to the ICRC volume on customary humanitarian law commented: "Opinions vary as to the reason for the increasing number of violations of international humanitarian law. Is it a lack of awareness of the rules on the part of those who should observe them? Is it the inadequacy of the rules even where they are known? Is it weak mechanisms for enforcing the rules? Or is it sheer disregard for the rules? To some extent, there is truth in each."[59]

58 Ibid, pp. xv-xvi.

59 Ibid, p. xii.

From the above, we are left with a situation in which the main international actor in the field of international humanitarian law, the ICRC, continues to provide invaluable humanitarian assistance work, to support the application and further development of the law, to engage in training and teaching in international humanitarian law, but chooses to contribute to the responsibility to prevent through its legal and training work. Is this a satisfactory state of affairs from the point of view of the responsibility to protect and the responsibility to prevent? There are issues for deep reflection here.

The best preventive strategy against violations of human rights and humanitarian law is to prevent armed conflicts in the first place. This underscores the importance of Secretary-General Boutros-Ghali's Agenda for Peace, launched in 1992. The activation of the concept of the responsibility to protect, and its endorsement by the General Assembly and the Security Council should be our starting point, with emphasis on the responsibility to prevent – especially genocide, ethnic cleansing, crimes against humanity and war crimes.

At the end of the day, the International Criminal Court is the bulwark institution. We should support the Prosecutor of the ICC and encourage him to bring more prosecutions against those responsible for international crimes. With more prosecutions, military and paramilitary commanders will be forced to think hard before committing atrocities.

Education and the dissemination of information to members of the armed forces, a long-standing strategy of the ICRC is a key prevention approach that should be continued and expanded.

Might it be, however, that an NGO or research institution should do an annual report on international crimes during armed conflict? This could serve as documentation for judicial processes nationally, regionally and internationally and would be one way of helping to discharge the responsibility to prevent in the area of international humanitarian law. This is a proposal that we would offer for discussion.

VIII. *Jus Cogens* Rights and Rights That May Never Be Suspended or Abrogated

The concept of peremptory norms of international law is that "certain overriding principles of international law exist, forming a body of *jus cogens*."[60] Examples cited by Brownlie include the prohibition of aggression, the prohibition of genocide, the principle of racial non-discrimination,

60 Brownlie, Second Edition, op. cit., p. 499.

crimes against humanity and the rules prohibiting trade in slaves.[61] The concept of *jus cogens* was included by the International Law Commission in its final draft on the law of treaties in 1966. Article 50 of that draft provided that "a treaty is void if it conflicts with a peremptory norm of general international law from which no derogation is permitted and which can be modified only by a subsequent norm of general international law having the same character."

The Vienna Conference on the Law of Treaties included a provision similar to that drafted by the Commission. The Vienna Convention on the Law of Treaties defined a peremptory norm as 'a norm accepted and recognized by the international community as a whole as a norm from which no derogation is permitted and which can be modified only by a subsequent norm of general international law having the same character."

Authoritative bodies of the international community have provided some guidance as to what norms of *jus cogens* are. In the Barcelona Traction case (Second Phase), the majority judgment of the International Court of Justice, supported by twelve judges, drew a distinction between obligations of a State arising vis-à-vis another State and obligations 'towards the international community as a whole'. The Court said:

> "Such obligations derive, for example, in contemporary international law, from the outlawing of acts of aggression, and of genocide, as also from the principles and rules concerning the basic rights of the human person, including protection from slavery and discrimination."[62]

In the Sixth Edition of his Principles of Public International Law, Ian Brownlie took the view that the notion of *delicta juris gentium*, as opposed to torts as reparation obligations between tortfeasor and claimant, takes four forms: (1) that of high illegality or breach of *jus cogens*, as in the case of genocide; (2) reference to cases where international law recognizes a general competence to exercise jurisdiction to apprehend, and perhaps to punish, irrespective of the nationality of the wrongdoer, as in the case of piracy; (3) acts which harm all states indiscriminately and which are difficult to trace to particular tortfeasors, as in the case of successive nuclear tests in the atmosphere; (4) acts infringing principles of law creating rights the beneficiaries of which do not have legal personality or, more correctly, do not have presently effective means of protecting their rights,

61 Ibid, p. 500.

62 ICJ Reports (1970), 3 at p. 32.

as for example, non-self-governing peoples and the populations of mandate or trust territories.[63]

In our submission, the domestic law of every Member State must incorporate peremptory norms of international law or norms of *jus cogens*. Under no circumstances should any Member State or its agents, including its courts, act at variance with peremptory norms of international law. There is a fundamental duty of care on the part of governments as well as their courts to be in compliance with such norms and to take special care not to act at variance with them.

The European Court of Human Rights, in the Al-Adsani case of 21 November, 2001 affirmed the peremptory character of the prohibition of torture.[64] The Inter-American Commission of Human Rights has had occasion to invoke the existence of jus cogens obligations in international human rights treaty law. In the case of Michael Domingues, which dealt with the issue whether the death penalty could be carried out on someone who was below the age of 18 at the time of the commission of the offence, the Court declared:

> "It has been proved that this norm has been recognized as a norm with sufficiently inalienable character as to constitute a *jus cogens* norm, evolution foreseen by the Commission in its Roach and Pinkerton decisions. As was pointed out, almost all the States have rejected the imposition of the death penalty to persons under 18 years, in its more explicit form through the ratification of the CCPR, the CRC and the American Convention, treaties in which this proscription was recognized as non-derogable. The acceptance of this norm covers the political and ideological frontiers and the attempts to run away from these norms have been strongly condemned by members of the international community as non-permissible according to contemporaneous norms of human rights .... Under this basis, the Commission considers that the United States is bound by a norm of *jus cogens* not to impose the death penalty to persons who had under 18 years at the moment of the commission of a felony. As a norm of *jus cogens*, this proscription obligates the international community, including the United States. The norm cannot be validly derogated whether by treaty or objection of a State, persistent or not."[65]

63 Brownlie, Sixth Edition, pp. 486-487.

64 Al-Adsani v. United Kingdom, Judgment of 5 November 2001, 34 EHRR 273.

65 CIDH, Case of Michael Domingues v. United States, Report 62/02, Case 12, 285 of 22 October, 2001. Annual Report of the Inter-American Commission, 2002.

IX. The Progressive Development of International Human Rights Treaty Law

The practice of international human rights treaty bodies has evidence of ground-breaking progressive developments of international human rights treaty law. As examples, one can cite the development, through practice, of interim measures of protection, interpretative general comments, concluding observations following the examination of States reports, the shift from the expression of views on petitions to findings of violations by States parties, holdings that, for example, it would breach the International Covenant on Civil and Political Rights to extradite someone to a country where the persons would be in danger of inhumane treatment. One can also cite the growing practice of NGO involvement in treaty procedures, the practice of Chairpersons of human rights treaty bodies reporting to the UN General Assembly, and the holding of annual meetings of Chairpersons of human rights treaty bodies.

Conclusion

This chapter has brought out that international human rights treaty obligations must be supervised within a framework of the supremacy of international law, the existence of norms of *jus cogens* (some of which are reflected in human rights treaties), the human rights obligations under the UN Charter and the existence of norms of international customary law reflected in human rights and humanitarian law treaties.

We sought, while acknowledging the broader international law of treaties, (notably the Vienna Convention on the Law of Treaties) to ground the principles of international human rights law in the jurisprudence of the International Court of Justice and other international judicial and quasi-judicial organs, which is particularly relevant in assessing the nature of international human rights law. We also sought to recall a fundamental tenet of international law, namely the inherent supremacy of international obligations over contradictory national laws. It is the latter that must give way to the former. We then proceeded to offer a presentation of the relationship between international law and domestic law that moves beyond doctrines of monism and dualism to a doctrine of responsibility for the implementation of international obligations made in good faith. The recent universal affirmation of the Responsibility to Protect makes this inevitable.

We looked next at the essential nature of treaty obligations and recalled the obligations of nearly all Member States of the United Nations to uphold the human rights obligations they have undertaken by adhering to the UN Charter. We looked next at mandatory decisions of the Security Council, which are binding upon every Member State of the UN and, some would say, upon all States. We discussed the relationship between treaties and international customary law, noting that treaty provisions often do correspond to rules of international customary law or may give rise to them over time. We paid particular attention to the cardinal nature of *jus cogens* rights, which may never be rescinded or derogated from. We also saw that human rights treaty bodies sometimes contribute to the progressive development of international human rights treaty law, sometimes introducing new rules that even enter the body of international customary law. Against this background we proceed in the next chapter to discuss a core requirement of international human rights treaty law, namely the need for a national protection system in every State party.

Chapter Two

The Requirement of a National Protection System

Introduction

In this chapter we shall seek to define the scope of the national responsibility to protect human rights based on international and regional human rights treaties. We shall begin with some observations on the responsibility to protect, then consider the recommendations of human rights treaty bodies on the need for a national protection system, discuss the dimensions of a national protection system and then proceed to discuss the implications of international human rights law for a national protection system, the prevention of human rights violations, remedies for human rights violations, the role of the courts, the role of law enforcement agencies, the role of national human rights institutions, the role of human rights education, and the role of national human rights plans of action. These and some additional propositions on the concept of a national protection system will be summarized in the concluding part of the chapter.

I. The National Responsibility to Protect

It is a widely held view in the world today that national, regional, and international activities should be geared towards the respect, realization, and protection of internationally agreed norms of human rights. By human rights are meant all rights, civil and political as well as economic, social and cultural[66]. In the UN Millennium Declaration[67] leaders the world over committed themselves to values for the twenty-first century which give priority to respect for human rights and fundamental freedoms. The Millennium Development Goals[68] sought to halve the number of people living in poverty in the world by 2015

66 See, the Universal Declaration of Human Rights (1948). International Covenant on Civil and Political Rights (1966); International Covenant on Economic, Social and Cultural Rights (1966).

67 UN General Assembly resolution 55/2.

68 UN General Assembly resolution, Millennium Development Goals, 2000.

In a follow-up summit five years later, in 2005, world leaders committed themselves to the concept of the responsibility to protect and pledged to take action against genocide, ethnic cleansing, war crimes and crimes against humanity. The responsibility to protect, as presented by an independent international commission in December, 2001, entails the responsibility to prevent violations of human rights, the responsibility to react and remedy them, and the responsibility to rebuild societies devastated by conflict and gross violations of human rights.

Much attention has been given in international discussions to the implementation of the responsibility to protect at the international level, and the concept continues to be treated with caution by some countries, particularly developing ones, which fear intervention into their affairs by powerful countries. But far less attention has been given to the national responsibility to protect, where the debate needs to be. For it is at home, in each country, that we should seek to build up the protection of human rights.

Whatever debates take place over the international dimensions of the responsibility to protect, there can be no doubt that there is a national responsibility to protect that rests with every Government in the world. This is by virtue of their acceptance of international human rights obligations under the United Nations Charter and international human rights instruments, and their overwhelming affirmations of the universality of human rights in major world gatherings such as the Vienna World Conference on Human Rights, 1993, the Millennium Summit, and the Summit of World Leaders, 2005.

The primary responsibility for the prevention of violations of human rights lies with the national protection system of each State. As has been correctly noted, the first obligation of a Government is to respect and to ensure to all individuals within its territory and subject to its jurisdiction the rights recognized in international human rights treaties.[69] A state complies with the obligation to respect the recognized rights by not violating them. The duty to ensure imposes an affirmative duty on the state and calls for specific activities by the state to enable individuals to enjoy the recognized rights.[70]

The second obligation is for the state to take the necessary steps, in accordance with its constitutional processes and with the provisions of international human rights treaties it has ratified to adopt such legislative

69 N. Jayawickrama, The Judicial Application of Human Rights Law: National, Regional and International Jurisprudence. (2003), p. 46.

70 Ibid, p. 48. We discuss these concepts further in a later chapter.

or other measures as may be necessary to give effect to these rights and freedoms.[71] The third obligation is to ensure that any person whose rights or freedoms are violated shall have an effective remedy, notwithstanding that the violation has been committed by persons acting in an official capacity; to ensure that any person claiming such a remedy shall have his right thereto determined by competent judicial, administrative, or legislative authorities, or by the legal system, and to develop the possibilities of judicial review; and to ensure that the competent authorities shall enforce such remedies when granted.[72]

Interpreting article 13 of the European Convention on Human Rights, which requires that everyone whose rights are violated 'shall have an effective remedy before a national authority', the European Court of Human Rights has observed that the authority referred to may not necessarily be a judicial authority, but, if it is not, its powers and the guarantees which it affords are relevant in determining whether the remedy before it is effective. For a remedy to be 'effective', it is not sufficient that it be provided for by the constitution or by law or that it be formally recognized; it must be truly effective in establishing whether there has been a violation of a right and in providing redress.

Human rights treaty bodies have provided significant recommendations on different aspects of the national responsibility to protect human rights that we shall set out next.

II. The Recommendations of Human Rights Treaty Bodies

Human rights treaty bodies have stressed the importance of the national protection of human rights and of the role that national human rights institutions can play in this process.

A. Implementation at the National Level (General Comment No. 3 (1981) of the Human Rights Committee)

The Human Rights Committee, in General Comment No. 3 (1981), noted that article 2 of the International Covenant on Civil and Political Rights (ICCPR) generally left it to the States Parties concerned to choose their method of implementation in their territories within the framework set out in that article. The Committee recognized, in particular, that implementation does not depend solely on constitutional or legislative enact-

71 Ibid, p. 49.

72 Ibid, p. 49-50.

ments, which in themselves are not *per se* sufficient. The Committee drew the attention of States Parties to the fact that the obligation under the Covenant is not confined to the respect of human rights, but that States Parties have also undertaken to ensure the enjoyment of these rights to all individuals under their jurisdiction. This aspect called for specific activities by the States Parties to enable individuals to enjoy their rights. In principle this obligation relates to all rights set forth in the Covenant.

In a later General Comment, 31 (2004), which we looked at in the previous chapter, the Human Rights Committee recalled that Article 2, paragraph 3 of the Covenant required that States Parties make reparation to individuals whose Covenant rights have been violated. Without reparation to individuals whose Covenant rights have been violated, the obligation to provide an effective remedy, which is central to the efficacy of Article 2, paragraph 3, is not discharged. In addition to the explicit reparation required by articles 9, paragraph 5, and Article 14, paragraph 6, the Committee considers that the Covenant generally, entails appropriate compensation. The Committee noted that, where appropriate, reparation can involve restitution, rehabilitation and measures of satisfaction, such as public apologies, public memorials, guarantees of non-repetition and changes in relevant laws and practices, as well as bringing to justice the perpetrators of human rights violations.

In general, the purposes of the Covenant would be defeated without an obligation integral to article 2 to take measures to prevent the recurrence of a violation of the Covenant. Accordingly, it had been a frequent practice of the Committee, in its consideration of individual petitions, to include in its Views the need for measures, beyond a victim-specific remedy, to be taken to avoid recurrence of the type of violation in question. Such measures may require changes in the State Party's laws or practices.

B. Developing a Comprehensive National Strategy (General Comment No. 5 of the Committee on the Rights of the Child)

In General Comment No. 5 (2003), the Committee on the Rights of the Child dealt with general measures of implementation of the Convention on the Rights of the Child. Included in the General Comment was part A, Developing a comprehensive national strategy rooted in the Convention. The Committee pointed out that if Government as a whole and at all levels is to promote and respect the rights of the child, it needed to work on the basis of a unifying comprehensive and rights-based national strategy, rooted in the convention.[73] The Committee recommended the development of a comprehensive national strategy or national plan of action for children, built on the framework of the convention. The Committee expected States parties to take account of the recommendations in its concluding observations on their periodic reports when developing and/or reviewing their national strategies. If such a strategy is to be effective, it needed to relate to the situation of all children, and to all the rights in the Convention. It would need to be developed through a process of consultation, including with children and young people and those living and working with them.

To give the strategy authority, it would need to be endorsed at the highest level of government. Also, it needed to be linked to national development planning and included in national budgeting; otherwise, the strategy might remain marginalized outside key decision-making processes. Developing a national strategy was not a one-off task. Once drafted, the strategy would need to be widely disseminated throughout the Government and to the public. The strategy would need to include arrangements for monitoring and continuous review, for regular updating and for periodic reports to parliament and to the public.[74]

C. *The Role of National Human Rights Institutions in the Protection of Economic, Social and Cultural Rights (General Comment No. 10 (1998) of the CESCOR)*

The Committee on Economic, Social and Cultural Rights (CESCOR), in its General Comment No. 10, adopted on 3 December, 1998, considered it essential that national human rights institutions give full attention to economic, social and cultural rights in all of the relevant activities of these institutions. It drew up the following indicative list of the types of activities that could be, and in some instances already had been, undertaken by national institutions in relation to these rights:

(a) the promotion of educational and informational programmes designed to enhance awareness and understanding of economic, social and cultural rights both within the population at large and among particular groups such as the public service, the judiciary, the private sector and the labour movement;

(b) the scrutinising of existing laws and administrative acts as well as draft bills and other proposals to ensure that they are consistent

73 HRI/GEN/1Rev.9, pp. 428-430.

74 Ibid, p. 429.

with the requirements of the Covenant on Economic, Social and Cultural Rights;

(c) providing technical advice, or undertaking surveys in relation to economic, social and cultural rights, including when requested by the public authorities or other appropriate agencies;
(d) the identification of national level benchmarks against which the realization of Covenant obligations can be measured;
(e) conducting research and inquiries designed to ascertain the extent to which particular economic, social and cultural rights are being realised, either within the State as a whole or in areas or in relation to communities of particular vulnerability;
(f) examining complaints alleging violations of applicable economic, social and cultural rights standards within the State.

The Committee called upon States Parties to ensure that the mandates accorded to all national human rights institutions included appropriate attention to economic, social and cultural rights and requested States Parties to include details both of the mandates and the principal relevant activities of such institutions in their reports submitted to the Committee.

D. CERD General Recommendation XVII (1993) on the Establishment of National Institutions to Facilitate the Implementation of the Convention

The Committee on the Elimination of Racial Discrimination (CERD), convinced of the need to encourage further the establishment of national institutions to facilitate the implementation of the Convention, recommended that States Parties establish national commissions or other appropriate bodies, taking into account the Paris Principles, to serve, *inter alia*, the following purposes:

(a) To promote respect for the enjoyment of human rights without any discrimination, as expressly set out in article 5 of the ICERD;
(b) To review government policy towards protection against racial discrimination;
(c) To monitor legislative compliance with the provisions of the Convention;
(d) To educate the public about the obligations of States Parties under the Convention;
(e) To assist the Government in the preparation of reports submitted to the Committee.

CERD further recommended that, where such commissions had already been established, they should be associated with the preparation of reports and possibly included in government delegations in order to intensify the dialogue between the Committee and the State Party concerned.

E. *CEDAW General Recommendation 6 (1988) on Effective National Machinery and Publicity*

The Committee on the Elimination of Discrimination Against Women (CEDAW) has recommended that States Parties:

1. Establish and/or strengthen effective national machinery, institutions and procedures, at a high level of Government, and with adequate resources, commitment and authority to:
   (a) Advise on the impact on women of all government policies;
   (b) Monitor the situation of women comprehensively;
   (c) Help formulate new policies and effectively carry out strategies and measures to eliminate discrimination;
2. Take appropriate steps to ensure the dissemination of the Convention, the reports of the States Parties under article 18 and the reports of the Committee in the language of the States concerned.

F. *Other Treaty Bodies*

As we shall see in different parts of this work, other treaty bodies have made detailed recommendations for national preventive and protective arrangements, particularly for the prevention of genocide and torture.

The foregoing recommendations of human rights treaty bodies were tailored to the requirements of their respective treaty. It is necessary to go beyond them and to consider more comprehensively the concept of a national protection system, which we do in the following section.

I. The Concept of a National Protection System

The protection of human rights should take place in one's country, where one lives and comes face to face with authority or power. Every country should have in place an adequate and effective national protection system. This is a basic duty of governments, which exist to advance and protect the dignity and rights of their people. It was in this sense that Article 21 of the Universal Declaration of Human Rights affirmed that the will of the people shall be the basis of the authority of government. This will, shall be expressed in periodic and genuine elections which shall be by universal and equal suffrage and shall be held by secret vote or by equivalent free voting procedures. Article 25 of the International Covenant on Civil and Political Rights states that everyone shall have the right and the opportunity, without any of the distinctions mentioned in article 2 and without unreasonable restrictions (a) to take part in the conduct of public affairs, directly or through freely chosen representatives; (b) to vote and to be elected at genuine periodic elections which shall be by universal and equal suffrage and shall be held by secret ballot, guaranteeing the free expression of the will of the electors; (c) to have access, on general terms of equality, to public service in his or her country.

The concept of the national protection system is one of the most strategic for the universal realization of human rights. It is thus understandable that the Summit of world leaders, meeting on the occasion of the sixtieth anniversary of the United Nations in 2005, highlighted the right to be protected and that Secretary-General Kofi Annan, in his last report on conflict prevention, emphasized the responsibility to prevent gross violations of human rights.[75]

A national protection system has the following key dimensions that we shall discuss below: constitutional, legislative, judicial, institutional, educational, and preventive. In addition, it requires an independent and efficient judiciary and law enforcement systems, and human rights education. National human rights plans of action can also help reinforce a national protection system.

Constitutional Dimension

The constitutional structure of a country is a matter for the sovereign choice of its people. However, three issues require particular attention and scrutiny from the perspectives of international human rights law: first its fundamental human rights guarantees; second, its judicial institutions; and third, its national institutions for the protection of human rights.

Fundamental human rights guarantees in the constitution or the bill of rights, if there is one, should not be less but may be more than what is provided for in international human rights law. Each country should be able to show that it has done two things: first, that it has methodically made a comparison between the provisions of its fundamental human rights guarantees and those in the principal international human rights instruments; second that rights guaranteed in international customary law, particularly norms of *jus cogens*, are among its constitutional human rights guarantees.

75 A/61/891, 18 July, 1961.

The Second Restatement of the Foreign Relations Laws of the USA provides a good summary of rights that are guaranteed in international law:

> "A state is obliged to respect the human rights of persons subject to its jurisdiction that it has (a) undertaken to respect by international agreements;(b) that states generally are bound to respect as a matter of customary international law; and (c) that it is required to respect under general principles of law common to the major legal systems of the world"[76]

> "A state violates international customary law if, as a matter of state policy, it practices, encourages, or condones:
> (a) Genocide.
> (b) slavery or slave trade.
> (c) the murder or causing the disappearance of individuals.
> (d) torture or other cruel, inhuman or degrading treatment or punishment.
> (e) prolonged arbitrary detention
> (f) systematic racial discrimination, or
> (g) a consistent pattern of gross violations of internationally recognized human rights."[77]

Legislative Dimension

International law gives a discretion to States whether they would make treaties they have accepted to be bound by directly applicable in their legal systems or whether they would reflect the provisions of those treaties in national legislation. Whichever route a country chooses, there is an obligation to make sure that its national laws correspond to its legal commitments under international human rights law or international human rights treaties. National parliaments should exercise oversight over whether this obligation has been met and, where action is required, see to it that legislative changes or enactments are done. The human rights treaty bodies operating under particular international conventions often make suggestions for legislative updating and national parliaments should require regular reports from the Executive about the recommendations of the human rights treaty bodies. There is role for parliamentary oversight over Governmental compliance with international human

76 Article 701.

77 Article 702.

rights obligations. Each parliament should ideally establish a human rights committee to perform this role.

Judicial Dimension

The judicial dimension requires that courts be independent and effective. There are United Nations declarations and statements on the meaning of judicial independence and effectiveness, which we shall discuss later in this chapter. As already indicated, international law leaves it to the choice of a Government whether it makes a treaty directly applicable in its legal system or whether it enacts legislation incorporating the obligations under the treaty. It would be our submission, however, that international human rights norms of *jus cogens* status, and human rights norms that have the status of international customary law should be directly applicable in national courts.

International law makes it obligatory that each State provide adequate guarantees against human rights violations. This responsibility falls, in the first place, primarily upon the national judiciary. In the event that there is a failure to protect, there may be remedies under international law. The Second American Restatement, which we cited earlier, summarized these remedies as follows:

> "(1) A state party to an international human rights agreement has, as against any other state party violating the agreement, the remedies generally available for violation of an international agreement, as well as any special remedies provided by the agreement;
> (2) Any state may pursue international remedies against any other state for a violation of the customary international law of human rights;
> (3) An individual victim of a violation of human rights agreement may pursue any remedy provided by that agreement or by other applicable international agreements."[78]

It is of great importance that judges and legal practitioners be provided with access to the key decisions of international human rights bodies in local languages so that they may be aware of them and may draw upon them. This is a task with which international human rights organizations and NGOs may assist. But it would be important also that national ministries of justice, or their equivalent, pay attention to this matter so that judges may have access to the latest human rights precedents and reasoning.

78 Aticle 703.

Institutional Dimension

Experience has shown that, in addition to the courts, institutions such as national human rights commissions, national human rights commissioners or ombudspersons can be quite helpful in advancing and protecting human rights.[79] International law does not make such institutions mandatory but, as a matter of policy, a country should periodically assess its institutional arrangements, or lack thereof to see whether the establishment of national human rights bodies could be helpful for the protection of human rights.

The Paris Principles, which we shall discuss later, provided that national human rights institutions could perform, among others, key tasks such as: seeking an amicable settlement of human rights grievances through conciliation, binding decision or other means; informing the complainant of his or her rights and of available means of redress, and promoting access to such redress; hearing complaints or referring them to a competent authority; and making recommendations to the competent authorities, including proposals for amendment of laws, regulations, or administrative practices that obstruct the free exercise of rights.

Monitoring Dimension

The responsibility to protect and to prevent demands that every country monitor itself to detect situations of distress and to address them well before they erupt into violations of human rights or conflict.[80] This calls for independent bodies that will systematically watch out for such distress situations and draw attention to them. A national human rights commission could be given the mandate to do this. In multi-ethnic countries special arrangements may need to be devised. But the concept of self-monitoring is a vital part of a national protection system.

A national protection system should provide for adequate and effective remedies to prevent violations of human rights and to provide redress in cases of breach. The absence of a remedy available to test an arguable claim for breach amounts to a violation of human rights [81] The right to

79 See, generally, B.G. Ramcharan (Ed.), The Protection Roles of National Human Rights Institutions. Martinus Nijhoff, 2005. J.A. Mertus, Human Rights Matters. Local Politics and National Human Rights Institutions. Stanford, Stanford University Press, 2009.

80 See, generally, B.G. Ramcharan, Preventive Human Rights Strategies. London, Routledge, 2009.

81 See the Annual Report of the Human Rights Committee, 2001, Faure v. Australia.

an effective remedy may, in certain circumstances, require Governments to provide for, and implement, provisional or interim measures to avoid continuing violations and to endeavour to repair at the earliest possible opportunity any harm that may have been done.[82]

A national protection system should be particularly attentive to the risks of genocide, ethnic cleansing, crimes against humanity and war crimes and should provide effective guarantees against them. As the Human Rights Committee stated in its General Comment 6/16 of 27 July, 1982, States have the supreme duty to prevent wars, acts of genocide, and other acts of mass violence causing arbitrary loss of life. A national protection system should provide for a system of regular visits by national, regional or international bodies to all places of detention.

In the event of a violation of human rights the national protection system must provide for measures, beyond a victim-specific remedy, to be taken to avoid recurrence of the type of violation in question. Such measures may require changes in the State's laws or practices.[83]

A national protection system should provide for investigations of gross violations of human rights and for justice to the victims. A national protection system should provide for safeguards against deportation or extradition to a state where the deportee/extraditee may face serious risks of torture or arbitrary execution. A national protection system should be particularly protective of human rights defenders.

A national human rights system should give priority to the prevention of violations of human rights, to which we turn next.

II. The Prevention of Human Rights Violations

The national responsibility to protect entails prevention, reaction, remedies, and measures to prevent recurrence. National legal systems provide for preventive remedies such as judicial review, quashing orders (certiorari), mandatory orders (mandamus), prohibiting orders (prohibition), Habeas corpus, Statutory mechanisms of challenge, injunctions.[84] Section 6 of the Hong Kong Bill of Rights, for example, provides that a court or tribunal may grant such remedy or relief in respect of such a breach, violation, *or threatened violation* as it has power to make or grant and as it considers appropriate and just in the circumstances.

82 See General Comment 31 of the Human Rights Committee.

83 See General Comment 31 of the Human Rights Committee.

84 See, e.g. Clive Lewis, Judicial Remedies in Public Law. London, Sweet and Maxwell (2008)

The national responsibility to protect requires that Governments fulfil their obligations under international human rights treaties with preventive requirements such as: the Convention for the Prevention and Punishment of Genocide; the Convention against Torture; the Optional Protocol to the Convention against Torture (OPCAT),[85] which provides for regular visits by national bodies and by the Subcommittee for the Prevention of Torture to prisons and places of detention. There are also preventive obligations under other international human rights norms and jurisprudence that we discuss next.

A. *Preventive Protection of the Right to Life*

Article 6 of the International Covenant on Civil and Political Rights (1966) protects the right to life which the Human Rights Committee, the monitoring body established under the Covenant, has deemed 'the supreme right from which no derogation is permitted even in time of public emergency which threatens the life of the nation (article 4)'.[86] The Committee considers that

> "States have the supreme duty to prevent wars, acts of genocide and other acts of mass violence causing arbitrary loss of life. Every effort they make to avert the danger of war, especially thermo-nuclear war, and to strengthen international peace and security would constitute the most important condition and guarantee for the safeguarding of the right to life. In this respect the Committee noted, in particular, a connection between article 6 and article 20, which states that the law shall prohibit any propaganda for war or incitement to violence."[87]

The Committee continued:

> "The protection against arbitrary deprivation of life which is explicitly required by the third sentence of article 6(1) is of paramount importance. The

85 The European Convention for the Prevention of Torture also provides for a system of visits.

86 General Comment 6/16 of 27 July, 1982. Reproduced in M. Nowak, The International Covenant on Civil and Political Rights. A Commentary, Engel Publishers, 2006, p. 1092.

87 General Comment 6/16 of 27 July, 1982. Reproduced in M. Nowak, The International Covenant on Civil and Political Rights. A Commentary, Engel Publishers, 2006, p. 1092.

Committee considers that States parties should take measures not only to prevent and punish deprivation of life by criminal acts, but also to prevent arbitrary killing by their own security forces. The deprivation of life by the authorities of the State is a matter of the utmost gravity. Therefore, the law must strictly control and limit the circumstances in which a person may be deprived of his life by such authorities.

States parties should also take specific and effective measures to prevent the disappearance of individuals, something which unfortunately has become all too frequent and leads too often to arbitrary deprivation of life. Furthermore, States should establish effective facilities and procedures to investigate thoroughly cases of missing and disappeared persons in circumstances which may involve a violation of the right to life."[88]

B. Preventive Dimensions of the Right to an Effective Remedy

Professor Manfred Nowak has noted that whether a remedy is effective may ultimately be determined only on the basis of concrete cases, taking into consideration all relevant circumstances. In some cases, the formal chain of judicial appeals is the only possible effective protection; in others, informal, preventive measures (e.g., against the application of torture or against arbitrary executions) are much more effective than a subsequent determination by a constitutional court. On the other hand, when judicial case law functions well and is adhered to by administrative organs, it may in the long term be far more effective in preventing similar violations in the future than, e.g. large-scale efforts to train civil servants.[89]

Professor Nowak has raised the question whether the right to an effective domestic remedy requires that a violation of a treaty provision has occurred, albeit not yet officially determined, and at what point it can be said that a violation has taken place. Does violation of Article 13 of the ICCPR, for example, arise upon deportation, with detention prior to this, or when a residency prohibition is enacted? Is personal liberty violated with imprisonment or upon sentencing to incarceration? Is the result different in the case of the death penalty because it is irreversible, whereas a prison sentence is reversible.[90]

Does the right to an effective remedy, ensured by Art. 2, refer, as suggested by the formulation of para. 3(a), only to a repressive remedy after

88 Ibid.

89 Novak, op. cit., p. 65.

90 Ibid, p. 67.

violation of a substantive right has occurred, or are States parties also required to take preventive measures? The Human Rights Committee dealt extensively with this problem in C.F. et al v. Canada (No. 113/198). In implementing Art. 25 of the Covenant, the Quebec Election Act had been amended in 1979 to recognize the right of inmates to vote. However, the implementation of the specific voting procedures was made subject to an administrative agreement, which the Solicitor General initially refused to sign for federal inmates. As a result, three inmates filed a request for a temporary injunction with the Federal court of first instance to force the Solicitor-General to conclude the administrative agreement in time for the provincial elections, but this was denied.

The issue subsequently came before the Human Rights Committee. On the issue whether Article 2 afforded preventive remedies and whether a declaratory judgment in favour of the authors following the election would have been an effective remedy within the meaning of Article 2(3) of the Covenant and Art. 5(2) of the Optional Protocol, the Committee stated:

> "With respect to article 5, paragraph 2(b) of the Optional Protocol the Committee observed that, although the authors might not have been able to obtain a declaratory judgment before the elections of 13 April, 1981, a subsequent judgment could nevertheless in principle have been an effective remedy in the meaning contemplated by article 2,paragraph 3 of the Covenant and article 5 paragraph 2(b) of the Optional Protocol. The Covenant provides that a remedy shall be granted whenever a violation of one of the rights guaranteed by it has occurred; consequently, it does not generally prescribe preventive protection, but confines itself to requiring effective redress *ex post facto*."

Professor Nowak commented critically on this finding:

> "In other words, the Committee reached the problematic conclusion from Article 2(3)(a) that this provision is limited to *repressive remedies* and 'generally' does not require preventive protection. ... The reasoning behind this decision is so unjustifiably broad as to miss the purpose of providing individuals with effective remedies. Would the Committee have decided differently if – instead of the right to vote – a deportation, the right to personal liberty, the prohibition of torture or even the right to life had been affected? ..."

Novak noted, however, that following its General Comment on the right to life, the Committee subsequently made it known in *Herrera Rubio v. Colombia* that as regards this right, Art. 2 also required preventive measures, such as deterring the disappearance of persons.

It may also be recalled that in its General Comment 31, which we discussed in the previous chapter, the Committee stated the following:

> "The right to an effective remedy may in certain circumstances require States Parties to provide for and implement provisional or interim measures to avoid continuing violations and to endeavour to repair at the earliest possible opportunity any harm that may have been caused by such violations."

C. *Interim Measures of Protection*

Interim measures of protection are a valuable method of preventive protection practiced by international judicial and human rights bodies, including the International Court of Justice, the European Court of Human Rights, the Inter-American Court of Human Rights, the UN Human Rights Committee, the United Nations Committee against Torture, and the Inter-American Commission on Human Rights. In the words of one scholar,

> "An author of interim measures may require that the State take positive action, such as providing protection for human rights activists or journalists, or it may call upon the State to refrain from taking action, such as not extraditing a person or delaying the execution of prisoners until their cases have been resolved before the international body. The purpose of interim measures in international human rights law is most often to protect the persons involved in a case from urgent danger of grave and irreparable injury."

The author continues that, in general, many States have accepted the decisions of international courts that interim measures are binding on the States that are parties to the applicable treaties. However some States have not. The author contends that interim measures are implied in the constituent documents that provide the right of individual petition and must be considered to be binding on States that are parties.[91]

91 J.M. Pasqualucci, Interim Measure in International Human Rights: Evolution and Harmonization, Vanderbilt Journal of International Law, January, 2005.

D. *Deportation and Extradition to Countries Where There is Risk of Serious Violation of Human Rights: Preventive Protection*

The jurisprudence of international and regional human rights bodies provides for preventive protection in the event that a potential deportee/extradite would be liable to suffer inhuman treatment, for example political persecution in the country to which they are to be sent, or the death penalty.[92] In the Soering case, decided by the European Court of Human Rights, Jens Soering, a German national, was 18 when he and his girl friend were alleged to have killed her parents in Virginia in the USA. Soering was subsequently arrested in England and his extradition was sought to the United States. The State of Virginia had the death penalty for murder, and it was usual for prisoners to spend between six and eight years on death row before being executed. Were he to be extradited, Soering might face the death penalty and death row phenomenon. An extradition order obtained in the English courts was put into suspense pending determination of Soering's application to the then European Commission on Human Rights.

The case eventually reached the European Court of Human Rights, which apparently took into consideration that Soering could have been extradited to Germany, his country of nationality. The Court held:

> "(H)aving regard to the very long period of time spent on death row in such extreme conditions, with the ever present and mounting anguish of awaiting execution of the death penalty, and to the personal circumstances of the applicant, especially his age and mental state at the time of the offence, the applicant's extradition to the United States would expose him to a real risk of treatment going beyond the threshold set by Article 3. A further consideration of relevance is that in the particular instance the legitimate purpose of extradition could be achieved by another means which would not involve suffering of such exceptional intensity or duration."[93]

The Court therefore held that the UK Secretary of State's decision to extradite Soering to the United States would, if implemented, give rise to a breach of Article 3 of the European Convention on Human Rights.

---

92 See F. Jacobs, et al., The European Convention on Human Rights, Fourth Edition, Oxford, Oxford University Press, 2006, p. 101.

93 See F. Jacobs, et al., The European Convention on Human Rights, op. cit., p. 103.

With regard to prevention strategies in the future, it would be advisable that every country, once every five years or so, commission an analysis of threats of gross violations of human rights with a view to taking preventive action. Such an analysis could be done by the national human rights commission, where it exists. National human rights commissions in existence should include a threat assessment in their annual reports. Poverty alleviation strategies should, in the future, be built on preventive approaches, with the accent being on preventing poverty where this could be done using existing resources within a country. At the end of the day, this is a task of efficient governance.

With new threats and challenges facing the world, national prevention systems should also have in view the human rights dimensions of issues such as

- Climate change
- Water shortage
- Pandemics
- Mass migration

It is also important for national prevention systems to be vigilant in respect of

- Violence against women, trafficking
- Breaches of human rights and humanitarian law during armed conflicts.
- Gross violations of human rights.[94]

III. Remedies for Human Rights Violations

The World Conference on Human Rights (1993) expressed grave concern about continuing human rights violations in all parts of the world in disregard of standards as contained in international human rights instruments and international humanitarian law and about the lack of sufficient and effective remedies for the victims."[95] This situation, unfortunately, has not changed.

Remedies for violations of human rights may be found in the areas of constitutional law, public law, criminal law and the law of torts. The constitution may provide for remedies for breach and, in Commonwealth jurisdictions, the courts will review an exercise of power to ensure that

94 See, generally, B.G. Ramcharan, Preventive Human Rights Strategies. Routledge, 2010.

95 Vienna Declaration (1993), para. 29.

a public body has not made an error of law; has considered all relevant factors, and not taken into account any irrelevant factors; has acted for a purpose expressly or impliedly authorized by statute; has not acted in a way that is so unreasonable that no reasonable public body would act in that way; and that the public body has observed statutory procedural requirements and the common law principles of natural justice or procedural fairness. These grounds were summarized by Lord Diplock as illegality, irrationality, and procedural impropriety.[96]

As indicated earlier, judicial review may take the form of a quashing order, a mandatory order, a prohibiting order, a declaration or injunction, damages, restitution, or recovery of money. The prerogative writ of habeas corpus is still available in Commonwealth countries as a means of challenging the legality of the detention of an individual by a public body. Furthermore, Statute may provide a means by which the legality of decisions of public bodies may be challenged in the courts.[97] There may also be remedies in tort for human rights abuses.[98]

We discuss remedies more fully later in the chapter on redress.

IV. The Role of the Courts and of Law Enforcement Agencies

We have already alluded to the foundation importance of the role of the courts and of law enforcement agencies. In this section we shall touch on the essentiality of these institutions upholding and conforming to international human rights standards. The Basic Principles on the Independence of the Judiciary, endorsed by the United Nations General Assembly on 13 December, 1985,[99] called for the independence of the judiciary to be guaranteed by the State and enshrined in the Constitution or law of the country. It is the duty of governmental and other institutions to respect and observe the independence of the judiciary. The judiciary, for its part, shall decide matters before them impartially, on the basis of the facts and in accordance with the law, without any restrictions, improper influences, inducements, pressures, threats or interferences, direct or indirect, from any quarter or for any reason.

96 See Clive Lewis, Judicial Remedies in Public Law. London, Sweet and Maxwell, 2008.

97 Ibid.

98 See on this, G.P. Fletcher, Tort Liability for Human Rights Abuses. Oxford, Hart Publishing, 2008.

99 UN General Assembly resolution 40/32.

The judiciary shall have jurisdiction over all issues of a judicial nature and shall have exclusive authority to decide whether an issue submitted for its decision is within its competence as defined by law. There shall not be any inappropriate or unwarranted interference with the judicial process, nor shall judicial decisions by the courts be subject to revision. Everyone shall have the right to be tried by ordinary courts or tribunals using established legal procedures. Tribunals that do not use the duly established procedures of the legal process shall not be created to displace the jurisdiction belonging to the ordinary courts of judicial tribunals.

The principle of the independence of the judiciary entitles and requires the judiciary to ensure that judicial proceedings are conducted fairly and that the rights of the parties are respected. It is the duty of each Government to provide adequate resources to enable the judiciary to properly perform its functions.

The Code of Conduct for Law Enforcement Officials adopted by the UN General Assembly on 17 December, 1979[100] states that law enforcement officials shall at all times fulfil the duty imposed upon them by law, by serving the community and by protecting all persons against illegal acts, consistent with the high degree of responsibility required by their profession. In the performance of their duty, they shall respect and protect human rights and maintain and uphold the human rights of all persons. They may use force only when strictly necessary and to the extent required for the performance of their duty. Matters of a confidential nature in the possession of law enforcement officials shall be kept confidential, unless the performance of duty or the needs of justice strictly require otherwise.

No law enforcement official may inflict, instigate or tolerate any act of torture or other cruel, inhuman or degrading treatment or punishment, nor may any law enforcement official invoke superior orders or exceptional circumstances such as a state of war or a threat of war, a threat to national security, internal political instability or any other public emergency as a justification of torture or other cruel, inhuman or degrading treatment or punishment.

Law enforcement officials shall ensure the full protection of the health of persons in their custody and, in particular, shall take immediate action to secure medical attention whenever required. Law enforcement officials shall not commit any act of corruption. They shall also rigorously oppose and combat all such acts. Law enforcement officials shall respect the law and the principles in the Code of Conduct. They shall also, to the

100 UN General Assembly resolution 34/169.

best of their ability, prevent and rigorously oppose any violations of them. Law enforcement officials who have reasons to believe that a violation of the Code has occurred or is about to occur shall report the matter to their superior authorities and, where necessary, to other appropriate authorities or organs vested with reviewing or remedial power.

It is sad to admit that the Basic Principles on the Independence of the Judiciary and the Code of Conduct for Law Enforcement Officials are violated in numerous countries. That, however, does not diminish their validity, and it is precisely the challenge of all national protection systems to strive to live up to them.

V. The Role of National Human Rights Institutions

Even before the adoption of the Universal Declaration of Human Rights, the UN Economic and Social Council, in 1946, had recognized that national implementation arrangements and human rights information and education would be essential to take forward the task of implementing the provisions of the Declaration universally. The Council invited Member States to consider the desirability of establishing information groups or local human rights committees to collaborate with them in furthering the work of the Commission on Human Rights. The former Commission on Human Rights, early on, highlighted these two aspects and decided to give them particular attention.

The attention given to both subjects, however, would be spasmodic in subsequent years. The Commission did call for reports from the Secretariat on the topic and also mandated the organization of world-wide seminars on the role of national institutions in the promotion and protection of human rights. A UN Seminar on National Institutions for the Promotion and Protection of Human Rights, held in 1978, put forward a set of helpful guidelines for the functioning of national human rights institutions. Those guidelines were further built upon in the Principles relating to the Status of National Institutions (The Paris Principles), which were endorsed by the General Assembly in its resolution 48/134 of 20 December, 1993.

The Paris Principles called for national institutions to have responsibilities such as: submitting recommendations, proposals and reports on matters relating to human rights to the Government, Parliament, or other competent bodies; promoting conformity of national laws and practices with international human rights standards; encouraging ratification and implementation of international standards; contributing to the reporting procedure under international instruments; assisting in formulating and executing human rights teaching and research programmes and increasing public awareness of human rights through information and education; and cooperating with the United Nations, regional institutions and national institutions of other countries.

In 2003, the then High Commissioner for Human Rights wrote to all Governments inviting them to provide concise summaries of their national protection systems under the following headings: 1. In what ways are the provisions of the principal human rights instruments and treaties reflected in the constitution of the country? 2 Is there an oversight process on the reflection of international human rights norms in national legislation? 3. What is the experience of the judiciary in drawing upon the provisions of international human rights norms when considering cases before them? 4. Are there any specific arrangements to promote human rights education in the country? 5. What specialized national human rights institutions are in existence and which of their good practices can be highlighted? 6. Are there arrangements to detect and anticipate threats to human rights of groups at risk?

A report that the Office of High Commissioner submitted to the Commission in 2004 summarized the replies of some three dozen countries. It showed that each country had positive experiences to report but that few of them had previously thought methodically about the six questions in their policy and governmental frameworks. The aim of the exercise was precisely to encourage each country to consider the six questions as a policy framework and, eventually, to publish a world report on the national protection systems of each country.[101]

As part of his reform programme, and as suggested by the Office of High Commissioner, Secretary-General Kofi Annan had called on the different parts of the United Nations system to concert their efforts to support the efforts of Governments to develop, or enhance, their national protection systems. Pursuant to this decision, a programme of cooperation was worked out, which is still continuing, to help support the enhancement of national protection systems. The aim of the process was two-fold: to respond positively to requests by Governments for support in strengthening their national protection systems; and to follow the recommendations of the human rights treaty bodies and the human rights special procedures and to see discreetly in what areas a government

101 UN doc. E/CN.4/2004/12/Add. 1: Progress report on support for the strengthening of national human rights protection systems. See, generally, B.G. Ramcharan (Ed.), The Protection Roles of National Human Rights Institutions. Martinus Nijhoff, 2005.

might be in need of assistance. A national protection system, as advanced by the Office of High Commissioner and by the Secretary-General, has six dimensions, that we discussed earlier in this chapter.

National human rights institutions are an essential component of a national protection system. Each National Commission could map and analyze the human rights history of the country and the contemporary and future challenges of protection. Each National Commission could do a study on the state of economic, social and cultural rights and identify issues and situations of concern. National Commissions could do a study of situations where there is evidence of a consistent pattern of gross violations of human rights. National Commissions could do a study of population groups at risk. National Commissions could offer policy recommendations for the advancement of women's rights. National Commissions could offer policy recommendations for the advancement of children's rights. National Commissions could maintain, as a principal focus, policies and strategies for the prevention of gross violations of human rights. National Commissions could encourage and support the work of judges in the protection of human rights. National Commissions could disseminate the core international human rights norms and jurisprudence to judges and magistrates. National Commissions could develop a policy for the spread of human rights education in schools and higher institutions of learning. National Commissions could enhance their cooperation with protection partners.

The Ninth International Conference of National Institutions for the Promotion and Protection of Human Rights held in Nairobi from 21-24 October, 2009, adopted the Nairobi Declaration in which they underlined that the State has the primary responsibility to protect, promote and respect human rights and ensure that the administration of justice is in full compliance with both international and domestic obligations. They felt that National Institutions can support Governments in the application of international standards and follow-up.

They considered that the Rule of law and administration of justice were of fundamental importance and saw an important role for the judiciary in applying human rights norms and in the development of a strong national system for human rights protection. They thought that National Institutions can help in ensuring an effective administration of justice, in particular with regard to access to justice. The rule of law should be based on a Constitution and national legislation, consistent with international standards and principles.

They considered that NHRIs should play an oversight role over law enforcement agencies and seek to protect the rights of prisoners and detainees. They felt that National institutions should monitor their Government's obligation to respect, protect and fulfil the rights of all people in detention, especially vulnerable or marginalized groups, and support their reintegration within society. NHRIs should strive to strengthen the correctional system and its personnel. They supported the role of NHRIs in receiving cases of human rights violations and assisting victims. They also supported the role of NHRIs in seeking informal legal redress mechanisms through conciliation or through binding decisions.

They saw for themselves a role in publicizing the findings of treaty bodies and human rights rapporteurs of the UN Human Rights Council. They also saw a role in promoting incorporation of international norms into national law. Furthermore they saw a role in providing recommendations to strengthen the legal system and judiciary and in promoting adherence and compliance of the judiciary with international human rights norms, including through amicus briefs and legal education.

They thought they could help in encouraging and supporting the establishment of legal aid centres.

The Preventive Role of National Human Rights Institutions

For the most part, national human rights institutions remain fledgling institutions, especially in developing countries. Their protection role is still largely undeveloped.[102] Their explicit prevention role is even thinner. However, as with all human rights activities, one can always claim that promotional work is meant to serve the cause of prevention, in the here and now and in the future.

One can say that national human rights institutions nowadays contribute to prevention in one or more of the following ways:

- Undertaking surveys and studies of issues and making recommendations on them.
- Drawing attention to problems in their annual reports or in periodic statements they might issue.
- Undertaking historical analysis of the experience of a country with regard to human rights and drawing lessons from the analysis.
- Undertaking visits to prisons and places of detention.
- Calling for the enactment of laws to correct problems in the society.
- Engaging in good offices activities with governments and law enforcement agencies.

102 See on this, B.G. Ramcharan (Ed.), The Protection Roles of National Human Rights Institutions. Martinus Nijhoff, 2005.

However, much more preventive work is required inside all countries. National institutions should undertake regular risk analysis from the perspectives of human rights. The following checklist of issues could be kept in mind when undertaking risk assessment through human rights lens:

a. What is the ethnic composition of the country? Is there a minority population? Is there an indigenous population? Is there a migrant population?
b. Is there a unifying vision of the country?
c. What is the state of governance? Is there a functioning democracy?
d. What is the state of the rule of law and the courts?
e. Is there an effective national protecting system?
f. Are there major grievances within the population?
g. Is there an internal system of early warming and alert to head off grievances?
h. Is there a *de jure* or *de facto* state of emergency?
i. Are there gross violations of human rights?
j. What is the state of human rights of women?
k. Is there a problem of human trafficking in the country?
l. What is the state of respect for the rights of the child?
m. What is the state of the freedoms of expression, religion or belief?
n. What is the national security doctrine of the state?
o. What are the UN human rights treaty bodies and the UN human rights investigators reporting about the country?
p. What are the leading international human rights organizations reporting about the country?
q. Are there reputable human rights NGOs in the country and what are they reporting?
r. Are perpetrators of gross violations of human rights being brought to justice?

VI. The Role of Human Rights Education in a National Protection System

Human rights education in primary and secondary schools, in universities and other higher institutions of learning, and in professional education of law enforcement personnel can help instil respect for a culture of human rights in each country and lay the foundations for societies aspiring to, and living up to international, regional, and national human rights norms. While there are courses on human rights in some law schools and other university departments, there is still a sad lack of human rights education in all countries. It is vital to remedy this situation.

The UN Human Rights Council has initiated the process of drafting a declaration on human rights education. One idea behind this project is to work towards the conclusion of an international convention on human rights education.[103] Such a process would have in mind some simple objectives: every teacher at the primary, secondary or university level should be provided with a teaching manual, in local languages, so that she or he might discuss the core human rights ideas with students and thereby impart the values of the Universal Declaration. This may appear a modest objective. But it is not. Human rights education is very infrequent world-wide. Countries struggling with economic and social problems do not normally think of allocating the resources needed to provide human rights teaching aids to instructors. A convention on human rights education would eventually help make the case for priority in the allocation of resources. World-wide human rights education will help spread a universal culture of human rights. It will help shape tomorrow's leaders by instilling in them an understanding that the purpose of government is to strive for the realization of the economic, social and cultural rights of their people while respecting, protecting and ensuring their civil and political rights. Human rights education thus has a powerful strategic objective. Another strategic objective must be to push more and more for national human rights action plans in all countries.

VII. The Role of National Human Rights Plans of Actions in National Protection Systems

The Vienna World Conference on Human Rights recommended that each State consider the desirability of drawing up a national action plan identifying steps whereby that State would improve the promotion and protection of human rights. According to a UN Handbook on National Human Rights Plans of Action[104], the fundamental purpose of a national

103 This author, when serving in the position of UN High Commissioner for Human Rights, called for a Convention on Human Rights Education in his address at the opening of the then Commission on Human Rights in 2004. He has subsequently supported the proposal for a declaration on human rights education.

104 Office of the High Commissioner for Human Rights, Professional Training Series No. 10, Handbook on National Human Rights Plans of Action. United Nations. New York and Geneva, 29 August, 2002.

human rights action plan is to improve the promotion and protection of human rights in a particular country. It does this by placing human rights improvements in the context of public policy, so that governments and communities can endorse human rights improvements as practical goals, devise programmes to ensure the achievement of these goals, engage all relevant sectors of government and society, and allocate sufficient resources. The benefits of this approach, the Handbook continues, include the following:

a. A national action plan should stimulate a more comprehensive assessment of needs in the country concerned and, by making plans explicit both to the government itself and to the general public, can generate a commitment to achievement that would otherwise not exist;
b. National action plans are practical in orientation: they set achievable targets and propose realistic activities aimed at reaching these objectives;
c. National action plans can be a tool of sound public administration and governance leading to a stronger rule of law, enhancing management of the State and economic performance as well as the rights of citizens; promotion of national cohesion by encouraging an environment of tolerance, harmony and common purpose even where there is diversity; effective promotion of programmes in areas such as education, health, housing, nutrition, social services and administration of justice, thereby enhancing the quality of life for all; reduced risk of catastrophic unrest and conflict that can have long-lasting adverse impacts on the State and its people;
d. A national action plan necessarily mobilizes a wide range of people and organizations in support of human rights activity. It therefore raises awareness and positive interest both with government and in the wider community;
e. A comprehensive and structured approach is more likely to ensure that the concerns of specific or vulnerable groups, such as women, children, minorities and indigenous peoples, are more effectively addressed;
f. A national action plan can facilitate the mobilization of domestic and international resources, including through United Nations and other programmes of technical cooperation, for countries that need resources, training and expertise to achieve their human rights goals;
g. National action planning takes an essentially non-confrontational approach to the consideration of human rights issues. By avoiding

the recriminations that sometimes make human rights work more difficult, it may be possible to achieve their human rights goals.

The Handbook continued that more specific purposes are:

- To provide guidance to government officials, non-governmental organizations (NGOs), professional groups, educators, advocates and other members of civil society regarding the tasks that need to be accomplished to ensure that human rights are effectively observed and to promote cooperation among these groups;
- To establish or strengthen national or issue-specific institutions dealing with human rights;
- To promote the universal ratification of international human rights treaties, facilitate the effective observance by governments of their obligations and promote conformity of national legislation with international standards;
- To promote wider awareness of human rights standards and mechanisms, including among those whose actions are particularly critical, such as police, security forces, prison staff and politicians as well as government officials and other workers in social fields;
- To promote and maintain a high level of awareness of the state of human rights observance in the country;
- To develop programmes specifically directed towards alleviating the human rights situations of vulnerable groups in society;
- To emphasize the role of human rights in national development.[105]

Conclusion

To conclude this chapter, we may offer the following recapitulation of essential elements for the adequate and effective protection of human rights inside each country. A national protection system, while anchored in national law, should be consistent with, and reflective of, international human rights law. A national protection system functions best under democracy and the rule of law. The legislature, the executive, the judiciary, the legal profession, dedicated institutions such as national human rights commission, and NGOs, all have roles to play in the efficient design and performance of the national protection system.

The national constitution should include provisions reflecting international human rights norms of public policy (jus cogens), such as the total prohibition of torture in any circumstance. National legislation should

105 Ibid, pp. 9-11.

incorporate all international human rights obligations of the State under international customary law, international treaties, and under mandatory decisions of the United Nations Security Council.

The national protection system should provide for effective safeguards against violations of international human rights norms from which no derogation is permissible under international law, such as the absolute prohibition of slavery. The judiciary should be able to invoke international human rights norms as reflected in international customary law, international treaties binding on the State, or general principles of law.[106]

The law enforcement system should be efficient and should observe and protect human rights. In the words of the UN Code of Conduct for Law Enforcement Officials, "In the performance of their duty, law enforcement officials shall respect and protect human dignity and maintain and uphold the human rights of all persons."[107]

Human rights education should be provided in all schools and higher institutions of learning. Human rights education should be viewed as an integral part of a national protection system. Human rights action plans should also be seen as an integral part of a national protection system. In periodic human rights action plans a society sets priority goals for achievement in the area of human rights and should work assiduously to achieve them.

A national protection system should include institutions such as a national commission on human rights or an ombudsperson. With a national commission on human rights a country gives a signal that it wishes to work methodically for the promotion, protection and realization of human rights.

A national protection system should include arrangements to detect potential gross violations of human rights or conflicts and to prevent them. Prevention arrangements are particularly important in multi-ethnic societies.

A national protection system should provide for adequate and effective remedies to prevent violations of human rights and to provide redress in cases of breach. The absence of a remedy available to test an arguable claim for breach amounts to a violation of human rights.[108] The

106 See on this, Article 38 of the Statute of the International Court of Justice.

107 Code of Conduct for Law Enforcement Officials, adopted by UN General Assembly resolution 34/169 of 17 December 1979.

108 See on this the case of Faure v. Australia in the Human Rights Committee, 2001; Annual Report of the Human Rights Committee, 2001.

right to an effective remedy may, in certain circumstances, require Governments to provide for and implement provisional or interim measures to avoid continuing violations and to endeavour to repair at the earliest possible opportunity any harm that may have been done.[109]

A national protection system should be particularly attentive to the risks of genocide, ethnic cleansing, war crimes and crimes against humanity, and should provide effective guarantees against them. As the Human Right Committee stated in its General Comment 6/16 of 27 July, 1982, States have the supreme duty to prevent wars, acts of genocide, and other acts of mass violence causing arbitrary loss of life. The Summit Outcome Document adopted by world leaders at the United Nations in 2005 affirmed the commitment of the international community to the responsibility to protect, especially in respect of genocide, ethnic cleansing, war crimes, and crimes against humanity. A national protection system should provide for a system of regular visits by national, regional or international bodies to all prisons and places of detention.[110]

In the event of a violation of human rights, the national protection system should provide for measures, beyond a victim-specific remedy, to be taken to avoid recurrence of the type of violation in question. Such measures may require changes in the State's laws or practices.[111] A national protection system should provide for investigations of gross violations of human rights and for justice to the victims. A national protection system should provide for safeguards against deportation or extradition to a state where the deportee/extradite may face serious risks of torture or arbitrary execution.

A national protection system should be particularly protective of human rights defenders. A country should be constantly reviewing and updating its national protection system so as to ensure that it provides the highest standard of protection of human rights and protection systems. After all, Governments are meant to serve the people and to protect their dignity and rights, not to trample on them.

109 General Comment 31 of the Human Rights Committee, supra.

110 See on this, The Optional Protocol to the Convention against Torture (OP-CAT), which provides for such a system of regular visits.

111 See General Comment 31 of the Human Rights Committee, Annex I below.

Chapter Three

Democracy and the Rule of Law

Introduction

In this chapter we discuss the law and practice of human rights treaty bodies on two issues of the greatest importance for the universal realization of human rights : democracy and the rule of law. In this regard it will be recalled that article 21 of the Universal Declaration of Human Rights proclaimed that the will of the people shall be the basis of the authority of government. This will shall be expressed in periodic and genuine elections which shall be by universal and equal suffrage and shall be held by secret vote or by equivalent free voting procedures.

Article 25 of the International Covenant on Civil and Political Rights states that everyone shall have the right and the opportunity, without any of the distinctions mentioned in article 2 and without unreasonable restrictions (a) to take part in the conduct of public affairs, directly or through freely chosen representatives; (b) to vote and to be elected at genuine periodic elections which shall be by universal and equal suffrage and shall be held by secret ballot, guaranteeing the free expression of the will of the electors; (c) to have access, on general terms of equality, to public service in his or her country.

Provisions on democracy and the rule of law are likewise to be found in the Inter-American Convention on Human Rights, the African Charter on Human and Peoples Rights, and the European Convention on Human Rights and Fundamental Freedoms, which calls for an effective political democracy.

The human rights treaty bodies have given guidance on the legal content of democracy and the rule of law and we look at some of these next.

I. The European Court of Human Rights

In the case of Zdanoka v. Latvia, the European Court of Human Rights captured the relationship between democracy and human rights superbly:

> "Democracy constitutes a fundamental element of the 'European public order'. That is apparent, firstly, from the Preamble to the Convention, which establishes a very clear connection between the Convention and democracy by stating that the maintenance and further realisation of human rights and fundamental freedoms are best ensured on the one hand by an effective political democracy and on the other by a common understanding and observance of human rights. The Preamble goes on to affirm that European countries have a common heritage of political traditions, ideals, freedom and the rule of law. This common heritage consists in the underlying values of the conventions: thus, the Court has pointed out on many occasions that the Convention was in fact designed to maintain and promote the ideals and values of a democratic society. In other words, democracy is the only political model contemplated by the Convention and, accordingly, the only one compatible with it."[112]

The words of the Court have universal significance for, in fact, the European Convention on Human Rights and Fundamental Freedoms was based on the early draft of the International Covenant on Human Rights then being considered at the United Nations. The Council of Europe decided to go ahead of the UN and adopt the European Convention based on the UN draft. The spirit of the European Convention and the International Covenants on Human Rights are thus identical.

II. General Comment No. 25 of the Human Rights Committee (1996)

General Comment No. 25 of the Human Rights Committee dealt with the issues of participation in public affairs and the right to vote. Recalling that Article 25 of the International Covenant on Civil and Political Rights recognized and protected the right of every citizen to take part in the conduct of public affairs, the right to vote and to be elected, and the right to have access to public service, the Committee commented that whatever form of constitution or government is in force, the Covenant required

112 Judgment of 16 March, 2006 (Grand Chamber – GC).

States to adopt such legislative and other measures as may be necessary to ensure that citizens have an effective opportunity to enjoy the rights it protects. The Committee stated: "Article 25 lies at the core of democratic government based on the consent of the people and in conformity with the principles of the Covenant."[113]

It added that any conditions which apply to the exercise of the rights protected by article 25 should be based on objective and reasonable criteria. The exercise of these rights by citizens may not be suspended except on grounds which are established by law and which are objective and reasonable.

III. General Comment No. 12 of the Human Rights Committee

In its General Comment No. 12 on the right to self determination, the Human Rights Committee stated: 'The article imposes on all States parties corresponding obligations. This right and the corresponding obligations concerning its implementation are interrelated with other provisions of the Covenant and rules of international law.' Other provisions of the Covenant include, particularly, Article 25. 'Every citizen shall have the right and the opportunity … (a) To take part in the conduct of public affairs, directly or through freely chosen representatives; (b) to vote and to be elected at genuine periodic elections which shall be by universal and equal suffrage, and shall be held by secret ballot, guaranteeing the free expression of the will of the electors; (c) To have access, on general terms of equality, to public service in his country.'

The jurisprudence of the Human Right Committee, which supervises the implementation of the Covenant and considers cases brought before it under its Optional Protocol, is that the provisions of article 1 of the Covenant, on the right to self-determination, while not covered by the individual petitions procedure under the Optional Protocol, 'may be relevant in the implementation of other rights protected by the Covenant' (Case No, 547/1991, Apirana Mahuika et al. v. New Zealand). In case No. 932/2000, (Marie-Helene Gillot et al. v. France), the Human Rights Committee stated:

> "Although the Committee does not have the competence under the Optional Protocol to consider a communication alleging violation of the right to self-determination protected in article 1 of the Covenant, it may interpret article 1, when this is relevant, in determining whether rights protected in

113 HRI/GEN/1/Rev.9, p. 217.

> parts II and III of the Covenant have been violated. The Committee is of the view, therefore, that, in this case, it may take article 1 into account in interpretation of article 25 of the Covenant."[114]

In this case, which concerned New Caledonia, the Human Rights Committee used the standard of 'reasonable criteria' in judging electoral arrangements under Article 25 in the light of Article 1:

> "The Committee recalls that, in the present case, article 25 of the Covenant must be considered in conjunction with article 1. It therefore considers that the criteria established are reasonable to the extent that they are applied strictly and solely to ballots held in the framework of a self-determination process. Such criteria, therefore, can be justified only in relation to Article 1 of the Covenant ..."

In this case, participation in the referendum had been limited to persons 'concerned' by the future of New Caledonia who had proven, sufficiently strong ties to that territory.

IV. Democracy and Human Rights

Professor Louis Henkin has argued that

> "The human rights ideology and the law of human rights represented in the International Covenant (on Civil and Political Rights) include, I believe, a right to democracy in the sense of constitutional democracy and its elements – authentic popular sovereignty, respect for individual rights, the rule of law, due process of law and commitment to the principle of justice. I think that these principles of justice were what those who drafted the Covenant contemplated and what states that became parties to the Covenant committed themselves to abide by."[115]

The World Conference on Human Rights (1993) had already declared that democracy, development and respect for human rights were interdependent and mutually reinforcing. It emphasised that 'The international community should support the strengthening and promoting of democ-

114 HRC Annual Report 2002, Vol. II, Annex IX, Sect GG, para. 13.4.

115 Commemorative Volume on the Occasion of the Twenty-Fifth Anniversary of the Human Rights Committee, N. Ando (Ed.), p. 176. Professor Larry Diamond has also asserted the universal right to democratic governance.

racy, development and respect for human rights and fundamental freedoms of the entire world.'

The Universal Declaration on Democracy adopted without a vote by the Inter-Parliamentary Council of the IPU in Cairo on 16 December, 1997 affirmed:

> "5. A state of democracy ensures that the processes by which power is acceded to, wielded and alternates allow for free political competition and are the product of open, free and non-discriminatory participation by the people, exercised in accordance with the rule of law, in both letter and spirit.
>
> 6. Democracy is inseparable from the rights set forth in the international instruments...
>
> 7. Democracy is founded on the primacy of the rule of law and the exercise of human rights. In a democratic State, no one is above the law and all are equal before the law."

The Inter-American Commission on Human Rights, early on, underlined that the right to take part in the government and participate in honest, periodic, free elections by secret ballot was of fundamental importance for safeguarding the human rights dealt with in the Inter-American instruments on human rights. The reason for this lay in the fact that, as historical experience had shown, governments derived from the will of the people, expressed in free elections, were those that provided the soundest guarantee that the basic human rights will be observed and protected.[116]

The right to political participation, the Commission has noted, left room for a wide variety of forms of government; there were many constitutional alternatives as regards the degree of centralization of the powers of the state or the election and attributes of the organs responsible for the exercise of those powers. However, a democratic framework was an essential element for establishment of a political society where human values could be fully realized. The right to political participation made possible the right to organize parties and political associations, which through open discussion and ideological struggle, could improve the social level and economic circumstances of the masses and prevent a monopoly of power by any one group or individual. At the same time, it

116 Inter-American Commission on Human Rights. Ten Years of Activities, 1971-1981. Washington, OAS, p. 334. 1978, El Salvador Report, p. 140.

could be said that democracy was a unifying link among the nations of the American Hemisphere.[117]

The Commission has noted that the American States had reaffirmed in the Charter of the Organization of American States that one of the guiding principles upon which their solidarity was based required that the political organization of those States be based on the effective exercise of representative democracy. Other international instruments on human rights, such as the Pact of San Jose of Costa Rica, had recognized the right of every citizen to take part in the conduct of public affairs, to vote and to be elected in genuine periodic elections, which shall be by universal equal suffrage and by secret ballot that guaranteed the free expression of the will of the voters. At the same time, the General Assembly of the OAS, at its Tenth Regular Session, had reiterated to its Member States that had not yet done so to re-establish or perfect the democratic system of government, in which the exercise of power derived from the legitimate and free expression of the will of the people, shall be in accordance with the particular characteristics and circumstances of each country.

For its part, the Commission has maintained that within the alternative forms of government that constitutional law recognized, the framework of a democratic regime should be the fundamental structure for the full exercise of human rights. In this context, governments had, in the face of political rights and the right to political participation, the obligation to permit and guarantee: the organization of all political parties and other associations, unless they were constituted to violate human rights; open debate of the principal themes of socioeconomic development; the celebration of general and free elections with all the necessary guarantees so that the results represented the popular will. As demonstrated by historical experience, the denial of political rights or the alteration of the popular will might lead to a situation of violence.[118] A political system in the Americas organized on the basis of the effective exercise of representative democracy was one of the principles enshrined in the Charter of the OAS that had the most direct relationship with the observance of human rights.[119]

117 Ten Years, op. cit., p. 334. Annual Report of the IACHR, 1979-80, p. 151.

118 Ten Years, op. cit., p. 335. Annual Report of the IACHR, 1980-81, pp. 122–123.

119 TenYears, op. cit., p. 335, Annual Report of the IACHR, 1978, p. 24. See, generally, the subsequent Inter-American Democratic Charter.

V. The Content of Democracy

On 16 September 1997, the Council of the Inter-Parliamentary Union, meeting in Cairo, adopted a Universal Declaration on Democracy in which it expressed its conviction that the strengthening of the democratization process and representative institutions would greatly contribute to the achievement of peace and development in the world. The Universal Declaration contained principles of democracy, the elements of democratic government and the international dimension of democracy.

On the principles of democracy the Declaration stated that democracy is a universally recognized ideal as well as a goal, which is based on common values held by peoples throughout the world community irrespective of cultural, political, social and economic differences. It is thus a basic right of citizenship to be exercised under conditions of freedom, equality, transparency and responsibility, with due respect for the plurality of views, and in the interest of the polity.

Democracy, the declaration continued, is both an ideal to be pursued and a mode of government to be applied according to modalities which reflect the diversity of experiences and cultural particularities without derogating from internationally recognized principles, norms and standards. It is thus a constantly perfected and always perfectible state or condition whose progress will depend upon a variety of political, social, economic and cultural factors.

As an ideal, democracy aims essentially to preserve and promote the dignity and fundamental rights of the individual, to achieve social justice, foster the economic and social development of the community, strengthen the cohesion of society and enhance national tranquility, as well as to create a climate that is favorable for international peace. As a form of government, democracy is the best way of achieving these objectives; it is also the only political system that has the capacity for self-correction.

The achievement of democracy presupposed a genuine partnership between men and women in the conduct of the affairs of society in which they work in equality and complementarity, drawing mutual enrichment from their differences.

A state of democracy ensured that the processes by which power is acceded to, wielded and alternates allow for free political competition and are the product of open, free and non-discriminatory participation by the people, exercised in accordance with the rule of law, in both letter and spirit.

Democracy was inseparable from international human rights. Those rights must therefore be applied effectively and their proper exercise must be matched with individual and collective responsibilities. Democracy was founded on the primacy of the law and the exercise of human rights. In a democratic state, no one is above the law and all are equal before the law. Peace and economic, social and cultural development were both conditions for and fruits of democracy. There was thus interdependence between peace, development, respect for and observance of the rule of law and human rights.

On the elements and exercise of democratic government the declaration added that democracy was based on the existence of well-structured and well-functioning institutions, as well as on a body of standards and rules and on the will of society as a whole, fully conversant with its rights and responsibilities. It was for democratic institutions to mediate tensions and maintain equilibrium between the competing claims of diversity and uniformity, individuality and collectivity, in order to enhance social cohesion and solidarity.

Furthermore, democracy was founded on the right of everyone to take part in the management of public affairs; it therefore required the existence of representative institutions at all levels and, in particular, a Parliament in which all components of society are represented and which has the requisite powers and means to express the will of the people by legislating and overseeing government action.

The key element in the exercise of democracy was the holding of free and fair elections at regular intervals enabling the people's will to be expressed. These elections must be held on the basis of universal, equal and secret suffrage so that all voters can choose their representatives in conditions of equality, openness and transparency that stimulate political competition. To that end, civil and political rights are essential, and more particularly among them, the rights to vote and to be elected, the rights to freedom of expression and assembly, access to information and the right to organize political parties and carry out political activities. Party organization, activities, finances, funding and ethics must be properly regulated in an impartial manner in order to ensure the integrity of the democratic processes.

It was an essential function of the state to ensure the enjoyment of civil, cultural, economic, political and social rights to its citizens. Democracy thus goes hand in hand with an effective, honest and transparent government, freely chosen and accountable for its management of public affairs.

Public accountability, which was essential to democracy, applied to all those who held public authority, whether elected or non-elected, and to all bodies of public authority without exception. Accountability entails a public right of access to information about the activities of government, the right to petition government and to seek redress through impartial administrative and judicial mechanisms.

Public life as a whole must be stamped by a sense of ethics and by transparency, and appropriate norms and procedures must be established to uphold them. Individual participation in democratic processes and public life at all levels must be regulated fairly and impartially and must avoid any discrimination, as well as the risk of intimidation by state and non-state actors.

Judicial institutions and independent, impartial and effective oversight mechanisms are the guarantors for the rule of law on which democracy is founded. In order for these institutions and mechanisms fully to ensure respect for the rules, improve the fairness of the processes and redress injustices, there must be access by all to administrative and judicial remedies on the basis of equality as well as respect for administrative and judicial decisions both by the organs of the state and representatives of public authority and by each member of society.

While the existence of an active civil society was an essential element of democracy, the capacity and willingness of individuals to participate in democratic processes and make governance choices could not be taken for granted. It was therefore necessary to develop conditions conducive to the genuine exercise of participatory rights, while also eliminating obstacles that prevent, hinder or inhibit this exercise. It was therefore indispensable to ensure the permanent enhancement of, inter alia, equality, transparency and education and to remove obstacles such as ignorance, intolerance, apathy, the lack of genuine choices and alternatives and the absence of measures designed to redress imbalances or discrimination of social, cultural, religious and racial nature, of for reasons of gender.

A sustained state of democracy thus required a democratic climate and culture constantly nurtured and reinforced by education and other vehicles of culture and information. Hence; a democratic society must be committed to education in the broadest sense of the term, and more particularly civic education and the shaping of a responsible citizenry.

Democratic process were fostered by a favourable economic environment; therefore, in its overall effort for development, society must be committed to satisfying the basic economic needs of the most disadvantaged, thus ensuring their full integration in the democratic process. The state of democracy presupposed freedom of opinion and expression; this right implies freedom to hold opinions without interference and to seek, receive and impart information and ideas through any media and regardless of frontiers.

The institutions and processes of democracy must accommodate the participation of all people in homogenous as well as heterogeneous societies in order to safeguard diversity, pluralism and the right to be different in a climate of tolerance. Democratic institutions and processes must also foster decentralized local and regional government and administration, which is a right and a necessity, and which makes it possible to broaden the base of public participation.[120]

VI. The Rule of Law

Ever since its inception, the International Commission of Jurists has elaborated a series of principles that provided guidance on the practical meaning of the rule of law. These included the following:

A. *Essential Requirements of a Society Under the Rule of Law*

- The legislative power must be effectively exercised by an appropriate organ, freely elected by the citizens. The laws and other legal measures taken by the legislature cannot be abolished or restricted by a governmental measure.
- The Rule of Law can only reach its highest expression and fullest realization under representative government. By representative government is meant a government deriving its power and authority from the people, in which power and authority are exercised through representatives freely chosen and responsible to them. Free periodic elections are therefore important to representative government.

B. *The Legislature and the Rule of Law*

- The function of the legislature in a free society under the Rule of Law is to create and maintain the conditions which will uphold the dignity of the human being as an individual. This dignity requires not only the recognition of his or her civil and political rights but also the establishment of the social, economic, educational and cultural conditions which are essential to the full development of his or her personality. Every legislature in a free society under the Rule of Law should endeavour to give full effect to the principles enunciated in the Universal Declaration of Human Rights.

120 IPU, *Democracy: Its Principles and Achievement* (Geneva: IPU, 1998), iv.-vii.

C. *The Executive and the Rule of Law*

- In general, the acts of the executive which directly and injuriously affect the person or property or rights of the individual should be subject to review by the courts.
- It will further the Rule of Law if the executive is required to formulate its reasons when reaching its decisions of a judicial or administrative character and affecting the rights of individuals and at the request of a party concerned to communicate them to him.

D. *The Criminal Process and the Rule of Law*

- It is always important that the definition and interpretation of the law should be as certain as possible, and this is of particular importance in the case of the criminal law, where the citizen's life or liberty may be at stake.

E. *The Judiciary and the Rule of Law*

- An independent judiciary is an indispensable requisite of a free society under the Rule of Law.

F. *The Legal Profession and the Rule of Law*

- It is essential to the maintenance of the Rule of Law that there should be an organized legal profession free to manage its own affairs. But it is recognized that there may be general supervision by the courts and that there may be regulations governing the admission to and pursuit of the legal profession.
- Lawyers should refuse to collaborate with any authority in any action which violates the Rule of Law. Lawyers should endeavour to promote knowledge of and to inspire respect for the Rule of Law, and an appreciation by all people of their rights under the law.

G. *Economic and Social Development*

- It is essential to economic and social development to overcome inequality arising from birth or wealth and discrimination.

VII. The Role of the Courts and of Law Enforcement Agencies

As we saw in the preceding chapter, the Basic Principles on the Independence of the Judiciary, endorsed by the United Nations General Assembly on 13 December, 1985,[121] called for the independence of the judiciary to be guaranteed by the State and enshrined in the Constitution or law of the country. The Code of Conduct for Law Enforcement Officials adopted by the UN General Assembly on 17 December, 1979[122] states that law enforcement officials shall at all times fulfill the duty imposed upon them by law, by serving the community and by protecting all persons against illegal acts, consistent with the high degree of responsibility required by their profession.

VIII. The European Court of Human Rights and the Rule of Law

In Annex V below we reproduce a report on the Council of Europe and the Rule of Law.[123] As will be seen from it, the European Court of Human Rights has provided detailed guidance on the meaning and thrust of the rule of law. We present below the central tenets of the court. The detailed references to the case law of the Court which are the basis for the statements made may be consulted in the original document.

The European Court of Human Rights has noted that the notion of separation of powers, notably between the political organs of the state (executive, legislature) and the judiciary has assumed a growing importance in the Court's case-law. The Court is careful to protect the judicial process from interferences by the legislature or the executive. The role of the judiciary is essential in a state based on the rule of law. It is the guarantor of justice, a fundamental value in a law-governed state. In criminal matters its role in the prevention and repression of crime, in particular when committed by State agents, is linked to the notion of the rule of law notably when procedural obligations under Articles 2 (right to life) and 3 (prohibition of torture) of the ECHR are at stake. Impunity, *de jure* or *de facto,* for violations of these Articles, is incompatible with the principle of the rule of law. In this context, the Court has repeatedly stressed the

121 UN General Assembly resolution 40/32.

122 UN General Assembly resolution 34/169.

123 We are grateful to Jeroen Schokkenbroek, Head of the Human Rights Development Department of the Directorate General of Human Rights and Legal Affairs of the Council of Europe for having made this document available to us. He was the author of the document.

importance of maintaining public confidence in the authorities' adherence to the rule of law and preventing any appearance of the authorities' tolerance of or collusion in unlawful acts. A state based on the rule of law has the duty to employ the necessary measures to uphold the law on its territory and to ensure the security of all as well as the enjoyment of human rights As one element of a state subject to the rule of law, prosecuting authorities must show the necessary diligence in the implementation of criminal law in order to prevent and repress crime and protect the citizens.

Article 6 § 1 ECHR requires that a tribunal must always be established by law. This reflects the principle of the rule of law inherent in the whole ECHR system. Legislation on the establishment and competence of judicial organs must be enacted by parliament, failing which a tribunal would lack the necessary legitimacy in a democratic society to hear the cases of individuals.

More generally as regards the legislature, the Court has systematically described the right to vote and stand for election as a right "central to democracy and the rule of law", thus illustrating the interdependence between these notions.

The Court has emphasized the duty of the state, notably the executive, to respect and apply the law, including the duty to enforce final domestic judgments. The Court has highlighted the importance of administrative courts which the Court views as one of the most conspicuous achievements of a state based on the rule of law, in particular because the jurisdiction of those courts to adjudicate on acts of the administrative authorities was not accepted without a struggle.

The principle of legality (sometimes referred to as supremacy of the law) forms a traditional core part of the rule of law concept. The rule of law requires that the state act on the basis of, and in accordance with, the law. This offers essential legal protection of the individual vis-à-vis the state and its organs and agents. Many ECHR provisions reflect this principle through references to the notion of "law", in most cases in the form of a requirement that interference with human rights must be lawful.[124]

124 Articles 2,5,6,7,8,9,10,11, 1 of Protocol No.1, 2 of Protocol No. 4, Protocol No. 7.

- **Principle of lawfulness**

The notion of law systematically used by the Court is a material or substantive one.[125] It covers not only statute law but also unwritten law (case-law) and regulations. The Court assesses whether domestic law as a whole has been complied with in the context of interferences with ECHR rights. In the context of deprivation of liberty (Article 5), the Court stresses the importance of the lawfulness of the detention, both procedurally and substantively, requiring scrupulous adherence to the rule of law. Non-compliance with domestic law leads to a violation of Article 5. In some cases, even where the law may have been formally respected, the Court has found a breach of the requirements of lawfulness on the ground that the authorities have attempted to circumvent the applicable legislation.

The state is not only obliged to respect and apply, in a foreseeable and consistent manner, the laws it has enacted, but also, as a corollary of this duty, to ensure the legal and practical conditions for their implementation.

The notion of "law" in the ECHR does not merely refer back to domestic law but also relates to the quality of the law, requiring it to be compatible with the rule of law. In particular, the law must be sufficiently accessible and foreseeable. These requirements have been developed in a rich case-law. Foreseeability means that the law must be foreseeable as to its effects, that is formulated with sufficient precision to enable the individual to regulate his conduct. In this context, a law which confers a discretion to a state authority must indicate the scope of that discretion. It would be contrary to the rule of law for the legal discretion granted to the executive to be expressed in terms of an unfettered power. Consequently, the law must indicate the scope of any such discretion and the manner of its exercise with sufficient clarity, to give the individual adequate protection against arbitrariness.

The principle of legality takes on a special importance in criminal matters. Article 7, ECHR enshrines two principles essential to the rule of law: a criminal conviction must be based on a norm which existed at the time of the act or omission (*nullum crimen sine lege*), and no heavier penalty may be imposed than the one applicable at the time the offence was committed (*nulla poena sine lege*). Neither is it permissible to apply new, more severe legislation to an ongoing situation that arose before the legislation came into force. In addition, the authority applying the criminal law may not interpret it extensively, for example by analogy,

125 With the exception of the right to a tribunal "established by law" (Article 6 § 1) dealt with under A above.

to the accused's detriment. The offence must be clearly defined in law. Here, too, requirements of accessibility and foreseeability apply. This is also true in respect of the penalty imposed. These principles all serve to offer essential safeguards against arbitrary prosecution, conviction and punishment.

- **Principle of legal certainty**

This principle is one of the basic elements of the rule of law. It can be linked to some of the principles and requirements set out above (such as lawfulness and foreseeability). The state has a duty to respect and apply, in a foreseeable and consistent manner, the laws it has enacted.

Legal certainty requires respect for the principle of *res judicata*. Final judgments by domestic courts should not be called into question; systems which allow for the quashing of final judgments for an indefinite period of time are incompatible with the principle of legal certainty.

The rule of law, in particular the principles of legality and legal certainty, also require that final court judgments be enforced. In private disputes, enforcement of final judgments may require the assistance of the police in order to avoid any risk of "private justice" contrary to the rule of law. The administration of the state's obligation to execute final domestic judgments is an essential feature of a state founded on the rule of law and the principle of legal certainty. Violations of this obligation are sanctioned under different ECHR provisions.

Likewise, authorities are obliged to respect final decisions ordering the release of a person from detention. A practice of detaining a person without the basis of a concrete legal provision or judicial decision is itself contrary to the principle of legal certainty.

The existence of conflicting decisions within a supreme court is contrary to the principle of legal certainty. It is therefore required that the courts, especially the highest courts, establish mechanisms to avoid conflicts and ensure the coherence of their case-law. The principle of legal certainty is essential to the public's confidence in the judicial system and the rule of law.

The principle of legal certainty may also justify certain limitations of rights, notably in the form of time-limits for lodging appeals or the use of statutory limitations. However, the ECHR may still be violated in case of particularly strict interpretations or rigid application of time-limits regardless of individual circumstances.

- **Principle of equality before the law**

The principle that all are equal before the law is reflected in various ways in the ECHR. Article 1 requires states to secure ECHR rights to "everyone" within their jurisdiction, and most ECHR rights are similarly framed: "Everyone has the right ...". In addition, Article 14 prohibits any discrimination in the enjoyment of ECHR rights, and Article 1 of Protocol No. 12 prohibits discrimination generally, including as regards the enjoyment of any right set forth by law and any other discrimination by a public authority. Equality before the law and non-discrimination are human rights principles as much as they are rule of law principles, and the Court's case-law tends to apply the prohibition of discrimination without there being a special need to refer to it as a rule of law principle, although there is some recognition that equality in rights and duties of all human beings before the law is an aspect of the rule of law.[126]

C. *Due process: Judicial Review, Access to Courts and Remedies, Fair Trial*

The principle of the rule of law implies that an interference by the executive authorities with an individual's rights should be subject to an effective control which should normally be assured by the judiciary, at least in the last resort, judicial control offering the best guarantees of independence, impartiality and a proper procedure (*Klass and Others*, 6.9.1978, § 55); This principle of judicial control of the executive was reaffirmed in more recent cases. As regards deprivation of liberty, the requirements of Article 5 §§ 3 and 4 ECHR, with their emphasis on promptitude and judicial control, assume a particular importance in the context of secret detentions and disappearances. What is at stake is both the protection of the physical liberty of individuals as well as their personal security in a context which, in the absence of safeguards, could result in a subversion of the rule of law and place detainees beyond the reach of the most rudimentary forms of legal protection.

The due process aspect of the rule of law entails certain positive obligations of the state in the form of procedural requirements and safeguards (such as the right to be heard and have one's views considered,

126 *Refah Partisi and Others*, Chamber judgment of 31.7.2001. The *GC judgment* of 13.2.2003 did not refer to equality but to the principle of secularism. The principle of equality before the law is also expressed through specific ECHR requirements concerning judicial proceedings such as equality of arms and impartiality of the judge (Article 6 ECHR).

e.g. for a pregnant woman concerning the therapeutic termination of her pregnancy.

The right of access to a court was established on the basis of the rule of law principle. In the *Golder judgment* (21.2.1975, § 35), the Court rejected an interpretation of Article 6 § 1 which would allow states to abolish their courts, take away their jurisdiction to decide certain classes of civil actions and entrust it to organs dependent on the government. Individuals must have a clear, practical opportunity to challenge an act that interferes with their rights. This right may imply an obligation to provide for legal aid in civil disputes. or to exempt actions for damages from high and inflexible court fees. The right of access to court may be subject to certain limitations, but these, in turn, are themselves subject to certain requirements.

The right to an effective remedy (Article 13 ECHR) for any arguable claim about violation of ECHR rights is also closely linked to the rule of law. Referring to that principle, the Court has established that, in expulsion cases, Article 13 may require a remedy with an automatic suspensive effect especially where there is a serious risk of torture or ill-treatment in case of deportation.

The right to a fair trial enshrined in Article 6 ECHR reflects the fundamental principle of the rule of law and occupies a prominent place in a democratic society. Unsurprisingly, the notion of the rule of law is used in the interpretation and application of the different guarantees of Article 6, such as the presumption of innocence, the rights of the defence and the right to a fair trial within a reasonable time.[127] In the Golder judgment, attention was drawn to the important danger that exists for the rule of law within national legal orders when excessive delays in the administration of justice occur in respect of which litigants have no domestic remedy. Article 6 also applies to the execution of a judicial decision: where authorities fail to execute such a decision, the fair trial guarantees enjoyed by a litigant during the proceedings are rendered devoid of purpose. This again illustrates the relevance of enforcement of the law as a rule of law principle.

127 The requirements concerning judicial independence are dealt with under point A. in Annex V below.

IX. Democracy and Freedom of Association in the Jurisprudence of ILO Supervisory Bodies

In a chapter in a book in honour of the highly regarded late Nicolas Valticos, Karen Curtis of the Norms and Standards Department of the ILO traced the jurisprudence and practice of ILO supervisory bodies on democracy and freedom of association. She wrote:

> "Over more than half a century, the ILO supervisory bodies have examined numerous cases where freely chosen, independent workers' organizations became dynamic agents for change in the political, social and economic life of countries where the bedrock of democracy, and often the accompanying civil liberties had not been ensured.
>
> ...
>
> Indeed, no one would hesitate to say that freedom of association is by definition contrary to the model of single party rule and totalitarianism. So, in countries where representative political parties cannot develop, it has often been observed that workers' organizations have become the channel for expressing public discontent and the sole organized form of representation, whether lawful or not. While a democratic system is a necessary prerequisite for the full respect of trade union rights, trade unions may nevertheless take their liberties in hand, demand respect for basic rights and become catalysts for an overall political transformation to democracy."[128]

She traced the jurisprudence and practice of ILO supervisory bodies in respect of Cuba, China, Myanmar, Poland, South Africa, Sudan, Swaziland and Zimbabwe. The ILO Committee of Experts on the Application of Conventions and Recommendations, dealing with the situation in Cuba, had held that a system in which a single party and a single central trade union organization existed, and where the statutes of such an organization established the objective of following the policy of the Party, was likely to lead to excessive interference in trade union independence and the election of trade union leaders, and was incompatible with ILO standards.[129]

The ILO Fact-Finding and Conciliation Commission on Freedom of Association had held that 'in the land of *apartheid,* many liberties

---

128 K. Curtis, Democracy, freedom of association and the ILO, in ILO, Les norms internationals du travail: un patrimoine pour l'avenir. Melanges en l'honneur de Nicolas Valticos, ILO, 2004, pp. 89-106, at p. 91.

129 Ibid, p. 99.

counted as normal in a democratic society were diminished or lost altogether'[130] The Committee on Freedom of Association, dealing with the situation in Zimbabwe, had held that freedom of association by definition meant that everyone had the right to think differently, to hope for other policy options and to make those hopes known in a peaceful and a law-abiding manner. Trade union activities could not be restricted solely to occupational matters since government policies and choices were generally bound to have an impact on workers.[131]

ILO supervisory bodies critized a Decree in Swaziland that banned all political parties, restricted constitutional freedoms, and imposed substantial restrictions on the right of organizations to hold meetings and demonstrations, thereby suppressing trade union rights.[132] Dealing with Chinese restrictions on attempts by workers to form workers' organizations independent from the monopolistic officially backed unions, the Committee on Freedom of Association, in 2002, held:

> "On a more general note, and giving full consideration to the context of transition described by the Government and its determination to achieve simultaneous development in economic and social fields, the Committee considers that it is precisely within this context that the only durable solution to the apparently increasing social conflict experienced in the country is through full respect for the right of workers to establish organizations of their own choosing by ensuring, in particular, the effective possibility of forming, in a climate of full security, organizations independent both of those which exist already and of any political party... The Committee strongly believes that the development of free and independent organizations and negotiation with all those involved in social dialogue is indispensable to enable a government to confront its social and economic problems and resolve them in the best interests of the workers and the nation. Indeed, a balanced economic and social development requires the existence of strong and independent organizations which can participate in the process of development."[133]

130 Ibid, p. 94.

131 Ibid, p. 98.

132 Ibid, p. 104.

133 Ibid, p. 101. 350th Report of the Freedom of Association Committee, Case No. 2189, paras. 465-466.

Dealing with the situation in Myanmar, the Committee of Experts on the Application of Conventions and Recommendations stated the following in its Report for 2008:

> "The Committee recalls once again that respect for civil liberties is essential for the exercise of freedom of association and that workers and employers should be able to exercise their freedom of association rights in a climate of complete freedom and security, free from violence and threats and that a climate of violence, in which murders and disappearances of trade union leaders go unpunished, constitutes an extremely serious obstacle to the exercise of trade union rights and that such acts require severe measures to be taken by the authorities. The authorities should not seize on legitimate trade union activities as a pretext for arbitrary arrest or detention.
>
> ...
>
> The Committee ... requests the Government to communicate any steps taken towards the adoption of the Constitution and provide the text of the fundamental principles for the drawing up of the Constitution as well as any further relevant draft laws, orders, or instructions made to guarantee freedom of association so that it may examine their conformity with the provisions of the Convention. Finally, the Committee requests the Government to indicate the manner in which the elements of civil society were involved in the adoption of the fundamental principles."[134]

X. The Jurisprudence and Practice of Other Treaty Bodies

In human rights treaty case law we find important expressions of the links between democracy and human rights. We saw the important pronouncement of the European Court in the Zdanoka case at the beginning of this chapter. In the Handyside Case, the Court considered as characteristics of a democratic society the notions of pluralism, tolerance, and broad-mindedness. In the Klass case the Court considered that one of the fundamental principles of a democracy is the rule of law. Justice is best served by constitutional democracy under the rule of law.

The Human Rights Committee has held that the principle of legality and the rule of law require that fundamental requirements of fair trial must be respected during a state of emergency.[135] The European Court of

134 International Labour Conference, 97th Session, 2008. Report of the Committee of Experts on the Application of Conventions and Recommendations, Report III (Part 1 A), ILO, 2008, pp. 162-163.

135 Digest of Decisions of the Human Rights Committee, p. 40.

Human Rights has held that measures affecting fundamental rights must be subject to some form of adversarial proceedings before an independent and competent tribunal if they are to be considered valid.[136]

The Human Rights Committee, in Case No. 1134/2002 (Garji-Dinka v. Cameroon), invoked the standard of objectivity and reasonableness. The Committee observed that the exercise of the right to vote and to be elected may not be suspended or excluded except on grounds established by law that were objective and reasonable, and reiterated that persons who were deprived of their liberty but who had not been convicted should not be excluded from exercising the right to vote.

In the case of Peter Chiko Bwalya v. Zambia, the Human Rights Committee held that a violation of Article 25 of the Covenant had been committed when the author had been prevented from participating in a general election campaign as well as from preparing his candidacy for his party.[137] In the case of Touron v. Uruguay, a person had been convicted of subversive association and barred from taking part in the conduct of public affairs and from being elected for public office for a period of 15 years. The Human Rights Committee held that article 25 of the Covenant permitted only reasonable restrictions and found that the 15-year ban was not reasonable.[138]

In the case of Marshall v. Canada, the Human Rights Committee stated the following:

> "It must be beyond dispute that the conduct of public affairs in a democratic State is the task of representatives of the people, elected for that purpose, and pubic officials appointed in accordance with the law. Invariably, the conduct of public affairs affects the interest of large segments of the population or even the population as a whole, while in other instances it affects more directly the interest of more specific groups of society. Although prior consultations, such as pubic hearings or consultations with the most interested groups may often be envisaged by law or have evolved as pubic policy in the conduct of public affairs, article 25(a) of the Covenant cannot be understood as meaning that any directly affected group, large or small, has the unconditional right to choose the modalities of participation in the conduct

136 Al Nashif v. Bulgaria, Judgment of 20 June 2002.

137 See R.Hanski and M. Scheinin, Leading Cases of the Human Rights Committee, Institute for Human Rights, Turku, 2003, p. 400 ff.

138 Communication 518/1992, UN Doc. CCPR/C/12/D/32/1978 (1981), para. 11.

of pubic affairs. That, in fact, would be an extrapolation of the right to direct participation by the citizens, far beyond the scope of article 25(a)"[139]

Conclusion

In this chapter we considered the primordial link between human rights on the one hand, and democracy and the rule of law on the other. We then outlined the general comments of the Human Rights Committee on Articles 1 and 25 of the International Covenant on Civil and Political Rights. We looked next at the jurisprudence and practice of human rights treaty bodies in respect of democracy and the rule of law. We outlined the provisions of the important declaration of the Inter-Parliamentary Union on the content of democracy and then recapitulated the principles of the International Commission of Jurists on the meaning of the rule of law. We recounted the jurisprudence of the European Court of Human Rights and then recalled the solid practice of ILO supervisory bodies on the importance of democracy and the rule of law for the implementation of trade union and human rights we finally cited some of the case law of the human rights treaty bodies giving effect to democratic rights.

This chapter has indeed brought out that democracy and the rule of law are part of the fundamentals of international human rights treaty law. In the next chapter we turn to the principles of international human rights treaty law on human rights during times of crises and emergencies.

139 Marshall v Canada, Communication 205/1986, UN Doc. CCPR/C/43/D/205/1986 (1991), para. 5.5.

Chapter Four

Human Rights in Times of Crises or Emergencies

Introduction

The principle of international protection in situations of national declarations of emergency was superbly brought out by an ILO Commission of Inquiry in 1956. Responding to Greece's contention that it had proclaimed a state of emergency in accordance with its national law and that the Government was the sole judge of the need to proclaim a state of emergency, the Commission stated:

> "The Commission understands perfectly the argument that conformity with the Constitution would make the Government in the eyes of Greek law the sole judge of the need to proclaim a state of emergency. But it is an accepted principle of international law that a State cannot rely on the terms of its national law, or otherwise invoke the concept of national sovereignty, to justify non-performance of an international obligation. Any doubt concerning the extent of such an obligation must be determined by exclusive reference to the relevant principles of international law, whether made express by the parties to a treaty or derived from another source of international law, in particular, international custom and general principles of law."[140]

The Commission added:

> "All the main legal systems accept in some form the principle that pleas of justification on grounds such as self-defence are subject to legal review. If a plea of emergency is to be treated in international law as a legal concept

140 Report of the Commission Appointed under Article 26 of the Constitution of the ILO to Examine the Complaints concerning the Observance by Greece of the Freedom of Association and Protection of the Right to Organise Convention, 1948 (No.87) and of the Right to Organize and Collective Bargaining Convention, 1949 (No. 98), made by a number of delegates to the 52nd session of the International Labour Conference. ILO, Official Bulletin, Special Supplement, Vol. LIV. 1971, No. 2, pp. 25-26, paras. 102-112.

there similarly has to be appraisal by an impartial authority at the international level. It is for this reason that international tribunals and supervisory organs, when seized of such a plea, have invariably made an independent determination of whether the circumstances justified the claim, and have not allowed the State concerned to be the sole judge of the issue."[141]

I. The Core Provisions

A governmental leader or officer contemplating the declaration of an emergency must first have regard to the governing provisions under any relevant human rights treaty. The European Convention, the International Covenant on Civil and Political Rights, and the Inter-American Convention all have provisions on this topic. There is no matching provision in the African Charter but there is solid case law of the African Commission on Human and Peoples' Rights. The African Commission has stated, for example:

> "Governments should avoid restricting rights, and have special care with regard to those rights protected by constitutional and international human rights law. No situation justifies the wholesale violation of human rights. In fact, general restrictions on rights diminish public confidence in the rule of law and are often counter-productive ...
>
> According to Article 9(2) of the Charter, dissemination of opinions may be restricted by law. – This does not mean that national law can set aside the right to express and disseminate one's opinions, this would make the protection of the right to express one's opinions ineffective. To allow national law to have precedence over the international law of the Charter would defeat the purpose of the rights and freedoms enshrined in the Charter. International human rights standards must always prevail over contradictory national law. Any limitation on the rights of the Charter must be in conformity with the provisions of the Charter.
>
> In contrast to other international human rights instruments, the African Charter does not contain a derogation clause. Therefore limitations on the rights and freedoms enshrined in the Charter cannot be justified by emergencies or special circumstances.
>
> The only legitimate reasons for limitations to the rights and freedoms of the African Charter are found in Article 27(2), that is the rights of the Charter 'shall be exercised with due regard to the rights of others, collective security, morality and common interests' ...

141 Ibid.

The reasons for possible limitations must be founded in a legitimate State interest and the evils of limitations of rights must be strictly proportionate with and absolutely necessary for the advantages which are to be obtained ...

Even more important, a limitation may never have as a consequence that the right itself becomes illusory."[142]

A. *The European Convention*

Article 15 of the European Convention provides:

1. In time of war or other public emergency threatening the life of the nation any High Contracting Party may take measures derogating from its obligations under the Convention to the extent strictly required by the exigencies of the situation, provided that such measures are not inconsistent with its other obligations under international law.
2. No derogation from Article 2, except in respect of deaths resulting from lawful acts of war, or from Articles 3, 4 (paragraph 1) and 7 shall be made under this provision.
3. Any High Contracting Party availing itself of this right to derogation shall keep the Secretary-General of the Council of Europe fully informed of the measures which it has taken and the reasons therefor. It shall also inform the Secretary-General of the Council of Europe when such measures have ceased to operate and the provisions of the Convention are again being fully executed.

B. *The ICCPR*

Article 4 of the International Covenant on Civil and Political Rights provides:

1. In time of pubic emergency which threatens the life of the nation and the existence of which is officially proclaimed, the States Parties to the present Covenant may take measures derogating from their obligations under the present Covenant to the extent strictly required by the exigencies of the situation, provided that such measures are

142 Communications 105/93, 128/94 and 152/96, Media Rights Agenda and Constitutional Rights Project v. Nigeria, Media Rights Agenda and Constitutional Rights Project, Twelfth Activity Report 1998-1999, Annex V. See generally on Limitations, the Syracusa Principles and the Limburg Principles Annexed to this work.

not inconsistent with their other obligations under international law and do not involve discrimination solely on the ground of race, colour, sex, language, religion or social origin.

2. No derogation from articles 6, 7, 8 (paragraphs 1 and 2), 11, 15, 16 and 18 may be made under this provision.
3. Any State Party to the present Covenant availing itself of the right of derogation shall immediately inform the other States parties to the present Covenant, through the intermediary of the Secretary-General of the United Nations, of the provisions from which it has derogated and of the reasons by which it was actuated. A further communication shall be made, through the same intermediary, on the date on which it terminates such derogations.

C. *The American Convention*

Article 27 of the American Convention provides:

1. In time of war, public danger, or other emergency that threatens the independence or security of a State Party, it may take measures derogating from its obligations under the present Convention to the extent and for the period of time strictly required by the exigencies of the situation, provided that such measures are not inconsistent with its other obligations under international law and do not involve discrimination on the grounds of race, colour, sex, language, religion, or social origin.
2. The foregoing provision does not authorize any suspension of the following articles: Article 3 (Right to Juridical Personality), Article 4 (Right to Life), Article 5 (Right to Humane Treatment), Article 6 (Freedom from Slavery), Article 9 (Freedom from *Ex Post Facto* Laws), Article 12 (Freedom of Conscience and Religion), Article 17 (Rights of the Family), Article 18 (Right to a Name), Article 19 (Rights of the Child), Article 20 (Right to Nationality), and Article 23 (Right to Participate in Government), or of the judicial guarantees essential for the protection of such rights.
3. Any State Party availing itself of the right of suspension shall immediately inform the other States Parties, through the Secretary-General of the Organization of American States, of the provision the application of which it has suspended, the reasons that gave rise to the suspension, and the date set for the termination of such suspension.

It will be noted that the European Convention refers to a time of war or other public emergency threatening the life of the nation. The ICCPR refers to a time of pubic emergency which threatens the life of the nation and the existence of which is officially proclaimed. The Inter-American Convention refers to a time of war, public danger, or other emergency that threatens the independence or security of a State Party. The list of rights expressly excluded from derogation is longer in the Inter-American Convention.

II. 1968 Resolution of the Inter-American Commission on Human Rights

Already in 1968, the Inter-American Commission on Human Rights adopted and transmitted to Governments a ground-breaking *Resolution on the Protection of Human Rights in Connection with the Suspension of Constitutional Guarantees or the Stage of Siege.*[143] Because of the importance of this resolution we reproduce it fully below:

> "*The Inter-American Commission on Human Rights*
> *Declares*:
> That the suspension of constitutional guarantees or 'state of siege' is compatible with the system of representative democratic government only if enacted under the following conditions:
> (a) When officially decreed under the procedure established in the respective constitutions;
> (b) When established in a measure strictly limited to the exigencies of the situation and with application limited to the duration thereof;
> (c) When adopted in case of war or other serious public emergency threatening the life of the nation or the security of the State;
> (d) When it does not entail any discrimination based on reasons of race, color, sex, language, religion, political or other opinions, national or social origin, economic status, birth or any other social conditions;
> (e) When it does not in any manner presuppose the suspension of the right to life, liberty or personal security, the right to protection against arbitrary detention, the right to due process of law, and the right to freedom of thought, conscience and religion;

143 See Inter-American Yearbook on Human Rights, 1968. Washington D.C., 1973, p. 61.

(f) When it does not in any manner presuppose restriction of the rule of law, or the provisions of the constitution, or alteration of the scope of the Powers of the State or of the proper exercise of the police powers.

States

That the imposition of the state of siege or the suspension of instituted guarantees can be made the object, without prejudice to national sovereignty or the principle of non-intervention, of international control by means of the signing and ratification of a convention establishing the reciprocal undertaking."[144]

III. General Comment No. 29 of the Human Rights Committee

The International Covenant on Civil and Political Rights is the treaty that covers a far larger number of States Parties than any of the two regional instruments and its General Comment 29, which elaborates on the meaning of Article 4 of the ICCPR, has attracted broad-based support among Governments and international human rights lawyers. General Comment 29, drawing upon the case law of the Human Rights Committee, provides invaluable guidance on the substance of the law of derogations during emergencies. The Committee began by observing that Article 4 of the Covenant was of paramount importance for the system of protection of human rights under the Covenant.[145]

A. *Essential Requirements*

The Human Rights Committee underlined that measures derogating from the provisions of the Covenant must be of an exceptional, temporary nature. Before a State moves to invoke article 4, two fundamental conditions must be met: the situation must amount to a public emergency threatening the life of the nation, and the State party must have officially proclaimed a state of emergency. The latter requirement was essential for the maintenance of the principle of legality and rule of law at times when they were most needed. When proclaiming a state of emergency with consequences that could entail derogation from any provision of the Cov-

144 This paragraph is explained by the fact that it was only a year later, in 1969, that the Inter-American Convention would be concluded.

145 General Comment 29 is reproduced in UN doc. HRI/Gen/1/Rev. 9, pp. 234-241.

enant, States must act within their constitutional and other provisions of law that govern such proclamation and the exercise of emergency powers.

B. The Meaning of a Public Emergency

Not every disturbance or catastrophe qualifies as a public emergency which threatens the life of the nation, as required by article 4, paragraph 1. The Covenant required that even during an armed conflict measures derogating from the Covenant were allowed only if and to the extent that the situation constituted a threat to the life of the nation. If States parties consider invoking article 4 in other situations than an armed conflict, they should carefully consider the justification and why such a measure is necessary and legitimate in the circumstances.[146]

C. Proportionality

A fundamental requirement for any measure derogating from the Covenant is that such measures be limited to the extent strictly required by the exigencies of the situation. Derogation from some Covenant obligations in emergency situations is distinct from restrictions or limitations allowed even in normal times under several provisions of the Covenant. The obligation to limit any derogations to those strictly required by the exigencies of the situation reflected the principle of proportionality common to derogation and limitation powers. This condition requires that States parties provide careful justification not only for their decision to proclaim a state of emergency but also for any specific measures based on such a proclamation. The fact that some of the provisions of the Covenant have been listed in article 4 (para. 2), as not being subject to derogation does not mean that other articles in the Covenant may be subjected to derogations at will, even where a threat to the life of the nation exists.

D. Peremptory Norms

The Human Rights Committee considers that the enumeration of non-derogable provisions in article 4 is related to, but not identical with, the

146 In the Lawless Case, the European Court of Human Rights defined a public emergency as 'an exceptional situation of crisis or emergency which affects the whole population and constitutes a threat to the organized life of the community of which the State is composed.' Lawless v. Ireland, Judgment of 7 April, 1961, para. 28.

question whether certain human rights obligations bear the nature of peremptory norms of international law. The Committee considers that the proclamation of certain provisions of the Covenant as being of a non-derogable nature in article 4, paragraph 2, is to be seen partly as recognition of the peremptory nature of some fundamental rights ensured in treaty form in the Covenants (e.g., articles 6 and 7). The category of peremptory norms extends beyond the list of non-derogable provisions as given in article 4, paragraph 2. States parties may in no circumstances invoke article 4 of the Covenant as justification for acting in violation of humanitarian law or peremptory norms of international law, for instance by taking hostages, by imposing collective punishments, through arbitrary deprivation of liberty or by deviating from fundamental principles of fair trial including the presumption of innocence.[147]

E. *Crimes Against Humanity*

In assessing the scope of legitimate derogation from the Covenant, one criterion can, in the view of the Human Rights Committee, be found in the definition of certain human rights violations as crimes against humanity. If action conducted under the authority of a State constitutes a basis for individual criminal responsibility for a crime against humanity by the persons involved in that action, article 4 of the Covenant cannot be used as justification that a state of emergency exempted the State in question from its responsibility in relation to the same conduct. The recent codification of crimes against humanity, for jurisdictional purposes, in the Rome Statute of the International Criminal Court is of relevance to the interpretation of article 4 of the Covenant.

F. *Notification*

The Human Rights Committee has emphasized that the notification by States parties should include full information about the measures taken and a clear explanation of the reasons for them, with full documentation attached regarding their law. Additional notifications are required if the State party subsequently takes further measures under article 4, for instance by extending the duration of a state of emergency. The requirement of immediate notification applies equally in relation to the termination of derogation.

147 Ibid, para. 11.

IV. The Prohibition of Torture

By letter dated 11 October 2001, the then High Commissioner for Human Rights solicited the views of the Committee against Torture on how to ensure that the human rights covered by its mandate were maintained with a high visibility in the light of various State responses to the terrorist attacks in the United States of America on 11 September, 2001. In the spirit of that request the Committee against Torture decided to communicate directly with the States Parties with the following statement:

> "The Committee against Torture condemns utterly the terrorist attacks of September 11 and expresses its profound condolences to the victims, who were nationals of some 80 countries, including many State parties to the Convention against Torture and Other Cruel, Inhuman or Degrading Treatment or Punishment. The Committee is mindful of the terrible threat to international peace and security posed by these acts of international terrorism, as affirmed in Security Council resolution 1368. The Committee also notes that the Security Council in resolution 1373 identified the need to combat by all means, in accordance with the Charter of the United Nations, the threats caused by terrorist acts.
>
> The Committee against Torture reminds States parties to the Convention of the non-derogable nature of most of the obligations undertaken by them in ratifying the Convention.
>
> The obligations contained in Articles 2 (whereby "no exceptional circumstances whatsoever may be invoked as a justification of torture"), 15 (prohibiting confessions extorted by torture being admitted in evidence, except against the torturer), and 16 (prohibiting cruel, inhuman or degrading treatment or punishment) are three such provisions and must be observed in all circumstances.
>
> The Committee against Torture is confident that whatever responses to the threat to international terrorism are adopted by States Parties, such responses will be in conformity with the obligations undertaken by them in ratifying the Convention against Torture."[148]

V. Judicial Guarantees

The Inter-American Court of Human Rights has on several occasions clarified the law governing states of siege or emergency in terms that are

148 CAT/C/XXVII/Misc.7, 22 November, 2001.

applicable internationally. In 1985, for example, the Court advised as follows, advice it has subsequently repeated on different occasions:

> "In a democratic society, the rights and freedoms inherent in the human person, the guarantees applicable to them and the rule of law form a triad. Each component thereof defines itself, complements and depends on the others for its meaning
>
> ...
>
> When guarantees are suspended, some legal restraints applicable to the acts of public authorities may differ from those in effect under normal conditions. These restraints may not be considered to be non-existent, however, nor can the government be deemed thereby to have acquired absolute powers that go beyond the circumstances justifying the grant of such exceptional legal measures. The Court has already noted, in this connection, that there exists an inseparable bond between the principle of legality, democratic institutions and the rule of law."[149]

In an Advisory Opinion on Judicial Guarantees in States of Emergency (Art. 27(2), 25, and 8 American Convention on Human Rights)[150] the Inter-American Court affirmed the following:

- The general requirement that in any state of emergency there be appropriate means to control the measures taken, so that they are proportionate to the needs and do not exceed the strict limits imposed by the Convention or derived from it.
- States parties have an obligation to provide effective judicial remedies that must be substantiated in accordance with the rules of due process of law.
- The absence of an effective remedy to violations of the rights recognized by the Convention is itself a violation of the Convention by the State Party in which the remedy is lacking.
- The principles of due process of law cannot be suspended in states of exception insofar as they are necessary conditions for the procedural institutions regulated by the Convention to be considered judicial guarantees.
- The rule of law, representative democracy, and personal liberty are essential in the system for the protection of human rights contained in the American Convention.

149 Advisory Opinion OC-5785 of November 13, 1985, Series A. No. 5, para. 66.

150 Advisory Opinion OC-9/87 of October 6, 1987, Series A No. 9.

VI. Margin of Appreciation

In the case of *Ireland v. The United Kingdom* (1978), the ECHR declared:

> "It falls in the first place to each Contracting State, with its responsibility for 'the life of the nation, to determine whether that life is threatened by a public emergency. ... By reason of their direct and continuous contact with the pressing needs of the moment, the national authorities are in principle in a better position than the international judge, to decide ... on the presence of such an emergency. ... In this matter, article 15(1) leaves those authorities a wide margin of appreciation."[151]

This, however, is subject to international supervision.

VII. The Legality of Nuclear Weapons

In its general comment No. 6 (16) adopted at its 378th meeting on 27 July 1982, the Human Rights Committee observed that the right to life enunciated in the first paragraph of article 6 of the International Covenant on Civil and Political Rights is the supreme right from which no derogation is permitted even in time of public emergency. The same right to life is enshrined in article 3 of the Universal Declaration of Human Rights. It is basic to all human rights.

In general comment No. 6, the Committee observed that it is the supreme duty of States to prevent wars. War and other acts of mass violence continue to be a scourge of humanity and take the lives of thousands of innocent human beings every year.

In general comment No. 14 (23) adopted at its twenty-third session in 1984, the Human Rights Committee, while remaining deeply concerned by the toll of human life taken by conventional weapons in armed conflicts, noted that during successive sessions of the UN General Assembly representatives from all geographical regions had expressed their growing concern at the development and proliferation of increasingly awesome weapons of mass destruction, which not only threatened human life but also absorbed resources that could otherwise be used for vital economic and social purposes, particularly for the benefit of developing countries,

151 Ireland v. The United Kingdom, 18 January 1978, Series A, No.25; (1979-80) 2 *EHRR* 25, para. 207. See, similarly, Aksoy v. Turkey (App. 1987/93), Judgment of 18 December 1996; 23 EHRR, para. 68 of the judgment.

and thereby for promoting and securing the enjoyment of human rights for all.

The Committee associated itself with this concern and added that it was evident that the designing, testing, manufacture, possession, and deployment of nuclear weapons were among the greatest threats to the right to life which confronted mankind. This threat was compounded by the danger that the actual use of such weapons might be brought about, not only in the event of war, but even through human or mechanical error or failure.

Furthermore, the very existence and gravity of this threat generated a climate of suspicion and fear between States, which was in itself antagonistic to the promotion of universal respect for, and observance of, human rights and fundamental freedoms in accordance with the Charter of the United Nations and the International Covenants on Human Rights.

The production, testing, possession, deployment and use of nuclear weapons should therefore be prohibited and recognized as crimes against humanity. The Committee accordingly, in the interest of mankind, called upon all States, whether Parties to the Covenant or not, to take urgent steps, unilaterally and by agreement, to rid the world of this menace.

Conclusion

This chapter has sought to summarise the law on one of the most central human rights issues of our times: when can a Government lawfully declare a state of emergency in a time of crisis or emergency. This issue is especially important because it is during times of crises or emergencies that some of the worst violations of human rights occur. We began by setting out the core provisions of the human rights treaties and proceeded to recall a landmark resolution of the Inter-American Commission on Human Rights on this topic adopted as far back as 1968. We then fast-forwarded to set out the provisions of General Comment No. 29 of the Human Rights Committee, which is widely considered a summary of the state of international law on this topic. We recalled next the views of the Committee Against Torture on the absolute interdiction of torture in all circumstances, which is directly relevant to the great debates swirling around in our times over the use of torture in fighting terrorism. We then looked at the issue of judicial guarantees during states of emergency and recalled the core tenets of the doctrine of the margin of appreciation enjoyed by governments (of democracies) in assessing the nature of risks in the society and of how best to respond to them within the law. We then recalled the views of the Human Rights Committee on the legality of nuclear weapons, a topic that is now back in centre stage with the declared emphasis of leaders such as President Barrack Obama to work for the total elimination of nuclear weapons.

We proceed, in the next chapter, to discuss the issue of preventive strategies under human rights treaties.

Chapter Five

Preventive Strategies: Obligations to Prevent under International Human Rights Treaties and Jurisprudence

Introduction

In the Velasquez Rodriguez Case (1988), the Inter-American Court of Human Rights had a superb discussion of the duty of Governments to prevent human rights violations. The State has, the Court declared, the legal duty to take reasonable steps to prevent human rights violations and to use the means at its disposal to carry out a serious investigation of violations committed within its jurisdiction, to identify those responsible, to impose the appropriate punishment and to ensure the victim adequate compensation.[152]

The duty to prevent, the Court continued, includes all those means of a legal, political, administrative and cultural nature that promote the protection of human rights and ensure that any violations are considered and treated as illegal acts, which, as such, may lead to the punishment of those responsible and the obligation to indemnify the victims for damages. The Court clarified, however, that while the State is obligated to prevent human rights abuses, the existence of a particular violation did not, in itself, prove the failure to take preventive measures. On the other hand, subjecting a person to official, repressive bodies that practiced torture and assassination with impunity was itself a breach of the duty to prevent violations of the rights to life and physical integrity of the person, even if that particular person was not tortured or assassinated, or if those facts could not be proven in a concrete case.[153]

In this chapter we look at the obligations of governments to prevent violations of human rights under international treaties that set out requirements to prevent human rights violations and we also discuss strands in international human rights jurisprudence that emphasize the duty of Governments to prevent gross violations of human rights. We begin with general recommendations of the human rights treaty bodies

152 Inter-American Court of Human Rights, The Velasquez Rodriguez case, 4 Inter-Am. Ct. H.R. (ser. C), para. 174.

153 Ibid, para. 175.

I. General Recommendations of Treaty Bodies

Treaty bodies have given solid guidance on the necessity for preventive measures against violations of human rights.

A. *The Prevention of Torture*

In its General Comment No. 2 (2007), the Committee Against Torture commented at length on the content of the obligation to take effective measures to prevent torture. For a start, States parties must make the offence of torture punishable as an offence under its criminal law, at a minimum, with the elements of torture as defined in article 1 of the Convention against Torture, and the requirements of article 4. It warned that serious discrepancies between the Convention's definition and that incorporated into domestic law create actual or potential loopholes for impunity. It was essential to investigate and establish the responsibility of persons in the chain of command as well as that of the direct perpetrator(s).

By defining the offence of torture as distinct from common assault or other crimes, the Committee considered that States parties will directly advance the Convention's overarching aim of preventing torture and ill-treatment. Naming and defining this crime will promote the Convention's aim, inter alia, by alerting everyone, including perpetrators, victims and the public, to the special gravity of the crime of torture. Codifying the crime would also emphasize the need for appropriate punishment that takes into account the gravity of the offence; strengthen the deterrent effect of the prohibition itself; enhance the ability of responsible officials to track the specific crime of torture; and enable and empower the public to monitor and, when required, to challenge State action as well as State inaction that violates the Convention.

Preventive measures identified by the Committee included: maintaining an official register of detainees, the right of detainees to be informed of their rights, the right promptly to receive independent legal assistance, independent medical assistance, and to contact relatives, the need to establish impartial mechanism for inspecting and visiting places of detention and confinement, and the availability to detainees and persons at risk of torture and ill-treatment of judicial and other remedies that would allow them to have their complaints promptly and impartially examined, to defend their rights, and to challenge the legality of their detention or treatment. As new methods of prevention (e.g. videotaping all interrogations, utilizing investigative procedures such as the Istanbul Protocol of 1999, or new approaches to public education or the protection of minors) are discovered, tested and found effective, article 2 of the Convention provided authority to build upon the remaining articles and to expand the scope of measures required to prevent torture.[154]

B. Preventing Racial Discrimination in the Administration and Functioning of the Criminal Justice System

In its General Recommendation XXXI (2005), the Committee on the Elimination of Racial Discrimination provided guidance on strategies needed to prevent racial discrimination in the administration and functioning of the criminal justice system. States parties, it counselled, should pursue national strategies the objectives of which include the following:

(a) To eliminate laws that have an impact in terms of racial discrimination, particularly those which target certain groups indirectly by penalizing acts which can be committed only by persons belonging to such groups, or laws that apply only to non-nationals without legitimate grounds or which do not respect the principle of proportionality;

(b) To develop, through appropriate education programmes, training in respect for human rights, tolerance and friendship among racial or ethnic groups, as well as sensitization to intercultural relations, for law enforcement officials: police personnel, persons working in the system of justice, prison institutions, psychiatric establishments, social and medical services, etc;

(c) To foster dialogue and cooperation between the police and judicial authorities and the representatives of relevant groups in order to combat prejudice and create a relationship of trust;

(d) To promote proper representation of persons belonging to racial and ethnic groups in the police and the system of justice;

(e) To ensure respect for, and recognition of the traditional systems of justice of indigenous peoples, in conformity with international human rights law;

(f) To make the necessary changes to the prison regime for prisoners belonging to relevant groups so as to take into account their cultural and religious practices;

(g) To institute, in situations of mass population movements, the interim measures and arrangements necessary for the operation of the justice system in order to take account of the particularly vulnerable situation of displaced persons, in particular by setting up decentral-

154 HRI/GEN/1/Rev.9, p. 379.

ized courts at the places where the displaced persons are staying or by organizing mobile courts;

(h) To set up, in post-conflict situations, plans for the reconstruction of the legal system and the re-establishment of the rule of law throughout the territory of the countries concerned by availing themselves, in particular, of the international technical assistance provided by the relevant United Nations entities;

(i) To implement national strategies or plans of action aimed at the elimination of structural discrimination. These long-term strategies should include specific objectives and actions as well as indicators against which progress can be measured. They should include, in particular, guidelines for prevention, recording, investigation and prosecution of racist or xenophobic incidents, assessment of the level of satisfaction among all communities concerning their relations with the police and the system of justice, and recruitment and promotion in the judicial system of persons belonging to various racial or ethnic groups;

(j) To entrust an independent national institution with the task of tracking, monitoring and measuring progress made under the national plans of action and guidelines against racial discrimination, identifying undetected manifestations of racial discrimination and submitting recommendations and proposals for improvement.[155]

C. *Avoiding Discrimination Against Women in National Strategies for the Prevention of AIDS*

In its General Recommendation No. 15 (1990), the Committee on the Elimination of Discrimination Against Women recommended that States parties intensify their efforts in disseminating information to increase public awareness of the risk of HIV infection and AIDS, especially in women and children, and of its effect on them; that programmes to combat AIDS should give special attention to the rights and needs of women and children, and to the factors relating to the reproductive role of women and their subordinate position in some societies which make them especially vulnerable to HIV infection; that States parties ensure the active participation of women in primary health and take measures to enhance their role as care providers, health workers and educators in the prevention of infection with HIV; and that all States parties include in their reports under article 12 of the Convention on the Elimination of All Forms of Discrimination against Women information on the effects

155 Ibid, pp. 309-310.

of AIDS on the situation of women and on the action taken to cater to the needs of those women who are infected and to prevent specific discrimination against women in response to AIDS.[156]

D. *Preventing Deprivation of Liberty of Children and Treatment in Cases Thereof*

In General Comment No. 6, which dealt with the treatment of unaccompanied and separated children outside their country of origin, the Committee on the Rights of the Child provided guidance on a variety of measures for the prevention of trafficking and of sexual and other forms of exploitation, abuse and violence; prevention of military recruitment and protection against effects of war; and prevention of deprivation of liberty and treatment in cases thereof. In application of article 37 of the Convention on the Rights of the Child, and in accordance with the principle of the best interests of the child, the Committee counselled, unaccompanied or separated children should not, as a general rule, be detained. Detention could not be justified solely on the basis of the child being unaccompanied or separated, or on their migratory or residence status, or lack thereof. In the exceptional case of detention, conditions of detention must be governed by the best interests of the child.[157]

E. *Preventive Protection of the Right to Life*

Article 6 of the International Covenant on Civil and Political Rights (1966) protects the right to life which, the Human Rights Committee, the monitoring body established under the Covenant, has deemed 'the supreme right from which no derogation is permitted even in time of public emergency which threatens the life of the nation (article 4)'. In General Comment 6/16 of 27 July, 1982. the Human Rights Committee advised that

> "States have the supreme duty to prevent wars, acts of genocide and other acts of mass violence causing arbitrary loss of life. Every effort they make to avert the danger of war, especially thermo nuclear war, and to strengthen international peace and security would constitute the most important condition and guarantee for the safeguarding of the right to life. In this respect the Committee notes, in particular, a connection between article 6 and ar-

156 Ibid, pp. 327-328.

157 Ibid, pp. 455-459.

ticle 20, which states that the law shall prohibit any propaganda for war or incitement to violence."

The Committee continued:

> "The protection against arbitrary deprivation of life which is explicitly required by the third sentence of article 6(1) is of paramount importance. The Committee considers that States parties should take measures not only to prevent and punish deprivation of life by criminal acts, but also to prevent arbitrary killing by their own security forces. The deprivation of life by the authorities of the State is a matter of the utmost gravity. Therefore, the law must strictly control and limit the circumstances in which a person may be deprived of his life by such authorities.
>
> States parties should also take specific and effective measures to prevent the disappearance of individuals, something which unfortunately has become all too frequent and leads too often to arbitrary deprivation of life. Furthermore, States should establish effective facilities and procedures to investigate thoroughly cases of missing and disappeared persons in circumstances which may involve a violation of the right to life."

II. The Convention on the Prevention and Punishment of the Crime of Genocide

On 11 December 1946, the General Assembly declared that Genocide was a crime under International Law, which the world condemned and that those guilty of it, whoever they were and for whatever reason they had committed it, were punishable. The Assembly invited member States to enact the necessary legislation for the prevention and punishment of this crime and called for international cooperation towards this end.

On 9 December 1948, the day before it adopted the Universal Declaration of Human Rights, the General Assembly approved the Convention on the Prevention and Punishment of the Crime of Genocide which entered into force on 12 January 1951. Article I of the convention states that genocide, whether committed in time of peace or in time of war, is a crime under international law. The International Court of Justice has subsequently affirmed that the principles underlying the Convention have the character of *jus cogens*.

Article II of the convention defined the crime of genocide as acts aimed at destroying a national, ethnical, racial or religious group as such. Article IV provides that guilty persons shall be punished, whether they are constitutionally responsible rulers, public officials or private individuals. Article VI provides that persons charged with genocide shall be tried by a competent tribunal of the State in the territory of which the act was committed or by such international penal tribunal as may have jurisdiction with respect to those Contracting Parties that have accepted its jurisdiction. In this regard it is worth noting that the statute of the International Criminal Court also covers the crime of genocide.

Article VIII provided that any Contracting Party may call upon the competent organs of the United Nations to take such action under the Charter that they consider appropriate for the prevention and suppression of acts of genocide or any of the proscribed acts enumerated in the Convention.

Since the General Assembly adopted the Convention in 1948, many genocides have undoubtedly taken place.[158] The question deserves to be asked, to what extent if any did the member States, the Security Council, the General Assembly, or the Secretary General marshal diplomatic resources to highlight the crime of genocide and to prevent it from taking place? The unfortunate answer to this question is that during the period of the Cold War – and even for most of the post-Cold War period – there is little evidence of special diplomatic activity to warn of the dangers of genocide. As we know, in Rwanda and Darfur mass killings have taken place under the very eyes of the International Community.

To be fair, the human rights programme of the United Nations did attempt to place the spotlight on the dangers of genocide within the then Sub-Commission on Prevention of Discrimination and Protection of Minorities. A global study on genocide was issued in 1979 and a second study updated two decades later. The author of the first study recommended that the Commission on Human Rights consider the setting up of *ad hoc* committees to inquire into allegations of genocide brought to the knowledge of the Commission by a Member State or an international organization and supported by sufficient *prima facie* evidence. The Special Rapporteur also called on the General Assembly to continue consideration of the question of an international criminal jurisdiction.

There has been the occasional inquiry into allegations of genocide such as the one prepared by Mr. Abdelwahab Bouhdiba, member of the

158 See S. Power, *Problem from Hell.* See also D. Hamburg, *No More Killing Fields: Preventing Deadly Conflict* (New York: Rowman & Littlefield Publishers, Inc., 2002) and D. and A. Hamburg, *Learning to Live Together: Preventing Hatred and Violence in Child and Adolescent Development.* (Oxford: Oxford University Press, 2004).

Sub-Commission, into the crimes committed under the Pol Pot regime in Cambodia. Three decades later, a court has been established in Cambodia to try some of those responsible for what has been described as "auto genocide" in Cambodia.

After years of efforts, the Rome Statute of the International Criminal Court was adopted on 17 July 1998 and is now in force. The Statute vests jurisdiction in the International Criminal Court to deal with accusations against persons charged with genocide. The International Criminal Tribunals on the Former Yugoslavia and on Rwanda have had accusations of genocide brought before them and the Rwanda tribunal has even handed down a verdict of genocide in one case.

When it comes to diplomacy *per se*, there is not much practice to go on. However, a spectacular case of preventive diplomacy in the form of mitigatory action did take place under Secretary General U Thant in relation to the events in the then East Pakistan in 1971.[159] The scale of the killings and other atrocities committed in East Pakistan was of such magnitude that many considered it comparable with a genocidal situation.

III. Convention against Torture and Other Cruel, Inhuman or Degrading Treatment or Punishment[160]

Article 1 of the Convention defines "torture" as any act by which severe pain or suffering, whether physical or mental, is intentionally inflicted on a person for such purposes as obtaining from him or a third person information or a confession, punishing him for an act he or a third person has committed or is suspected of having committed, or intimidating or coercing him or a third person, or for any reason based on discrimination of any kind, when such pain or suffering is inflicted by or at the instigation of or with the consent or acquiescence of a public official or other person acting in an official capacity. It does not include pain or suffering arising only from, inherent in or incidental to lawful sanctions. Article 2 requires each State Party to take effective legislative, administrative, judicial or other measures to prevent acts of torture in any territory under its jurisdiction. No exceptional circumstances whatsoever, whether a state of war or a threat of war, internal political in stability or any other public

159 See on this, B.G. Ramcharan, *Humanitarian Good Offices in International Law* (The Hague: Martinus Nijhoff, 1983).

160 Adopted and opened for signature, ratification and accession by General Assembly resolution 39/46 of 10 December 1984.
Entry into force 26 June 1987, in accordance with article 27 (1).

emergency, may be invoked as a justification of torture. An order from a superior officer or a public authority may not be invoked as a justification of torture.

Under Article 3, no State Party shall expel, return ("refouler") or extradite a person to another State where there are substantial grounds for believing that he would be in danger of being subjected to torture. For the purpose of determining whether there are such grounds, the competent authorities shall take into account all relevant considerations including, where applicable, the existence in the State concerned of a consistent pattern of gross, flagrant or mass violations of human rights.

Article 4 requires that each State Party shall ensure that all acts of torture are offences under its criminal law. The same shall apply to an attempt to commit torture and to an act by any person which constitutes complicity or participation in torture. Each State Party shall make these offences punishable by appropriate penalties which take into account their grave nature. Furthermore, under Article 5, each State Party shall take such measures as may be necessary to establish its jurisdiction over the offences referred to in article 4 in the following cases: (a) When the offences are committed in any territory under its jurisdiction or on board a ship or aircraft registered in that State; (b) When the alleged offender is a national of that State; (c) When the victim is a national of that State if that State considers it appropriate.

Each State Party shall likewise take such measures as may be necessary to establish its jurisdiction over such offences in cases where the alleged offender is present in any territory under its jurisdiction and it does not extradite him pursuant to article 8 to any of the States mentioned in paragraph I of this article.

Furthermore, each State Party shall keep under systematic review interrogation rules, instructions, methods and practices as well as arrangements for the custody and treatment of persons subjected to any form of arrest, detention or imprisonment in any territory under its jurisdiction, with a view to preventing any cases of torture.

Under Article 12 each State Party shall ensure that its competent authorities proceed to a prompt and impartial investigation, wherever there is reasonable ground to believe that an act of torture has been committed in any territory under its jurisdiction.

Article 13 provides that each State Party shall ensure that any individual who alleges he has been subjected to torture in any territory under its jurisdiction has the right to complain to, and to have his case promptly and impartially examined by, its competent authorities. Steps shall be taken to ensure that the complainant and witnesses are protected against all ill-treatment or intimidation as a consequence of his complaint or any evidence given.

Each State Party, under Article 14, shall ensure in its legal system that the victim of an act of torture obtains redress and has an enforceable right to fair and adequate compensation, including the means for as full rehabilitation as possible. In the event of the death of the victim as a result of an act of torture, his dependants shall be entitled to compensation. Nothing in this article shall affect any right of the victim or other persons to compensation which may exist under national law.

Article 15 requires that each State Party shall ensure that any statement which is established to have been made as a result of torture shall not be invoked as evidence in any proceedings, except against a person accused of torture as evidence that the statement was made.

Article 16 states that each State Party shall undertake to prevent in any territory under its jurisdiction other acts of cruel, inhuman or degrading treatment or punishment which do not amount to torture as defined in article I, when such acts are committed by, or at the instigation of, or with the consent or acquiescence of, a public official or other person acting in an official capacity. In particular, the obligations contained in articles 10, 11, 12 and 13 shall apply with the substitution for references to torture of references to other forms of cruel, inhuman or degrading treatment or punishment. The provisions of the Convention are without prejudice to the provisions of any other international instrument or national law which prohibits cruel, inhuman or degrading treatment or punishment or which relates to extradition or expulsion.

Under Article 17 there is established a Committee against Torture consisting of ten experts of high moral standing and recognized competence in the field of human rights, who serve in their personal capacity. If the Committee receives reliable information which appears to it to contain well-founded indications that torture is being systematically practised in the territory of a State Party, the Committee shall, under article 20 invite that State Party to co-operate in the examination of the information and to this end to submit observations with regard to the information concerned. Taking into account any observations which may have been submitted by the State Party concerned, as well as any other relevant information available to it, the Committee may, if it decides that this is warranted, designate one or more of its members to make a confidential inquiry and to report to the Committee urgently. If an inquiry is made in accordance with this article, the Committee shall seek the co-operation of the State Party concerned. In agreement with that State Party, such an inquiry may include a visit to its territory.

After examining the findings of its member or members submitted in accordance with paragraph 2 of this article, the Committee shall transmit these findings to the State Party concerned together with any comments or suggestions which seem appropriate in view of the situation. All the proceedings of the Committee shall be confidential , and at all stages of the proceedings the co-operation of the State Party shall be sought. After such proceedings have been completed with regard to an inquiry made in accordance with paragraph 2, the Committee may, after consultations with the State Party concerned, decide to include a summary account of the results of the proceedings in its annual report made in accordance with article 24.

Article 21 provides that a State Party to the Convention may at any time declare that it recognizes the competence of the Committee to receive and consider communications to the effect that a State Party claims that another State Party is not fulfilling its obligations under the Convention. Such communications may be received and considered according to the procedures laid down in this article only if submitted by a State Party which has made a declaration recognizing in regard to itself the competence of the Committee. No communication shall be dealt with by the Committee under this article if it concerns a State Party which has not made such a declaration. Communications received under this article shall be dealt with in accordance with the following procedure: (a) If a State Party considers that another State Party is not giving effect to the provisions of this Convention, it may, by written communication, bring the matter to the attention of that State Party. Within three months after the receipt of the communication the receiving State shall afford the State which sent the communication an explanation or any other statement in writing clarifying the matter, which should include, to the extent possible and pertinent, reference to domestic procedures and remedies taken, pending or available in the matter; (b) If the matter is not adjusted to the satisfaction of both States Parties concerned within six months after the receipt by the receiving State of the initial communication, either State shall have the right to refer the matter to the Committee, by notice given to the Committee and to the other State; (c) The Committee shall deal with a matter referred to it under this article only after it has ascertained that all domestic remedies have been invoked and exhausted in the matter, in conformity with the generally recognized principles of international law. This shall not be the rule where the application of the remedies is unreasonably prolonged or is unlikely to bring effective relief to the person who is the victim of the violation of this Convention; (d) The Committee shall hold closed meetings when examining communications under this article; (e)Subject to the provisions of subparagraph (c), the Committee shall make available its good offices to the States Parties concerned with a view to a friendly solution of the matter on the basis of respect for the obligations provided for in the Convention. For this purpose, the Committee may, when appropriate, set up an *ad hoc* conciliation commission; (f) In any matter referred to it under this article, the Committee may call upon the States Parties concerned, referred to in subparagraph (b), to supply any relevant information; (g) The States Parties concerned, referred to in subparagraph (b), shall have the right to be represented when the matter is being considered by the Committee and to make submissions orally and/or in writing; (h) The Committee shall, within twelve months after the date of receipt of notice under subparagraph (b), submit a report: (i) If a solution within the terms of subparagraph (e) is reached, the Committee shall confine its report to a brief statement of the facts and of the solution reached; (ii) If a solution within the terms of subparagraph (e) is not reached, the Committee shall confine its report to a brief statement of the facts; the written submissions and record of the oral submissions made by the States Parties concerned shall be attached to the report. In every matter, the report shall be communicated to the States Parties concerned.

Under Article 22, a State Party to the Convention may at any time declare under this article that it recognizes the competence of the Committee to receive and consider communications from or on behalf of individuals subject to its jurisdiction who claim to be victims of a violation by a State Party of the provisions of the Convention. No communication shall be received by the Committee if it concerns a State Party which has not made such a declaration. The Committee is required to bring any communications submitted to it under this article to the attention of the State Party to the Convention which has made a declaration under paragraph I and is alleged to be violating any provisions of the Convention. Within six months, the receiving State shall submit to the Committee written explanations or statements clarifying the matter and the remedy, if any, that may have been taken by that State.

The Committee considers communications received under this article in the light of all information made available to it by or on behalf of the individual and by the State Party concerned.

IV. Optional Protocol to the Convention against Torture and other Cruel, Inhuman or Degrading Treatment or Punishment[161]

This Protocol recalls that the effective prevention of torture and other cruel, inhuman or degrading treatment or punishment requires education and a combination of various legislative, administrative, judicial and other measures, and that the World Conference on Human Rights firmly had declared that efforts to eradicate torture should first and foremost be concentrated on prevention and called for the adoption of an optional protocol to the Convention, intended to establish a preventive system of regular visits to places of detention,

The objective of the Protocol, as stated in Article 1, is to establish a system of regular visits undertaken by independent international and national bodies to places where people are deprived of their liberty, in order to prevent torture and other cruel, inhuman or degrading treatment or punishment. Article 2 provides for the establishment of a Subcommittee on Prevention of Torture and Other Cruel, Inhuman or Degrading Treatment or Punishment of the Committee against Torture.

The Subcommittee on Prevention is required to carry out its work within the framework of the Charter of the United Nations and to be guided by the Purposes and Principles thereof, as well as the norms of the United Nations concerning the treatment of people deprived of their liberty. The Subcommittee on Prevention shall be guided by the principles of confidentiality, impartiality, non-selectivity, universality and objectivity.

Each State Party, under Article 3, shall set up, designate or maintain at the domestic level one or several visiting bodies for the prevention of torture and other cruel, inhuman or degrading treatment or punishment (hereinafter referred to as the national preventive mechanism). Furthermore, in accordance with Article 4, each State Party shall allow visits by the mechanisms referred to in articles 2 and 3 to any place under its jurisdiction and control where persons are or may be deprived of their liberty, either by virtue of an order given by a public authority or at its instigation or with its consent or acquiescence (places of detention). These visits shall be undertaken with a view to strengthening, if necessary, the protection of these persons against torture and other cruel, inhuman or degrading treatment or punishment. Deprivation of liberty means any

161 Adopted on 18 December 2002 at the fifty-seventh session of the General Assembly of the United Nations by resolution A/RES/57/199.
Entered into force on 22 June 2006.

form of detention or imprisonment or the placement of a person in a public or private custodial setting which that person is not permitted to leave at will by order of any judicial, administrative or other authority.

The Subcommittee on Prevention, as specified in Article 5, consist of ten members. After the fiftieth ratification of or accession to the Protocol, the number of the members of the Subcommittee on Prevention shall increase to twenty-five. The members of the Subcommittee on Prevention shall be chosen from among persons of high moral character, having proven professional experience in the field of the administration of justice, in particular criminal law, prison or police administration, or in the various fields relevant to the treatment of persons deprived of their liberty.

Under Article 11, The Subcommittee on Prevention shall:

(a) Visit the places referred to in article 4 and make recommendations to States Parties concerning the protection of persons deprived of their liberty against torture and other cruel, inhuman or degrading treatment or punishment;

(b) In regard to the national preventive mechanisms:

 (i) Advise and assist States Parties, when necessary, in their establishment;

 (ii) Maintain direct, and if necessary confidential, contact with the national preventive mechanisms and offer them training and technical assistance with a view to strengthening their capacities;

 (iii) Advise and assist them in the evaluation of the needs and the means necessary to strengthen the protection of persons deprived of their liberty against torture and other cruel, inhuman or degrading treatment or punishment;

 (iv) Make recommendations and observations to the States Parties with a view to strengthening the capacity and the mandate of the national preventive mechanisms for the prevention of torture and other cruel, inhuman or degrading treatment or punishment;

(c) Cooperate, for the prevention of torture in general, with the relevant United Nations organs and mechanisms as well as with the international, regional and national institutions or organizations working towards the strengthening of the protection of all persons against torture and other cruel, inhuman or degrading treatment or punishment.

In order to enable the Subcommittee on Prevention to comply with its mandate as laid down in article 11, the States Parties undertake under Article 12:

(a) To receive the Subcommittee on Prevention in their territory and grant it access to the places of detention as defined in article 4 of the present Protocol;
(b) To provide all relevant information the Subcommittee on Prevention may request to evaluate the needs and measures that should be adopted to strengthen the protection of persons deprived of their liberty against torture and other cruel, inhuman or degrading treatment or punishment;
(c) To encourage and facilitate contacts between the Subcommittee on Prevention and the national preventive mechanisms;
(d) To examine the recommendations of the Subcommittee on Prevention and enter into dialogue with it on possible implementation measures.

Article 13 calls for the Subcommittee on Prevention to establish, at first by lot, a programme of regular visits to the States Parties in order to fulfil its mandate as established in article 11. After consultations, the Subcommittee on Prevention shall notify the States Parties of its programme in order that they may, without delay, make the necessary practical arrangements for the visits to be conducted. The visits shall be conducted by at least two members of the Subcommittee on Prevention. These members may be accompanied, if needed, by experts of demonstrated professional experience and knowledge in the fields covered by the present Protocol who shall be selected from a roster of experts prepared on the basis of proposals made by the States Parties, the Office of the United Nations High Commissioner for Human Rights and the United Nations Centre for International Crime Prevention. In preparing the roster, the States Parties concerned shall propose no more than five national experts. The State Party concerned may oppose the inclusion of a specific expert in the visit, whereupon the Subcommittee on Prevention shall propose another expert. If the Subcommittee on Prevention considers it appropriate, it may propose a short follow-up visit after a regular visit.

In order to enable the Subcommittee on Prevention to fulfil its mandate, the States Parties undertake in Article 14 to the Protocol to grant it:

(a) Unrestricted access to all information concerning the number of persons deprived of their liberty in places of detention as defined in article 4, as well as the number of places and their location;

(b) Unrestricted access to all information referring to the treatment of those persons as well as their conditions of detention;
(c) Subject to paragraph 2 below, unrestricted access to all places of detention and their installations and facilities;
(d) The opportunity to have private interviews with the persons deprived of their liberty without witnesses, either personally or with a translator if deemed necessary, as well as with any other person who the Subcommittee on Prevention believes may supply relevant information;
(e) The liberty to choose the places it wants to visit and the persons it wants to interview.

Objection to a visit to a particular place of detention may be made only on urgent and compelling grounds of national defence, public safety, natural disaster or serious disorder in the place to be visited that temporarily prevent the carrying out of such a visit. The existence of a declared state of emergency as such shall not be invoked by a State Party as a reason to object to a visit.

As provided for in Article 15, no authority or official shall order, apply, permit or tolerate any sanction against any person or organization for having communicated to the Subcommittee on Prevention or to its delegates any information, whether true or false, and no such person or organization shall be otherwise prejudiced in any way.

Article 16 provides that the Subcommittee on Prevention shall communicate its recommendations and observations confidentially to the State Party and, if relevant, to the national preventive mechanism. The Subcommittee on Prevention shall publish its report, together with any comments of the State Party concerned, whenever requested to do so by that State Party. If the State Party makes part of the report public, the Subcommittee on Prevention may publish the report in whole or in part. However, no personal data shall be published without the express consent of the person concerned. The Subcommittee on Prevention shall present a public annual report on its activities to the Committee against Torture.

If the State Party refuses to cooperate with the Subcommittee on Prevention according to articles 12 and 14, or to take steps to improve the situation in the light of the recommendations of the Subcommittee on Prevention, the Committee against Torture may, at the request of the Subcommittee on Prevention, decide, by a majority of its members, after the State Party has had an opportunity to make its views known, to make a public statement on the matter or to publish the report of the Subcommittee on Prevention.

Article 17 deals with national preventive mechanisms. It provides that each State Party shall maintain, designate or establish, at the latest one year after the entry into force of the Protocol or of its ratification or accession, one or several independent national preventive mechanisms for the prevention of torture at the domestic level. Mechanisms established by decentralized units may be designated as national preventive mechanisms for the purposes of the Protocol if they are in conformity with its provisions. The States Parties shall, under Article 18, guarantee the functional independence of the national preventive mechanisms as well as the independence of their personnel. The States Parties shall take the necessary measures to ensure that the experts of the national preventive mechanism have the required capabilities and professional knowledge. They shall strive for a gender balance and the adequate representation of ethnic and minority groups in the country. The States Parties undertake to make available the necessary resources for the functioning of the national preventive mechanisms. When establishing national preventive mechanisms, States Parties shall give due consideration to the UN Principles relating to the status of national institutions for the promotion and protection of human rights.

The national preventive mechanisms shall, in accordance with Article 19, be granted at a minimum the power:

(a) To regularly examine the treatment of the persons deprived of their liberty in places of detention as defined in article 4, with a view to strengthening, if necessary, their protection against torture and other cruel, inhuman or degrading treatment or punishment;
(b) To make recommendations to the relevant authorities with the aim of improving the treatment and the conditions of the persons deprived of their liberty and to prevent torture and other cruel, inhuman or degrading treatment or punishment, taking into consideration the relevant norms of the United Nations;
(c) To submit proposals and observations concerning existing or draft legislation.

In order to enable the national preventive mechanisms to fulfil their mandate, the States Parties to the Protocol undertake in Article 20 to grant them:

(a) Access to all information concerning the number of persons deprived of their liberty in places of detention as defined in article 4, as well as the number of places and their location;
(b) Access to all information referring to the treatment of those persons as well as their conditions of detention;

(c) Access to all places of detention and their installations and facilities;
(d) The opportunity to have private interviews with the persons deprived of their liberty without witnesses, either personally or with a translator if deemed necessary, as well as with any other person who the national preventive mechanism believes may supply relevant information;
(e) The liberty to choose the places they want to visit and the persons they want to interview;
(f) The right to have contacts with the Subcommittee on Prevention, to send it information and to meet with it.

Article 21 stipulates that no authority or official shall order, apply, permit or tolerate any sanction against any person or organization for having communicated to the national preventive mechanism any information, whether true or false, and no such person or organization shall be otherwise prejudiced in any way. Confidential information collected by the national preventive mechanism shall be privileged. No personal data shall be published without the express consent of the person concerned.

The competent authorities of the State Party concerned are required under Article 22 to examine the recommendations of the national preventive mechanism and enter into a dialogue with it on possible implementation measures. The States Parties to the Protocol undertake in Article 23 to publish and disseminate the annual reports of the national preventive mechanisms.

V. European Convention for the Prevention of Torture and Inhuman or Degrading Treatment or Punishment[162]

The member States of the Council of Europe who subscribe to the Convention affirm their conviction that the protection of persons deprived of their liberty against torture and inhuman or degrading treatment or punishment could be strengthened by non-judicial means of a preventive character based on visits, They therefore agreed in Article 1 to the establishment of a European Committee for the Prevention of Torture and Inhuman or Degrading Treatment or Punishment ("the Committee") which shall, by means of visits, examine the treatment of persons deprived of their liberty with a view to strengthening, if necessary, the

162 Strasbourg, 26.XI.1987. Text amended according to the provisions of Protocols No. 1 (ETS No. 151) and No. 2 (ETS No. 152) which entered into force on 1 March 2002.

protection of such persons from torture and from inhuman or degrading treatment or punishment.

Each Party agrees in Article 2 to permit visits, in accordance with the Convention, to any place within its jurisdiction where persons are deprived of their liberty by a public authority. In the application of the Convention, the Committee and the competent national authorities of the Party concerned shall, in accordance with Article 3, co-operate with each other.

The Committee, in accordance with Article 4, consists of a number of members equal to that of the Parties. The members of the Committee shall be chosen from among persons of high moral character, known for their competence in the field of human rights or having professional experience in the areas covered by this Convention.

Article 6 provides that the Committee shall meet *in camera*. A quorum shall be equal to the majority of its members. Under Article 7, the Committee shall organise visits to places referred to in Article 2. Apart from periodic visits, the Committee may organise such other visits as appear to it to be required in the circumstances. As a general rule, the visits shall be carried out by at least two members of the Committee. The Committee may, if it considers it necessary, be assisted by experts and interpreters.

The Committee is required, under Article 8, to notify the Government of the Party concerned of its intention to carry out a visit. After such notification, it may at any time visit any place referred to in Article 2. A Party shall provide the Committee with the following facilities to carry out its task:

a access to its territory and the right to travel without restriction;
b full information on the places where persons deprived of their liberty are being held;
c unlimited access to any place where persons are deprived of their liberty, including the right to move inside such places without restriction;
d other information available to the Party which is necessary for the Committee to carry out its task. In seeking such information, the Committee shall have regard to applicable rules of national law and professional ethics;
e The Committee may interview in private persons deprived of their liberty;
f The Committee may communicate freely with any person whom it believes can supply relevant information;

g If necessary, the Committee may immediately communicate observations to the competent authorities of the Party concerned.

Article 9 states that in exceptional circumstances, the competent authorities of the Party concerned may make representations to the Committee against a visit at the time or to the particular place proposed by the Committee. Such representations may only be made on grounds of national defence, public safety, serious disorder in places where persons are deprived of their liberty, the medical condition of a person or that an urgent interrogation relating to a serious crime is in progress. Following such representations, the Committee and the Party shall immediately enter into consultations in order to clarify the situation and seek agreement on arrangements to enable the Committee to exercise its functions expeditiously. Such arrangements may include the transfer to another place of any person whom the Committee proposed to visit. Until the visit takes place, the Party shall provide information to the Committee about any person concerned.

After each visit, the Committee shall, in accordance with Article 10, draw up a report on the facts found during the visit, taking account of any observations which may have been submitted by the Party concerned. It shall transmit to the latter its report containing any recommendations it considers necessary. The Committee may consult with the Party with a view to suggesting, if necessary, improvements in the protection of persons deprived of their liberty. If the Party fails to co-operate or refuses to improve the situation in the light of the Committee's recommendations, the Committee may decide, after the Party has had an opportunity to make known its views, by a majority of two-thirds of its members to make a public statement on the matter.

The information gathered by the Committee in relation to a visit, its report and its consultations with the Party concerned shall, in accordance with Article 11, be confidential. The Committee shall publish its report, together with any comments of the Party concerned, whenever requested to do so by that Party. However, no personal data shall be published without the express consent of the person concerned.

Subject to the rules of confidentiality in Article 11, the Committee shall every year, in accordance with Article 12, submit to the Committee of Ministers a general report on its activities which shall be transmitted to the Consultative Assembly and to any non-member State of the Council of Europe which is a party to the Convention, and made public.

The members of the Committee, experts and other persons assisting the Committee are required, under Article 13, during and after their terms of office, to maintain the confidentiality of the facts or information of which they have become aware during the discharge of their functions.

Article 20 provides that the Committee shall not visit places which representatives or delegates of Protecting Powers or the International Committee of the Red Cross effectively visit on a regular basis by virtue of the Geneva Conventions of 12 August 1949 and the Additional Protocols of 8 June 1977 thereto.

Article 21 specifies that no reservation may be made in respect of the provisions of the Convention.

VI. Preventive Procedures of UN Human Rights Treaty Organs

In 1992/1993, the preventive role of human rights treaty bodies was discussed in various treaty bodies, as reflected in the following consideration taken from the Fourth meeting of Chairpersons of Human Rights treaty bodies:

> "the treaty bodies have an important role in seeking to prevent as well as to respond to human rights violations. It is thus appropriate for each treaty body to undertake an urgent examination of all possible measures that it might take, within its competence, both to prevent human rights violations from occurring and to monitor more closely emergency situations of all kinds arising within the jurisdiction of States parties. Where procedural innovations are required for this purpose, they should be considered as soon as possible."

The Committee on the Elimination of Racial Discrimination, taking into account the procedures adopted by other treaty bodies,[163] followed this recommendation, and decided to create an early warning and urgent action procedure. To this end, it adopted a working paper in 1993, presenting the legal basis of the procedure.[164] The working paper considered early warning measures as aimed at addressing existing structural problems so as to prevent these from escalating into conflicts and also include confidence building measures to identify and support structures to strengthen racial tolerance and solidify peace in order to prevent a relapse into conflict in situations where it has occurred. The criteria for the adoption of such measures included:

---

163 The Human Rights Committee, the Committee on Economic, Social and Cultural Rights and the Committee on the Rights of the Child.

164 A/48/18, annex I.

- the lack of an adequate legislative basis for defining and criminalizing all forms of racial discrimination;
- inadequate implementation or enforcement mechanisms, including the lack of recourse procedures;
- the presence of a pattern of escalating racial hatred and violence, or racist propaganda or appeals to racial intolerance by persons, groups or organizations, notably by elected or other officials;
- a significant pattern of racial discrimination evidenced in social and economic indicators;
- significant flows of refugees or displaced persons resulting from a pattern of racial discrimination or encroachment on the lands of minority communities.

The measures proposed to remedy such a situation were:

- to establish a follow-up mechanism to the suggestions and recommendations contained in its concluding observations;
- to offer to send to States parties one or more of its members in order to facilitate the implementation of international standards or technical assistance to establish a human rights institutional infrastructure;
- to recommend to States parties to avail themselves of the advisory services and technical assistance programme of the OHCHR;
- to submit information to the Secretary-General as a contribution to his early-warning mechanism; and
- to recommend greater cooperation at the regional level.

Various measures were proposed to enhance the effectiveness of the procedure:

- request the urgent submission of a special report concerning measures taken to prevent a serious a pattern of racial discrimination;
- designate a special Rapporteur to act as a focal point for monitoring critical situations and consult with the Chairman of the Committee to initiate the urgent action procedure and to follow up when decisions have been taken;
- expression concern, along with recommendations for actions to:
  - the State party concerned;
  - the Special Rapporteur on contemporary forms of racism, racial discrimination and xenophobia and related intolerance;
  - the UN Secretary-General;
  - the Security Council through the Secretary-General;
  - other relevant human rights bodies.

Conclusion

In this chapter we began by looking at solid pronouncements by human rights treaty bodies on the duty of States parties to act for the prevention of violations of human rights. We saw that major statements to this effect had been in general comments or recommendations of CAT, CERD, CEDAW, and the Committee on the Rights of the Child. We then looked at the jurisprudence of treaty bodies on preventive protection of the right to life, preventive dimensions of the right to an effective remedy, interim measures of protection, and deportation to countries where there is a risk of serious violation of human rights. We looked next at conventions with an express preventive purpose: The Convention against Genocide, The Convention against Torture, the Optional Protocol to this convention, and the European Convention for the Prevention of Torture. We then examined the preventive procedures of human rights treaty bodies, notably the CERD. The comment may be offered that while there are significant norms, jurisprudence and practice on prevention, there remains much scope still for the further development of preventive approaches in international human rights treaty bodies. Prevention must be highlighted in the duty to respect, protect and ensure, the topic of the next chapter.

Chapter Six

The Duty to Respect, Protect and Ensure

Introduction

The primary responsibility for the prevention of violations of human rights lies with the national protection system of each State. According to one author, the first obligation is to respect and to ensure to all individuals within its territory and subject to its jurisdiction the rights recognized in the ICCPR.[165] A state complies with the obligation to respect the recognized rights by not violating them. The duty to ensure imposes an affirmative duty on the state and calls for specific activities by the state to enable individuals to enjoy the recognized rights.[166] The second obligation is for the state to take the necessary steps, in accordance with its constitutional processes and with the provisions of the ICCPR to adopt such legislative or other measures as may be necessary to give effect to these rights and freedoms.[167] The third obligation is to ensure that any person whose rights or freedoms are violated shall have an effective remedy, notwithstanding that the violation has been committed by persons acting in an official capacity; to ensure that any person claiming such a remedy shall have his right thereto determined by competent judicial, administrative, or legislative authorities, or by the legal system, and to develop the possibilities of judicial review; and to ensure that the competent authorities shall enforce such remedies when granted.[168]

---

165 N. Jayawickrama, The Judicial Application of Human Rights Law. National, Regional, and International Jurisprudence. Cambridge, Cambridge University Press, 2002, p. 46.

166 Ibid, p. 48.

167 Ibid, p. 49.

168 Ibid, p. 49.

I. The Duty to Respect

In the Velasquez Rodriguez Case (1988), the Inter-American Court of Human Rights[169] dealt with Article l (1) of the American Convention on Human Rights which provides as follows: '1. The States Parties to this Convention undertake to respect the rights and freedoms recognized herein and to ensure to all persons subject to their jurisdiction the free and full exercise of those rights and freedoms, without any discrimination …' The Court held that according to Article 1(1), any exercise of public power that violates the rights recognized by the Convention is illegal. Whenever a State organ, official or public entity violates one of those rights, this constitutes a failure of the duty to respect the rights and freedoms set forth in the Convention. This conclusion was independent of whether the organ or official had contravened provisions of internal law or overstepped the limits of his authority; under international law a State was responsible for the acts of its agents undertaken in their official capacity and for their omissions, even when those agents acted outside the sphere of their authority or violated internal law.[170]

Furthermore, an illegal act which violated human rights and which was initially not directly imputable to a State (for example, because it was the act of a private person or because the person responsible had not been identified) could lead to international responsibility of the State, not because of the act itself, but because of the lack of diligence to prevent the violation or to respond to it as required by the Convention.[171] What was decisive was whether a violation of the rights recognized by the Convention had occurred with the support or the acquiescence of the government, or whether the State had allowed the act to take place without taking measures to prevent it or to punish those responsible.[172]

The State has, the Court continued, the legal duty to take reasonable steps to prevent human rights violations and to use the means at its disposal to carry out a serious investigation of violations committed within its jurisdiction, to identify those responsible, to impose the appropriate punishment and to ensure the victim adequate compensation.

169 4 Inter-Am. Ct. H.R. (ser C).

170 Ibid, para. 170.

171 Ibid, para. 172.

172 Ibid, para. 173.

II. The Duty to Protect

The notion of protection (initially domestic protection) may be traced back to very early times as organized human societies were emerging and notions of law and justice were evolving. In his study, *Freedom in the Ancient World,* H.J. Muller showed how law codes, written or unwritten, provided protection to the individual and he traced 'the efforts of kings to protect ordinary men against the abuses of power and privilege'.[173] Bello has found notions akin to protection in African customary humanitarian law and has reported that, while not generally the case, during armed conflicts in certain parts of Africa some tribes 'took pride in according respect and human rights to women, children and old persons'.[174] In Asia, Alexandrowicz found that there existed, historically, high standards of protection of foreigners irrespective of religion or civilization.[175]

In Europe the sixteenth century saw the development of the institution of 'Protecting Powers' as European powers obtained through capitulation treaties 'the right to exercise exclusive, extra-territorial jurisdiction over their nationals in the Ottoman Empire, and later on in the other independent countries of the Middle and Far East.' The institution of protecting powers, which could also be found in diplomatic and consular practice evolved, subsequently, and grew into the 'cornerstone of the system of implementation of the Geneva conventions' of 1949 on the laws of armed conflicts.[176]

The use of treaties providing for the protection of human rights, which was known even in the practice of the ancient Greeks, began to assume prominence in the seventeenth century. The Treaty of Westphalia (1648) sought to ensure equality of rights for Roman Catholics and Protestants in Germany. During the seventeenth century, some governments undertook in peace treaties to respect the rights of Roman Catholic subjects of Protestant princes. In 1774 Turkey undertook vis-à-vis Russia to

173 H.J. Muller, *Freedom in the Ancient World* (London: Secker and Warburg, 1962), 58-59. See also, J. Shotwell, *The Long Way to Freedom* (New York: Columbia University Press, 1960).

174 E. Bello, *African Customary Humanitarian law* (1980), 29.

175 C.H. Alexandrowicz, 'The Afro-Asian World and the Law of Nations (Historical Aspects)," 123, *R.C.A.D.I* (1968), I, 117-214, at 151.

176 For a concise and useful history of the institution of Protecting Power, see G. Abi-Saab, "The Implementation of Humanitarian Law" in A. Cassese (Ed.), *The New Humanitarian Law of Armed Conflict* (The Hague: Martinus Nijhoff, 1979), 310-348 at 311-318.

protect the Christian religion and its churches within its territory. The congress of Vienna of 1815 provided for the free exercise of religion and for equality, irrespective of religion, in various cantons of Switzerland as well as for the equality of Christian denominations in Germany. The Congress also contained provisions aiming at the improvement of the civil status of Jews.[177]

The doctrine and practice of "humanitarian intervention" may also be included among the antecedents of the concept of "international protection." In previous centuries, when the treatment by a state of its own population was so abusive and cruel that it shocked the conscience of humanity, other states claimed the right to threaten or use force in order to assist the oppressed persons. Setting aside the issue of the validity of such interventions in contemporary international law, the practice does at least offer guidance with regard to one set of circumstances when international protection would be warranted: when atrocities reach such a scale as to shock the conscience of humanity.

The concept of international protection may, furthermore, be traced in the movements for the abolition of slavery, for the establishment of international humanitarian law concerning the conduct of hostilities and the protection of human rights during periods of armed conflict, and for the development of international social and labor legislation which the ILO has pioneered since its establishment.

The institution of diplomatic protection, one of the hallowed institutions of international law, has also contributed to the development of the concept of international protection of human rights. Diplomatic protection proceeds from a state's right to protect its nationals abroad. As the Permanent Court of International Justice stated in the Mavrommatis Palestine Concession Case, "It is an elementary principle of international law that a state is entitled to protect its subjects, when injured by acts contrary to international committed by another state, from whom they have been unable to obtain satisfaction through the ordinary channels."[178] In traditional international law, the responsibility of states for damage done in their territory to the person or property of foreigners rested on the international standard of justice, and the principle of the equality of nationals and aliens. As the General Claims Commission held in the Neer Case, the propriety of governmental acts should be put to the test of international standards.

177 See E. Schwelb, "Human Rights," in *Encyclopedia Britannica*, Vol. 8, 1974, 1183-1189.

178 Mavrommatis Palestine Concessions Case, P.C.I.J., ser A. No.2 (1924), 12.

In an important submission, F.V. Garcia-Amador, former rapporteur of the International Law Commission, argued that what was formerly the object of these two principles – the protection of the person and of his property – is now intended to be accomplished by the international recognition of the essential rights of human beings.[179]

In some of the peace treaties, in special minorities treaties and in declarations made after World War I, some states of central and eastern Europe and a state in the Middle East (Iraq) accepted obligations towards their racial, linguistic and religious minorities to the effect that all of their nationals were to be equal before the law and were to enjoy the same civil and political rights without distinction as to race, language or religion. The relevant treaties provided that their provisions constituted obligations of international concern rather than domestic matters and all were placed under the guarantee of the League of Nations.

At the drafting of the United Nations Charter in San Francisco, the question arose expressly whether the Charter should define the role of the United Nations in terms of 'promotion' or 'protection'. The drafters opted for language calling for the achievement of international cooperation in promoting and encouraging respect for human rights and for fundamental freedoms. Notwithstanding the use of the term 'promotion', the practice of the United Nations has confirmed the competence of the Organization to act for the protection of human rights. As an authoritative commentator wrote in 1972:

> "In the actual practice of the various organs of the United Nations over the past 25 years the obstacles to taking action based on the human rights provisions of the Charter have proved to be far less formidable than the cleavage of theoretical opinions of scholars and of abstract statements by governments would lead one to assume. In the practice of the United Nations and its Members neither the vagueness and generality of the human rights clauses of the Charter nor the domestic jurisdiction clause have prevented the United Nations from considering, investigating, and judging concrete human rights situations, provided there was a majority strong enough and wishing strongly enough to attempt to influence the particular development ...".[180]

179 F.V. Garcia-Amador, "Report on State Responsibility," *Y.B.I.L.C.* 1956, Vol.II, 173-231, at 203.

180 E. Schwelb, "The International Court of Justice and the Human Rights Clauses of the Charter," 66 *A.J.I.L.* (1972), 337-351, at 341.

An expert on the ICRC, discussing the protection functions of the ICRC, placed them into two categories: direct protection and indirect protection. He submitted that each of the following three basic roles of the ICRC had a direct and an indirect dimension: (1) *ad hoc* diplomacy; (2) development of law; and (3) application of the law.[181] There is much merit in this frame of direct and indirect protection, which we believe offers a conceptual approach corresponding mostly closely to international protection as practiced in the United Nations. We discuss this further later in this chapter.

The Responsibility to Protect

The report of the International Commission on Intervention and state Sovereignty, launched the concept of the responsibility to protect.[182] In the Commissions view, the responsibility to protect embraced three specific responsibilities: the responsibility to prevent, namely, to address both the root causes and direct causes of internal conflict and other man-made crises putting populations at risk; the responsibility to react, namely, to respond to situations of compelling human need with appropriate measures, which may include coercive measures like sanctions and international prosecution, and in extreme cases military intervention; the responsibility to rebuild, namely, to provide, particularly after a military intervention, full assistance with recovery, reconstruction and reconciliation, addressing the causes of the harm the intervention was designed to halt or avert.

The Commission was firm in its view that prevention was the single most important dimension of the responsibility to protect. Prevention options should always be exhausted before intervention was contemplated, and more commitment and resources must be devoted to it. The exercise of the responsibility to prevent and react should always involve less intrusive and coercive measures before more coercive and intrusive ones are applied.

The United Nations Summit of world leaders, meeting to mark the organizations 60th anniversary in 2005 endorsed the responsibility to protect and declared their readiness, if need be, to refer to the UN Se-

181 D.P. Forsythe, *Humanitarian Politics: The International Committee of the Red Cross* (Baltimore: The Johns Hopkins University Press, 1977), 28-32.

182 International Commission on Intervention and State Sovereignty, *The Responsibility to Protect*, December 2001. See also *The Responsibility to Protect: Research, Bibliography, Background*, December 2001.

curity Council (UNSC) for its attention situations of genocide, crimes against humanity and war crimes.

Preventive, Curative and Remedial or Compensatory Protection

International protection may be grouped into three categories: anticipatory or preventive, mitigatory or curative, remedial or compensatory. *Preventive protection* means that the national authorities, regional organizations, or the United Nations, should try to anticipate and head off potential situations of gross violations of human rights before they occur. This is a newer thrust in the efforts of the human rights movement and prevention is still in its infancy.[183] Prevention should be an essential part of any national protection system.

Among the preventive measures taken by international bodies, mention may be made of urgent appeals addressed on behalf of victims or of interim measures undertaken on their behalf. On some occasions the UNSC has met to consider a situation and to bring its influence to bear on those involved. Special Procedures of the UN Human Rights Council (HRC) address urgent appeals to Governments in cases of concern. The UN High Commissioner for Human Rights may do likewise or may make public statements expressing concern. The Secretary-General may intercede if he considers that this could be helpful. In the European Commission and the Inter-American Commission on Human Rights, the secretaries of these organs have an established practice of interceding urgently with a government if, from the facts reported to them, they conclude that an individual is in serious danger of having irreparable harm done to them. The good offices of international officials such as the Director-General of the ILO may be called upon.[184]

Aside from these limited measures, such as appeals, interim measures, or the use of humanitarian good offices, the area of anticipation and prevention represents one of the major gaps in the arrangements for the international protection of human rights. Let us cite, in this regard, the following statement which was made by Dr. Theo C. van Boven, the then Director of the United Nations Division of Human Rights to the Commissioner on Human Rights (CHR) in 1980:

183 See, L-A Sicilianos, et al. (Eds.) *The Prevention of Human Rights Violations* (The Hague, New York: Martinus Nijhoff Publishers, 2001).

184 See B.G. Ramcharan, *Humanitarian Good Offices in International Law* (The Hague: Martinus Nijhoff, 1983).

> "We are frequently faced in the United Nations with serious and urgent problems of violations of human rights which arise in different parts of the world, but, apart from statements of the Secretary-General issued in a humanitarian spirit, or the exercise of his good offices in certain cases, the organization is mostly unable to take action in a situation where every day counts heavily notwithstanding the hope and expectations of the international community for such action. In the ILO, for example, the Director-General has been granted the competence, in urgent cases, to approach the government concerned to receive a mission from the organization urgently to look into allegations of violations of trade unions rights within the country in question. ... We, in the United Nations, similarly receive many complaints and disturbing reports about grave human rights problems in this as well as in other countries ... but there is no similar possibility for action open to us. In my view, this is a major deficiency in the arrangements."[185]

The situation has not changed markedly since then.

Curative protection involves efforts to mitigate and stop gross violations of human rights that may be taking place. The UNSC, the HRC, Special Procedures of the HRC, the United Nations High Commissioner for Human Rights, and the United Nations Secretary-General endeavors to engage in mitigatory and curative protection.

Various procedures exist within different international organizations, whose aims may be said to stop or to mitigate excesses being committed, or to cure or redress situations giving rise to such excesses. Among these may be mentioned: the United Nations procedures for dealing with complaints of violations of human rights; ILO's complaints procedures; UNESCO's complaints procedures; Inter-governmental complaints procedures, such as those under the European Convention on Human Rights, the American Convention on Human Rights or the International Covenant on Civil and Political Rights; investigation and fact-finding under various procedures in the United Nations, ILO, the Council of Europe and the OAS, visits on-the spot or the establishment of international presences; the activities of the ICRC, and the United Nations High Commissioner for Human Rights, the UN High Commissioner for Refugees (UNHCR); the activities of non-governmental organizatons; the exercise of good offices; and public denunciations of violations of human rights.

185 T.C. van Boven, *People Matter* (Meulenhoff, 1982), 73.

Some of the procedures within the different international organizations may be said to have the objective of providing protection through remedies or compensation. Of particular significance in this regard are the petition systems under the European and American Conventions on Human Rights and under the Optional Protocol to the International Covenant on Civil and Political Rights. Judicial measures of protection such as those provided by the European Court and the Inter-American Court of Human Rights are also relevant in this regard. Also related are the efforts currently being made within the United Nations to provide reconstruction assistance to countries which have experienced extensive violations of human rights, as well as to individuals who have been subjected to such violations.[186]

Remedial and compensatory protection involves processes of establishing the truth about what took place in a situation of gross violations of human rights, bringing perpetrators to justice where possible, and providing redress to victims of gross violations of human rights or to their families. Truth and reconciliation commissions are bodies that seek to ascertain and record what took place. National or hybrid courts may deal with justice issues. So might the ICC or *ad hoc* tribunals such as the International Criminal Tribunals for the Former Yugoslavia and Rwanda, the Sierra Leone Court and the Cambodia Court.

It should be pointed out that although we have referred to some procedures under the headings of preventive/anticipatory; curative/mitigatory and remedial/compensatory, many procedures in fact perform functions belonging to more than one of these categories.

Shades of Protection: Direct and Indirect

As discussed earlier in this chapter, the international protection of human rights in the contemporary world may be said to be direct or indirect. By direct international protection is meant the intercession of an international entity either at the behest of a victim or victims concerned, or by persons on their behalf, or on the volition of the international protecting agency itself to halt a violation of human rights. As examples of direct international protection mention may be made of the activities of the UN High Commissioner for Refugees, the UN High Commissioner for Human Rights, of the ICRC, or of the various petitions or complaints

186 A United Nations Fund for Victims of Torture has been in existence since 1991.

procedures such as that provided under the Optional Protocol to the International Covenant on Civil and Political Rights.

However, much of the protecting activities undertaken in the international community may be classified into the category of indirect protection. Among these may be included: the creation of an international environment which is conducive to the realization of human rights; the elaboration of norms and standards; education, teaching, training, research and the dissemination of information,[187] and the provision of advisory services in the field of human rights.

In the following section we examine how various organizations and procedures have approached the application of 'direct protection'.

Human rights treaty bodies monitor the implementation of international human rights norms and make an important contribution to reinforcing the international protection framework. The Human Rights Committee which operates under the International Covenant on Civil and Political Rights, in its General Comment No. 6, declared that the right to life in Article 6 of the Covenant is the supreme right from which no derogation is permitted even time of public emergency, and also, that it is the duty of States to prevent wars.

Furthermore, its General Comment No. 14 declared that nuclear weapons are among the greatest threats to the right to life that confront mankind today, and that the production, testing, possession, deployment and use of those weapons should be prohibited and recognized as crimes against humanity.

Human rights treaty bodies consider and comment on reports, may consider and pronounce upon petitions, and may make visits to countries. In all three instances human rights treaty bodies contribute to the clarification and implementation of the protection concept.

Some human rights treaty bodies have established a practice according to which, in times of emergency, they request emergency reports from States parties. The Human Rights Committee has, since 1991, developed a procedure applicable to emergency situations. Under the procedure the Committee has requested urgent reports from more than a dozen states. In most cases the States parties were requested to submit the reports within three months. Reports thus submitted have been considered by the Committee as soon as possible, usually at the next scheduled session.

---

187 See on this, the Report of the ILA Sub-Committee on the International Protection of Human Rights by the Mobilisation of Public Opinion, submitted to the ILA conference in 1976.

In 1995 a coalition of NGOs from one State party drew the attention of the Committee on Economic Social and Cultural Rights to imminent changes in the social welfare laws which might be construed as detrimental to implementation of the economic covenant in that country. The NGOs submitted written materials and sought and obtained the consent of the Committee to address it during the day of the session set aside for NGO submissions. The Committee agreed that its chairperson would communicate the allegations to the government and solicit its views on the matter (E/C.12/1995/SR 4 and 5).

III. The Duty to Ensure

In the Velasquez Rodriguez Case (1988), the Inter-American Court of Human Rights[188] dealt with Article l(1) of the Inter-American Convention on Human Rights which provides as follows: '1. The States Parties to this Convention undertake to respect the rights and freedoms recognized herein and to ensure to all persons subject to their jurisdiction the free and full exercise of those rights and freedoms, without any discrimination ...' The Court commented that in effect, this article charges the State Parties with the fundamental duty to respect and guarantee the rights recognized in the Convention. Any impairment of those rights which can be attributed under the rules of international law to the action or omission of any public authority constitutes an act imputable to the State, which assumes responsibility in the terms provided by the Convention.

The Court went on to clarify the meaning of the obligation 'to ensure'. The obligation of the State Party, it held, is to ensure the free and full exercise of the rights recognized by the Convention to every person subject to its jurisdiction. This obligation implies the duty of the States Parties to organize the governmental apparatus and, in general, all the structures through which public power is exercised, so that they are capable of juridically ensuring the free and full enjoyment of human rights. As a consequence of this obligation, the States must prevent, investigate and punish any violation of the rights recognized by the Convention and, moreover, if possible attempt to restore the right violated and provide compensation as warranted for damages resulting from the violation.

The State is obligated, the Court continued, to investigate every situation involving a violation of the rights protected by the Convention. If the State apparatus acted in such a way that the violation went unpunished and the victim's full enjoyment of such rights was not restored as

188 4 Inter-Am. Ct. H.R. (ser C).

soon as possible, the State had failed to comply with its duty to ensure the free and full exercise of those rights to the persons within its jurisdiction. The same was true when the State allowed private persons or groups to act freely and with impunity to the detriment of the rights recognized in the Convention.

In certain circumstances, the Court recognized, it might be difficult to investigate acts that violated an individual's rights. The duty to investigate, like the duty to prevent, was not breached merely because the investigation did not produce a satisfactory result. Nevertheless, it must be undertaken in a serious manner and not as a mere formality preordained to be ineffective. An investigation must have an objective and be assumed by the State as its own legal duty, not as a step taken by private interests that depended upon the initiative of the victim or his family or upon their offer of proof, without an effective search for the truth by the government. This was true regardless of what agent was eventually found responsible for the violation. Where the acts of private parties that violated the Convention were not seriously investigated, those parties were aided in a sense by the government, thereby making the State responsible on the international plain.

In the case of a disappeared person, for example, the duty to investigate the facts continued as long as there was uncertainty about the fate of the person who had disappeared.

IV. Violations of the Obligations to Respect, to Protect and to Fulfil

In a series of general comments, the Committee on Economic, Social and Cultural Rights has expounded on the duty to respect, protect and to fulfil particular rights in the Covenant on Economic, Social and Cultural Rights and on violations of these obligations. In General Comment No. 14, for example, dealing with the right to the highest attainable standard of health, the Committee reaffirmed what it had stated in General Comment No. 3 that States parties had a core obligation to ensure the satisfaction of, at the very least, minimum essential levels of each of the rights contained in the Covenant, including essential primary health care. The Committee proceeded to deal with violations of the obligations to respect, to protect and to fulfil in the following terms:

Violations of the obligation to respect

Violations of the obligation to respect are those State actions, policies or laws that contravene the standards set out in article 12 of the Covenant and are likely to result in bodily harm, unnecessary morbidity and preventable mortality.

Violations of the obligation to protect

Violations of the obligation to protect follow from the failure to take all necessary measures to safeguard persons within their jurisdiction from infringements of the right to health by third parties.

Violations of the obligation to fulfil

Violations of the obligation to fulfil occur through the failure of States parties to take all necessary steps to ensure the realization of the right to health.[189]

Conclusion

In this chapter we have examined some of the foundation concepts of international human rights treaty law which deserve special attention on the part of all those who are called upon to implement human rights treaties or to supervise their implementation. On the duty to respect, we saw landmark jurisprudence in cases such as that of Velasquez Rodriguez decided by the Inter-American Court of Human Rights. We looked at greater length at the responsibility to protect, which was underlined by the summit of world leaders meeting at the United Nations in 2005. On the duty to ensure observance of human rights treaty provisions we again took profit from the Velasquez Rodriguez case. We then saw groundbreaking recommendations from the Committee on Economic, Social and Cultural Rights on the responsibility of Governments for violations of the obligation to respect, protect, and fulfil human rights treaty obligations. Failure to fulfil the obligations to respect, protect and ensure give rise to the right to redress, which we discuss in the following chapter.

189 HRI/GEN/1Rev.9, pp 90-91. See similarly, p. 105 ff. on violations of the right to water; pp. 116-117 and 121-122 violations of article 3 on equal rights between men and women; pp. 133-134 on violations of article 15; pp. 147-148, violations of the right to work.

Chapter Seven

The Duty to Provide Redress

Introduction

In this chapter we look at the duty to provide redress as it has been expounded upon by human rights treaty bodies and as it has been codified in a set of UN principles endorsed by the UN General Assembly.

I. The Jurisprudence and Practice of Treaty Bodies

A. Inter-American Court of Human Rights

In its Advisory Opinion on Judicial Guarantees in States of Emergency[190] the Inter-American Court of Human Rights underlined the importance of the principle of effective judicial remedies to victims of human rights violations and declared as follows:

> "According to this principle, the absence of an effective remedy to violations of the rights recognized by the Convention is itself a violation of the Convention by the State Party in which the remedy is lacking. In that sense, it should be emphasized that, for such a remedy to exist, it is not sufficient that it be provided for by the Constitution or by law or that it be formally recognized, but rather it must be truly effective in establishing whether there has been a violation of human rights and in providing redress. A remedy which proves illusory because of the general conditions prevailing in the country, or even in the particular circumstances of a given case, cannot be considered effective. That could be the case, for example, when practice has shown its ineffectiveness, when the Judicial Power lacks the necessary independence to render impartial decisions or the means to carry out its judgments; or in any other situation that constitutes a denial of justice, as when there is an unjustified delay in the decision or when, for any reason, the alleged victim is denied access to a judicial remedy."[191]

---

190 Advisory Opinion OC-9/87 of October 6, 1987, Series A No. 9.

191 Para. 24.

B. Human Rights Committee

The Human Rights Committee, in its General Comment No. 31 provided the following guidance on the issue of remedies:

> "15. Article 2, paragraph 3, requires that in addition to effective protection of Covenant rights States parties must ensure that individuals also have accessible and effective remedies to vindicate those rights. Such remedies should be appropriately adapted so as to take account of the special vulnerability of certain categories of person, including in particular children. The Committee attaches importance to States parties' establishing appropriate judicial and administrative mechanisms for addressing claims of rights violations under domestic law. The Committee notes that the enjoyment of the rights recognized under the Covenant can be effectively assured by the judiciary in many different ways, including direct applicability of the Covenant, application of comparable constitutional or other provisions of law, or the interpretive effect of the Covenant in the application of national law. Administrative mechanisms are particularly required to give effect to the general obligation to investigate allegations of violations promptly, thoroughly and effectively through independent and impartial bodies. National human rights institutions, endowed with appropriate powers, can contribute to this end. A failure by a State party to investigate allegations of violations could in and of itself give rise to a separate breach of the Covenant. Cessation of an ongoing violation is an essential element of the right to an effective remedy."[192]

C. Committee on Economic, Social and Cultural Rights

The Committee on Economic, Social and Cultural Rights has taken the view that:

> "9. The right to an effective remedy need not be interpreted as always requiring a judicial remedy. Administrative remedies will, in many cases, be adequate and those living within the jurisdiction of a State party have a legitimate expectation, based on the principle of good faith, that all administrative authorities will take account of the requirements of the Covenant in their decision-making. Any such administrative remedies should be accessible, affordable, timely and effective. An ultimate right of judicial appeal from administrative procedures of this type would also often be appropri-

192 General Comment No. 31, HRI/GEN/Rev.9 p. 246.

ate. By the same token, there are some obligations, such as (but by no means limited to) those concerning non-discrimination in relation to which the provision of some form of judicial remedy would seem indispensable in order to satisfy the requirements of the Covenant. In other words, whenever a Covenant right cannot be made fully effective without some role for the judiciary, judicial remedies are necessary."[193]

D. *Committee on the Elimination of Discrimination Against Women (CEDAW)*

CEDAW has provided the following guidance:

> "Measures that are necessary to overcome family violence should include:
> - Criminal penalties where necessary and civil remedies in case of domestic violence;
> - Legislation to remove the defence of honour in regard to the assault or murder of a female family member;
> - Services to ensure the safety and security of victims of family violence, including refuges, counselling and rehabilitation programmes;
> - Rehabilitation programmes for perpetrators of domestic violence;
> - Support services for families where incest or sexual abuse has occurred."[194]

E. *Committee on the Elimination of Racial Discrimination (CERD)*

CERD has adopted the following position:

> "The Committee notifies States parties that, in its opinion, the right to seek just and adequate reparation or satisfaction for any damage suffered as a result of such discrimination, which is embodies in article 6 of the Convention, is not necessarily secured solely by the punishment of the perpetrator of the discrimination; at the same time, the courts and other competent authorities should consider awarding financial compensation for damage, material or moral, suffered by a victim, whenever appropriate."[195]

193 General Comment No. 9, HRI/GEN/Rev.9 p. 49.

194 General recommendation No. 19, HRI/GEN/Rev.9 p. 336.

195 General recommendation XXVI, HRI/GEN/REV.9, p. 288.

II. The UN Basic Principles and Guidelines

The Basic Principles and Guidelines which the UN General Assembly adopted in 2006 provide an authoritative statement of the duty of Governments to provide remedies for human rights violations. The adoption of the Basic Principles and Guidelines followed years of study by independent experts and governmental comments.[196] The Basic Principles and Guidelines contain thirteen chapters with core provisions of international human rights law. Because of the clarity and firmness of the statements in the document, we summarize key provisions below. The document is a magisterial summary of the contemporary international law of human rights generally and of the ideas of justice, redress and reparation in particular.

A. Obligation to Respect, Ensure Respect for and Implement International Human Rights Law and International Humanitarian Law

The Basic Principles and Guidelines recall that the obligation to respect, ensure respect for, and implement international human rights law and international humanitarian law as provided for under the respective bodies of law emanate from: treaties to which a State is a party; customary international law; the domestic law of each State. The document urges that if they have not already done so, States shall, as required under international law, ensure that their domestic law is consistent with their international legal obligations by: (a) Incorporating norms of international human rights law and international humanitarian law into their domestic law, or otherwise implementing them in their domestic legal system; (b) Adopting appropriate and effective legislative and administrative procedures and other appropriate measures that provide fair, effective and prompt access to justice; (c) Making available adequate, effective, prompt, and appropriate remedies, including reparation, as defined below; and (d) Ensuring that their domestic law provides at least the same level of protection for victims as required by their international obligations.

B. Scope of the Obligation

The Basic Principles and Guidelines specify that the obligation to respect, ensure respect for and implement international human rights law and in-

196 General Assembly resolution 60/147.

ternational humanitarian law as provided for under the respective bodies of law, includes, inter alia, the duty to: (a) Take appropriate legislative and administrative and other appropriate measures to prevent violations; (b) Investigate violations effectively, promptly, thoroughly and impartially and, where appropriate, take action against those allegedly responsible in accordance with domestic and international law; (c) Provide those who claim to be victims of a human rights or humanitarian law violation with equal and effective access to justice, as described below, irrespective of who may ultimately be the bearer of responsibility for the violation; and (d) Provide effective remedies to victims, including reparation, as described below.

C. *Gross Violations of International Human Rights Law and Serious Violations of International Humanitarian Law that Constitute Crimes under International Law*

The Basic Principles and Guidelines underline that in cases of gross violations of international human rights law and serious violations of international humanitarian law constituting crimes under international law, States have the duty to investigate and, if there is sufficient evidence, the duty to submit to prosecution the person allegedly responsible for the violations and, if found guilty, the duty to punish her or him. Moreover, in these cases, States should, in accordance with international law, cooperate with one another and assist international judicial organs competent in the investigation and prosecution of these violations.

To that end, where so provided in an applicable treaty or under other international law obligations, States shall incorporate or otherwise implement within their domestic law appropriate provisions for universal jurisdiction. Moreover, where it is so provided for in an applicable treaty or other international legal obligations, States should facilitate extradition or surrender offenders to other States and to appropriate international judicial bodies and provide judicial assistance and other forms of cooperation in the pursuit of international justice, including assistance to, and protection of, victims and witnesses, consistent with international human rights legal standards and subject to international legal requirements such as those relating to the prohibition of torture and other forms of cruel, inhuman or degrading treatment or punishment.

D. Statutes of Limitations

The Basic Principles and Guidelines specify that where so provided for in an applicable treaty or contained in other international legal obligations, statutes of limitations shall not apply to gross violations of international human rights law and serious violations of international humanitarian law which constitute crimes under international law. Domestic statutes of limitations for other types of violations that do not constitute crimes under international law, including those time limitations applicable to civil claims and other procedures, should not be unduly restrictive.

E. Victims of Gross Violations of International Human Rights Law And Serious Violations of International Humanitarian Law

The Basic Principles and Guidelines define victims as persons who individually or collectively suffered harm, including physical or mental injury, emotional suffering, economic loss or substantial impairment of their fundamental rights, through acts or omissions that constitute gross violations of international human rights law, or serious violations of international humanitarian law. Where appropriate, and in accordance with domestic law, the term "victim" also includes the immediate family or dependants of the direct victim and persons who have suffered harm in intervening to assist victims in distress or to prevent victimization. A person shall be considered a victim regardless of whether the perpetrator of the violation is identified, apprehended, prosecuted, or convicted and regardless of the familial relationship between the perpetrator and the victim.

F. Treatment of Victims

The Basic Principles and Guidelines specify that victims should be treated with humanity and respect for their dignity and human rights, and appropriate measures should be taken to ensure their safety, physical and psychological well-being and privacy, as well as those of their families. The State should ensure that its domestic laws, to the extent possible, provide that a victim who has suffered violence or trauma should benefit from special consideration and care to avoid his or her re-traumatization in the course of legal and administrative procedures designed to provide justice and reparation.

G. *Victims' Right to Remedies*

The Basic Principles and Guideline includes as remedies for gross violations of international human rights law and serious violations of international humanitarian law the victim's right to the following as provided for under international law: equal and effective access to justice; adequate, effective and prompt reparation for harm suffered; and access to relevant information concerning violations and reparation mechanisms.

H. *Access to Justice*

The Basic Principles and Guidelines register that a victim of a gross violation of international human rights law or of a serious violation of international humanitarian law shall have equal access to an effective judicial remedy as provided for under international law. Other remedies available to the victim include access to administrative and other bodies, as well as mechanisms, modalities and proceedings conducted in accordance with domestic law. Obligations arising under international law to secure the right to access justice and fair and impartial proceedings shall be reflected in domestic laws. To that end, States should:

(a) Disseminate, through public and private mechanisms, information about all available remedies for gross violations of international human rights law and serious violations of international humanitarian law;
(b) Take measures to minimize the inconvenience to victims and their representatives, protect against unlawful interference with their privacy as appropriate and ensure their safety from intimidation and retaliation, as well as that of their families and witnesses, before, during and after judicial, administrative, or other proceedings that affect the interests of victims;
(c) Provide proper assistance to victims seeking access to justice;
(d) Make available all appropriate legal, diplomatic and consular means to ensure that victims can exercise their rights to remedy for gross violations of international human rights law or serious violations of international humanitarian law.

In addition to individual access to justice, States should endeavour to develop procedures to allow groups of victims to present claims for reparation and to receive reparation, as appropriate. An adequate, effective and prompt remedy for gross violations of international human rights law or serious violations of international humanitarian law should include all available and appropriate international processes in which a person may have legal standing and should be without prejudice to any other domestic remedies.

I. Reparation for Harm Suffered

The Basic Principles and Guidelines stipulates that adequate, effective and prompt reparation is intended to promote justice by redressing gross violations of international human rights law or serious violations of international humanitarian law. Reparation should be proportional to the gravity of the violations and the harm suffered. In accordance with its domestic laws and international legal obligations, a State shall provide reparation to victims for acts or omissions which can be attributed to the State and constitute gross violations of international human rights law or serious violations of international humanitarian law. In cases where a person, a legal person, or other entity is found liable for reparation to a victim, such party should provide reparation to the victim or compensate the State if the State has already provided reparation to the victim.

States should endeavour to establish national programmes for reparation and other assistance to victims in the event that the party liable for the harm suffered is unable or unwilling to meet their obligations. States shall, with respect to claims by victims, enforce domestic judgments for reparation against individuals or entities liable for the harm suffered and endeavour to enforce valid foreign legal judgments for reparation in accordance with domestic law and international legal obligations. To that end, States should provide under their domestic laws effective mechanisms for the enforcement of reparation judgments.

In accordance with domestic law and international law, and taking account of individual circumstances, victims of gross violations of international human rights law and serious violations of international humanitarian law should, as appropriate and proportional to the gravity of the violation and the circumstances of each case, be provided with full and effective reparation, as laid out in principles 19 to 23, which include the following forms: restitution, compensation, rehabilitation, satisfaction and guarantees of non-repetition.

Restitution should, whenever possible, restore the victim to the original situation before the gross violations of international human rights law or serious violations of international humanitarian law occurred. Restitution includes, as appropriate: restoration of liberty, enjoyment of human rights, identity, family life and citizenship, return to one's place of residence, restoration of employment and return of property.

Compensation should be provided for any economically assessable damage, as appropriate and proportional to the gravity of the violation and the circumstances of each case, resulting from gross violations of international human rights law and serious violations of international humanitarian law, such as:

(a) Physical or mental harm;
(b) Lost opportunities, including employment, education and social benefits;
(c) Material damages and loss of earnings, including loss of earning potential;
(d) Moral damage;
(e) Costs required for legal or expert assistance, medicine and medical services, and psychological and social services.

Rehabilitation should include medical and psychological care as well as legal and social services. *Satisfaction* should include, where applicable, any or all of the following:

(a) Effective measures aimed at the cessation of continuing violations;
(b) Verification of the facts and full and public disclosure of the truth to the extent that such disclosure does not cause further harm or threaten the safety and interests of the victim, the victim's relatives, witnesses, or persons who have intervened to assist the victim or prevent the occurrence of further violations;
(c) The search for the whereabouts of the disappeared, for the identities of the children abducted, and for the bodies of those killed, and assistance in the recovery, identification and reburial of the bodies in accordance with the expressed or presumed wish of the victims, or the cultural practices of the families and communities;
(d) An official declaration or a judicial decision restoring the dignity, the reputation and the rights of the victim and of persons closely connected with the victim;
(e) Public apology, including acknowledgement of the facts and acceptance of responsibility;
(f) Judicial and administrative sanctions against persons liable for the violations;
(g) Commemorations and tributes to the victims;

(h) Inclusion of an accurate account of the violations that occurred in international human rights law and international humanitarian law training and in educational material at all levels.

Guarantees of non-repetition should include, where applicable, any or all of the following measures, which will also contribute to prevention:
(a) Ensuring effective civilian control of military and security forces;
(b) Ensuring that all civilian and military proceedings abide by international standards of due process, fairness and impartiality;
(c) Strengthening the independence of the judiciary;
(d) Protecting persons in the legal, medical and health-care professions, the media and other related professions, and human rights defenders;
(e) Providing, on a priority and continued basis, human rights and international humanitarian law education to all sectors of society and training for law enforcement officials as well as military and security forces;
(f) Promoting the observance of codes of conduct and ethical norms, in particular international standards, by public servants, including law enforcement, correctional, media, medical, psychological, social service and military personnel, as well as by economic enterprises;
(g) Promoting mechanisms for preventing and monitoring social conflicts and their resolution;
(h) Reviewing and reforming laws contributing to or allowing gross violations of international human rights law and serious violations of international humanitarian law.

J. Access to Relevant Information Concerning Violations and Reparation Mechanisms

The Basic Principles and Guidelines calls upon States to develop means of informing the general public and, in particular, victims of gross violations of international human rights law and serious violations of international humanitarian law of the rights and remedies addressed by these Principles and Guidelines and of all available legal, medical, psychological, social, administrative and all other services to which victims may have a right of access. Moreover, victims and their representatives should be entitled to seek and obtain information on the causes leading to their victimization and on the causes and conditions pertaining to the gross violations of international human rights law and serious violations of international humanitarian law and to learn the truth in regard to these violations.

K. *Non-Discrimination*

The Basic Principles and Guidelines underline that the application and interpretation of its provisions must be consistent with international human rights law and international humanitarian law and be without any discrimination of any kind or ground, without exception.

Transitional Justice

There is growing emphasis in the international human rights movement that victims of gross violations of human rights and/or their families have the right to a process that establishes the facts of what took place and draws lessons for the prevention of similar occurrences in the future. This is sometimes given the label of 'transitional justice'. According to the organization, Transitional Justice, the major approaches to transitional justice include the following:

- Domestic, hybrid, and international prosecutions of perpetrators of human rights abuse;
- Determining the full extent and nature of past abuses through truth-telling initiatives, including national and international commissions;
- Providing reparations to victims of human rights violations, including compensatory, restitutionary, rehabilitation, and symbolic reparations;
- Institutional reform, of which one measure is the vetting of abusive, corrupt, or incompetent officials from the police and security services, the military, and other public institutions including the judiciary. Vetting refers to the process of excluding from public employment those known to have committed human rights abuses or been involved in corrupt practices;
- Promoting reconciliation within divided communities, including working with victims on traditional justice mechanisms and forging social reconstruction;
- Constructing memorials and museums to preserve the memory of the past;
- Taking into account gendered patterns of abuse to enhance justice for female victims.[197]

197 See http://www.ictj.org/en/tj/, 16 May, 2005.

Conclusion

In this chapter on the duty to provide redress we looked at path-breaking general comments and recommendations of the Human Rights Committee, the Committee on Economic, Social and Cultural Rights, CEDAW, CERD, CAT, and the Committee on the Rights of the Child. We then looked at the provisions of the codificatory UN Basic Principles and Guidelines which provide a ready checklist to Government personnel and legal advisers, and to human rights treaty bodies. On this highly important topic of the duty of States parties to provide redress for violations of human rights. It would be fair to say that while human rights treaty bodies have rightly emphasized the duty of governments to provide redress for violations, in many instances redress is not forthcoming. This will hopefully change as governments participate more and more faithfully in reporting procedures and, thereby, give themselves the opportunity to benefit from the comments and observations of the human rights treaty bodies. In the next chapter we look at the essence of supervision in reporting systems.

Chapter Eight

The Essence of Supervision in Reporting Systems

Introduction

The essence of supervision in reporting systems was admirably brought out by the ILO Committee of Experts on the Application of Conventions and Recommendations in a report it submitted to the International Labour Conference in 1977. It affirmed that

> "... its function is to determine whether the requirements of a given Convention are being met, whatever the economic and social conditions existing in a given country. Subject only to any derogations which are expressly permitted by the Convention itself, these requirements remain constant and uniform of all countries. In carrying out this work, the Committee is guided by the standards laid down in the Convention alone, mindful, however, of the fact that the modes of their implementation may be different in different States. These are international standards, and the manner in which their implementation is evaluated must be uniform and must not be affected by concepts derived from any particular social or economic system."[198]

I. The Objectives of Reporting Systems

The Committee on Economic, Social and Cultural Rights has given superb guidance on the objectives of reporting systems. It has pointed out that the reporting obligations which are contained in part IV of the Covenant (IECSR) are designed principally to assist each State party in fulfilling its obligations under the Covenant and, in addition, to provide a basis on which the Council, assisted by the Committee, can discharge its responsibilities for monitoring States parties' compliance with their obligations and for facilitating the realization of economic, social cultural rights in accordance with the provisions of the Covenant. In accordance

198 International Labour Conference, 63rd Session, 1977, Report III, Part 4A, Report of the Committee of Experts on the Application of Conventions and Recommendations, ILO, Geneva, 1977, pp. 10-11, para. 31.

with the letter and spirit of the Covenant, the processes of preparation and submission of reports by States can, indeed should, serve a variety of objectives.

A first objective is to ensure that a comprehensive review is undertaken with respect to national legislation, administrative rules and procedures, and practices in an effort to ensure the fullest possible conformity with the Covenant. Such a review might, for example, be undertaken in conjunction with each of the relevant national ministries or other authorities responsible for policy-making and implementation in the different fields covered by the Covenant.

A second objective is to ensure that the State party monitors the actual situation with respect to each of the rights on a regular basis and is thus aware of the extent to which the various rights are, or are not, being enjoyed by all individuals within its territory or under its jurisdiction. A third objective of the reporting process is to enable the Government to demonstrate that principled policy-making has been undertaken in order to provide the basis for the elaboration of clearly-stated and carefully targeted policies, including the establishment of priorities which reflect the provisions of the Covenant.

A fourth objective of the reporting process is to facilitate public scrutiny of government policies with respect to economic, social and cultural rights and to encourage the involvement of the various economic, social and cultural sectors of society in the formulation, implementation and review of the relevant policies. A fifth objective is to provide a basis on which the State party itself, as well as the Committee, can effectively evaluate the extent to which progress has been made towards the realization of the obligations contained in the Covenant. For this purpose, it may be useful for States to identify benchmarks or goals against which their performance in a given area can be assessed.

A sixth objective is to enable the State party itself to develop a better understanding of the problems and shortcomings encountered in efforts to realize progressively the full range of economic, social and cultural rights. For this reason, it is essential that States parties report in detail on the 'factors and difficulties' inhibiting such realization. This process of identification and recognition of the relevant difficulties then provides the framework within which more appropriate policies can be revised.

A seventh objective is to enable the Committee and the States parties as a whole, to facilitate the exchange of information among States and to develop a better understanding of the common problems faced by States parties and a fuller appreciation of the type of measures which might be taken to promote effective realization of each of the rights contained in the Covenant. This part of the process also enables the Committee on ES-CRts to identify the most appropriate means by which the international community might assist States, in accordance with articles 22 and 23 of the Covenant.[199]

II. Cooperation of States Parties

In its General Comment No. 30, the Human Rights Committee noted that States parties had undertaken to submit reports in accordance with article 40 of the Covenant (ICCPR) within one year of its entry into force for the States parties concerned and, thereafter, whenever the Committee so requests. The Committee remarked that only a small number of States had submitted their reports on time. Most of them had been submitted with delays ranging from a few months to several years and some States parties were still in default, despite repeated reminders by the Committee. Other States had announced that they would appear before the Committee but had not done so on the scheduled date.

To remedy such situations, the Committee decided as follows:

- If the State party is represented by a delegation, the Committee will, in presence of the delegation, proceed with the examination on the date assigned;
- If the State party is not represented, the Committee may, at its discretion, either decide to proceed to consider the measures taken by the State party to implement the guarantees of the Covenant at the initial date or notify a new date to the State party.

The Committee would hold its meetings in pubic session if a delegation is present, and in private if a delegation was not present, and would follow the modalities set forth in the reporting guidelines and in the rules of procedure of the Committee. After the Committee has adopted concluding observations, a follow-up procedure would be employed in order to establish, maintain or restore a dialogue with the State party. For this purpose and in order to enable the Committee to take further action, the Committee would appoint a Special Rapporteur, who would report to the Committee.[200]

---

199 General Comment No. 1 (1989) of the Committee on Economic, Social and Cultural Rights.

200 General Comment No. 30 (2002) of the Human Rights Committee.

III. General Comments of Treaty Bodies

The general comments and recommendations adopted by the human rights treaty bodies provide invaluable guidance on the meaning of their respective treaties and on the obligations of States parties to give effect to them. General comments and recommendations have been adopted to date by six of the UN-based human rights treaty bodies: the Human Rights Committee, the Committee on Economic, Social and Cultural Rights, the Committee on the Elimination of Discrimination Against Women, the Committee on the Rights of the Child, the Committee on the Elimination of Racial Discrimination, and the Committee against Torture.[201] The Committee on Migrant Workers has so far not adopted any general recommendation. Treaty bodies in specialized agencies and in regional organizations make general recommendations in different forms, for example in their annual reports or in thematic statements adopted from time to time.

A. *The Range of General Comments*

The Committee on Economic, Social and Cultural Rights has so far adopted 19 general comments that deal with the following topics: reporting by States parties; international technical assistance; the nature of States parties obligations; the right to adequate housing; persons with disabilities; the economic, social and cultural rights of older persons; forced evictions; economic sanctions; the domestic application of the Covenant; the role of national human rights institutions; plans of action for primary education; the right to adequate food; the right to education; the right to health; the right to water; the equal rights of men and women; rights resulting from literary or artistic production; the right to work; and the right to social security.

The Human Rights Committee has so far adopted 34 general comments on: reporting obligations of States parties; reporting guidelines; implementation at the national level; equal rights of men and women; derogations; right to life; prohibition of torture; liberty and security of person; humane treatment of persons deprived of their liberty; freedom of opinion; advocacy of hatred; right to self-determination; administration of justice; the position of aliens; right to privacy; rights of the child; non-

201 For a collection of the general comments, see UN doc. HRI/GEN/1/Rev.9, 27 May, 2008.

discrimination; the family; prohibition of torture; freedom of thought, conscience or religion; rights of minorities; reservations; participation in public affairs and the right to vote; continuity of obligations; freedom of movement; the nature of the general legal obligation imposed on States parties to the Covenant; the right to equality before courts and tribunals and to a fair trial.

The Committee on the Elimination of Racial Discrimination has so far adopted 31 general recommendations on: States parties obligations; reporting by States parties; overdue reports; adoption of legislation; interpretation of article 1; application of article 8; technical assistance; non-citizens; successor states; training of law-enforcement officials; article 4; article 9; the establishment of national institutions; the establishment of an international tribunal to prosecute crimes against humanity; article 3; article 5; the right to self-determination; refugees and displaced persons; indigenous peoples; gender-related dimensions of racial discrimination; article 6; discrimination against Roma; and racial discrimination in the administration and functioning of the criminal justice system.

The Committee on the Elimination of Discrimination Against Women has so far adopted 25 general recommendations on: reporting obligations by States parties; education and public information campaigns; reservations; temporary special measures; effective national machinery and publicity; resources; article 8; technical advisory services for reporting obligations; violence against women; equal remuneration; female circumcision; avoidance of discrimination against women in national strategies for the prevention of AIDS; unpaid women workers in rural and urban family enterprises; the unremunerated domestic activities of women; disabled women; reservations; equality in marriage and family relations; political and public life; women and health.

The Committee Against Torture has so far adopted two general comment on refoulement and communications (article 3 of the Convention in the context of article 22), and another on the content of the obligation to prohibit torture.

The Committee on the Rights of the Child has adopted 10 general comments so far on: the aims of education; the role of independent national human rights institutions; HIV/AIDS; adolescent health and development; general measures of implementation; treatment of unaccompanied and separated children outside their country of origin; implementing child rights in early childhood; protection from corporal punishment; children with disabilities; and children's rights in juvenile justice.

B. The Purpose of General Comments

In the introduction to annex III (General comments) in its 1989 report to the Economic and Social Council, the Committee on Economic, Social and Cultural Rights explained the purpose of the general comments as follows:

> "The Committee endeavours, through its general comments, to make the experience gained so far through the examination of these reports available for the benefit of all States parties in order to assist and promote their further implementation of the Covenant; to draw the attention of the States parties to insufficiencies disclosed by a large number of reports; to suggest improvements in the reporting procedures and to stimulate the activities of the States parties, the international organizations and the specialized agencies concerned in achieving progressively and effectively the full realization of the rights recognized in the Covenant. Whenever necessary, the Committee may, in the light of the experience of States parties and of the conclusions which it has drawn therefrom, revise and update its general comments."[202]

C. The Spirit of Implementation

The Committee on Economic, Social and Cultural Rights has, on more than one occasion, indicated the spirit that should guide implementation. A good example of this was its General comment No. 4 on the right to adequate housing, which it adopted in 1991. Noting that there remained a disturbingly large gap between the standards set out in article 11(1) of the Covenant and the situation prevailing in many parts of the world, the Committee assessed the concept of adequacy in relation to: legal security of tenure; availability of services, materials, facilities and infrastructure; affordability; habitability; accessibility; location; and cultural adequacy.[203]

D. Domestic Application

In its General Comment No. 9 (1998) on the domestic application of the Covenant, the Committee on Economic, Social and Cultural Rights gave the following guidance on the standards of supervision on this issue:

202 See HRI/GEN/1/Rev.9, p. 1.

203 Ibid, pp. 11-17.

"Questions relating to the domestic application of the Covenant must be considered in the light of two principles of international law. The first, as reflected in article 27 of the Vienna Convention on the Law of Treaties, is that "(A) party may not invoke the provisions of its internal law as justification for its failure to perform a treaty". In other words, States should modify the domestic legal order as necessary in order to give effect to their treaty obligations. The second principle is reflected in article 8 of the Universal Declaration of Human Rights according to which "Everyone has the right to an effective remedy by the competent national tribunals for acts violating the fundamental rights granted him by the constitution or by law." The International Covenant on Economic, Social and Cultural Rights contains no direct counterpart to article 2,paragraph 3(b) of the International Covenant on Civil and Political Rights, which obligates States parties to, inter alia, 'develop the possibilities of judicial remedy'. Nevertheless, a State party seeking to justify its failure to provide any domestic legal remedies for violations of economic, social and cultural rights would need to show either that such remedies are not 'appropriate means' within the terms of article 2, paragraph 1,ofthe International Covenant on Economic, Social and Cultural Rights or that, in view of the other means used, they are unnecessary. It will be difficult to show this and the Committee considers that, in many cases, the other means used could be rendered ineffective if they are not reinforced or complemented by judicial remedies."[204]

Conclusion

In this chapter on the essence of supervision in reporting systems we looked at the practice of human rights treaty bodies on the objectives of reporting systems, the duty of States parties to cooperate in reporting procedures, and the general comments of human rights treaty bodies, the range of general comments, the purpose of general comments, the spirit of implementation, and the question of the domestic application of human rights treaty norms. There are, without doubt, serious continuing problems with respect to the effectiveness of reporting procedures and the extent to which States parties are participating in these procedures with the seriousness required. At the same time, for whatever reasons, many countries are mired in poverty, underdevelopment, conflicts, and unrepresentative governments. It is the mission of the human rights movement to help these and other countries along the road towards good

204 Ibid, p. 47.

faith implementation of human rights treaties. The guidance provided by human rights treaty bodies is intended to help in this endeavour. So are petitions and fact-finding procedures, topics to which we turn in the penultimate chapter of this work.

Chapter Nine

The Essence of Petitions and Fact-finding Procedures

Introduction

In this chapter we shall try to identify what monitoring and supervisory bodies have laid down as the essence of petitions and fact-finding procedures.

I. The Essence of Petitions Procedures

One can distil as the essence of petitions procedures the concept of international protection, the principle of equality of arms, the duty of States parties to cooperate in good faith in the examination of petitions, and the concept of the living law.

A. The Concept of International Protection

The United Nations' role in shaping the future world is greatest in the human rights jurisprudence it has developed to help build a world of human dignity and progress based on respect for human rights. At the forefront of this work has been the UN Human Rights Committee, which monitors the implementation of the International Covenant on Civil and Political Rights (1966).

It is striking how much the Human Rights Committee has influenced the human rights jurisprudence of the world. The first thing that stands out from the case law is that the Human Rights Committee is in the process of clarifying the constitutional or public order of the world and its corresponding legal norms. The Human Rights Committee is articulating the principle of international supervision of human rights, namely that what is legal or illegal is determined, in the final instance, by a UN Human Rights body. 111 States are at present bound by the petitions procedure operated by the Committee and, undoubtedly, the remaining States will do so when they see the light – as eventually they must if they are to do justice to their own citizens.

The second thing that stands out is that the Human Rights Committee is in the process of humanizing sovereignty. The Committee insists that governments are not at liberty to act as they see fit but must conform to international human rights standards. Of equal significance, third, the Human Rights Committee has held in a landmark case that the foremost United Nations organ, the Security Council, must comply with international human rights norms when its actions affect individuals. This is a breath-taking decision of the Human Rights Committee in the case of Sayadi and others v. Belgium (2008). In that case, Belgium argued that it was shielded from scrutiny because it was acting to implement a Security Council resolution. 'No', the Committee replied; Belgium must comply with its human rights obligations, which took precedence. The Security Council cannot act in breach of human rights.

Fourth, the Human Rights Committee has insisted that even in times of public emergency there can be no excuses for violating fundamental rights such as the right to life or not to be tortured. In a time when human rights are being flouted in the name of acting against terrorism, the Human Rights Committee holds aloft the banner of international human rights law and insists that no Government is above the law.

Fifth, among the legal precepts developed by the Human Rights Committee are the following:

- Governments are legally bound to take reasonable and appropriate measures to protect people within their jurisdiction or control.
- The law must strictly control and limit the circumstances in which a person may be deprived of his or her life by the authorities of the State.
- A State, by invoking the existence of exceptional circumstances, cannot evade the obligations it has undertaken under international human rights law by ratifying the Covenant.
- A situation in which the functions and competences of the judiciary and the executive are not clearly distinguishable or where the executive is able to control or direct the judiciary is incompatible with the notion of an independent and impartial judiciary.
- Governments are under a legal obligation to ensure that remedies for violations are effective. Expedition and effectiveness are particularly important in the adjudication of cases involving torture.
- Where violations have taken place Governments must take measures to ensure that similar violations do not take place in the future.
- Governments should take specific and effective measures to prevent the disappearance of individuals and establish effective facilities and

procedures to investigate thoroughly by an appropriate and impartial body, cases of missing and disappeared persons.
- Being subjected to incommunicado detention in an unknown location constitutes cruel and inhuman treatment.
- Women and men are entitled to equal treatment in the application of laws.

Andreas Mavrommatis, the first Chairperson of the Human Rights Committee, in an assessment of the jurisprudence of the Human Rights Committee, concluded that from the perspective of international constitutional and public law, as well as definitional paradigms of justice, the Human Rights Committee has laid down foundation building blocks of lasting importance and potential, including the following:
- The Committee has come out squarely in favour of democratic governance and the right to democratic participation in political processes.
- The Committee was a forerunner in the development of the concept of the responsibility to protect, particularly its preventive dimensions. In a series of cases, the Committee has registered that States parties have a duty of diligence to act for the prevention of violations of human rights, in particular the obligation to take effective remedies to ensure the security of the person.
- The Committee has provided important clarification of the meaning of the principles of equality and non-discrimination, not only with respect to civil and political rights, but autonomously with respect to all human rights.
- The Committee led the way at the outset in the development of a jurisprudence that upheld the primacy of human rights in grave unrest and situations of national emergency, already since the days of the Latin American military juntas.
- The Committee has consistently reaffirmed the principle of the non-derogability of fundamental human rights enumerated in article 4 of the Covenant.
- The Committee has clarified, elucidated and developed the meaning of the core rights contained in the Covenant.
- The Committee has insisted on the principles of justice, redress and compensation for violations of human rights and has rejected impunity for the violators.

- The Committee has made landmark contributions in the area of State responsibility for violations of human rights.[205]

The concept of international protection emerges clearly from a number of cases of international and regional monitoring bodies. In Hugo Rodriguez v. Uruguay, the Human Rights Committee held that amnesties for gross violations of human rights were unacceptable:

> "The Committee ... reaffirms its position that amnesties for gross violations of human rights and legislation (providing for it)...are incompatible with the obligations of the State party under the Covenant. The Committee notes with deep concern that the adoption of this law effectively excludes in a number of cases the possibility of investigation into past human rights abuses and thereby prevents the State party from discharging its responsibility to provide effective remedies to the victims of those abuses. Moreover, the Committee is concerned that, in adopting this law the State party has contributed to an atmosphere of impunity which may undermine the democratic order and give rise to further grave human rights violations."[206]

In Glenn Ashby v. Trinidad and Tobago, the Human Rights Committee had to deal with a situation in which it had asked the Government not execute Mr Ashby but it had gone ahead nevertheless. The Committee continued its consideration of the case and found a breach of article 6 of the ICCPR as well as of the State party's obligations under the Optional Protocol. The Committee stated:

> "With regard to Mr Ashby's execution, the Committee recalls its jurisprudence that apart from any violation of the rights under the Covenant, the State party commits a serious breach of its obligations under the Optional Protocol if it engages in any acts which have the effect of preventing or frustrating consideration by the Committee of a communication alleging any violation of the Covenant, or to render examination by the Committee moot and the expression of its Views nugatory and futile. The behaviour of the State party represents a shocking failure to demonstrate even the most elementary good faith required of a State party to the Covenant and of the

205 A. Mavrommatis, Foreword to J. Th. Moller and A. de Zayas, United Nations Human Rights Committee Case Law 1977-2008. N.P. Engel, Publisher, 2009, pp. xix-xxi.

206 Report of the Human Rights Committee, 1994, Vol. II, Annex IX, Sect. B., para. 12.4.

> Optional Protocol. The Committee finds that the State party breached its obligations under the Protocol, by proceeding to execute Mr Ashby before the Committee could conclude its examination of the communication, and the formulation of its Views. It was particularly inexcusable for the State party to do so after the Committee had acted under its Rule 86 requesting the State party to refrain from doing so. Flouting the Rule, especially by irreversible measures such as the execution of the alleged victim, undermines the protection of Covenant rights through the Optional Protocol."[207]

B. General Comment 33 of the Human Rights Committee

General Comment No 33 of the Human Rights Committee dealt with the obligations of States Parties under the Optional Protocol to the International Covenant on Civil and Political Rights. We present the contents of this important general comment below.

Recalling that Article 1 of the Optional Protocol provides that a State party to it recognizes the competence of the Committee to receive and consider communications from individuals subject to its jurisdiction who claim to be victims of a violation by that State party of any of the rights set forth in the Covenant, the Human Rights Committee has underlined that States parties are obliged not to hinder access to the Committee and to prevent any retaliatory measures against any person who has addressed a communication to the Committee.

Article 2 of the Optional Protocol requires that individuals who submit communications to the Committee must have exhausted all available domestic remedies. The Committee has advised that in its response to a communication, a State party, where it considers that this condition has not been met, should specify the available and effective remedies that the author of the communication has failed to exhaust.

The Human Rights Committee uses the description "author" to refer to an individual who has submitted a communication to the Committee under the Optional Protocol. The Committee uses the term "communication" contained in article 1 of the Optional Protocol instead of such terms as "complaint" or "petition", although the latter term is reflected in the current administrative structure of the Office of the High Commissioner for Human Rights, where communications under the Optional Protocol are initially handled by a section known as the Petitions Team.

207 Report of the Human Rights Committee, 2007, Vol. II, Annex VII, Section II, paras. 11.11.

Terminology similarly reflected the nature of the role of the Human Rights Committee in receiving and considering a communication. Subject to the communication being found admissible, after considering the communication in the light of all written information made available to it by the individual author and by the State party concerned, "the Committee shall forward its views to the State party concerned and to the individual."

The Committee notes that the first obligation of a State Party, against which a claim has been made by an individual under the Optional Protocol, is to respond to it within the time limit of six months set out in article 4 (2). Within that time limit, "the receiving State shall submit to the Committee written explanations or statements clarifying the matter and the remedy, if any, that may have been taken by the State." The Committee's Rules of Procedure amplify these provisions, including the possibility in exceptional cases of treating separately questions of the admissibility and merits of the communication.

In responding to a communication that appears to relate to a matter arising before the entry into force of the Optional Protocol for the State party (the ratione temporis rule), the State party should invoke that circumstance explicitly, including any comment on the possible "continuing effect" of a past violation.

In the experience of the Committee, States do not always respect their obligation. In failing to respond to a communication, or responding incompletely, a State which is the object of a communication puts itself at a disadvantage, because the Committee is then compelled to consider the communication in the absence of full information relating to the communication. In such circumstances, the Committee may conclude that the allegations contained in the communication are true, if they appear from all the circumstances to be substantiated.

While the function of the Human Rights Committee in considering individual communications is not, as such, that of a judicial body, the views issued by the Committee under the Optional Protocol exhibit some important characteristics of a judicial decision. They are arrived at in a judicial spirit, including the impartiality and independence of Committee members, the considered interpretation of the language of the Covenant, and the determinative character of the decisions.

The term used in article 5, paragraph 4 of the Optional Protocol to describe the decisions of the Committee is "views". These decisions state the Committee's findings on the violations alleged by the author of a communication and, where a violation has been found, state a remedy for that violation.

The views of the Committee under the Optional Protocol represent an authoritative determination by the organ established under the Covenant itself charged with the interpretation of that instrument. These views derive their character, and the importance which attaches to them, from the integral role of the Committee under both the Covenant and the Optional Protocol.

Under article 2, paragraph 3 of the Covenant, each State party undertakes "to ensure that any person whose rights or freedoms as herein recognised are violated shall have an effective remedy, notwithstanding that the violation has been committed by a person acting in an official capacity." This is the basis of the wording consistently used by the Committee in issuing its views in cases where a violation has been found:

> "In accordance with article 2, paragraph 3(a) of the Covenant, the State party is required to provide the author with an effective remedy. By becoming a party to the Optional Protocol the State party has recognized the competence of the Committee to determine whether there has been a violation of the Covenant or not and that, pursuant to article 2 of the Covenant, the State party has undertaken to ensure to all individuals within its territory or subject to its jurisdiction the rights recognized in the Covenant and to provide an effective and enforceable remedy in case a violation has been established. In this respect, the Committee wishes to receive from the State party, within 180 days, information about the measures taken to give effect to the Committee's views."

The character of the views of the Committee is further determined by the obligation of States parties to act in good faith, both in their participation in the procedures under the Optional Protocol and in relation to the Covenant itself. A duty to cooperate with the Committee arises from an application of the principle of good faith to the observance of all treaty obligations.

The Committee decided, in 1997, under its rules of procedure, to appoint a member of the Committee as Special Rapporteur for the Follow-Up of Views. That member, through written representations, and frequently also through personal meetings with diplomatic representatives of the State party concerned, urges compliance with the Committee's views and discusses factors that may be impeding their implementation. In a number of cases this procedure has led to acceptance and implementation of the Committee's views where previously the transmission of those views had met with no response.

The Committee noted that failure by a State party to implement the views of the Committee in a given case becomes a matter of public record through the publication of the Committee's decisions inter alia in its annual reports to the General Assembly of the United Nations.

The Committee further noted that some States parties, to which the views of the Committee have been transmitted in relation to communications concerning them, had failed to accept the Committee's views, in whole or in part, or had attempted to re-open the case. In a number of those cases these responses had been made where the State party took no part in the procedures, having not carried out its obligation to respond to communications under article 4, paragraph 2 of the Optional Protocol.

In other cases, rejection of the Committee's views, in whole or in part, had come after the State party had participated in the procedure and where its arguments had been fully considered by the Committee. In all such cases, the Committee regards dialogue between the Committee and the State party as ongoing with a view to implementation. The Special Rapporteur for the Follow-up of Views conducts this dialogue, and regularly reports on progress to the Committee.

The Committee recalled that measures may be requested by an author, or decided by the Committee on its own initiative, when an action taken or threatened by the State party would appear likely to cause irreparable harm to the author or the victim unless withdrawn or suspended pending full consideration of the communication by the Committee. Examples included the imposition of the death penalty and violation of the duty of non-refoulement. In order to be in a position to meet these needs under the Optional Protocol, the Committee established, under its rules of procedure, a procedure to request interim or provisional measures of protection in appropriate cases. Failure to implement such interim or provisional measures is incompatible with the obligation to respect in good faith the procedure of individual communication established under the Optional Protocol.

The Committee made the point that most States do not have specific enabling legislation to receive the views of the Committee into their domestic legal order. The domestic law of some States parties does, however, provide for the payment of compensation to the victims of violations of human rights as found by international organs. In any case, States parties must use whatever means lie within their power in order to give effect to the views issued by the Committee.

C. *Equality of Arms*

A special feature of petitions procedures is that they should place the individual and the State on an equal plane when it comes to participation in the procedure. This requires that written submissions of one side should be provided to the other side, which should have an opportunity to comment on it and that no side should be at any disadvantage when it comes to having access to the written papers before the examining body. There are some views that the petitioner or his or her representative should have an opportunity of appearing in person and being heard by the examining body. This idea could possibly be realised with the establishment, eventually, of a World Court of Human Rights.

D. *The Duty to Cooperate in the Examination of Petitions*

The Committee Against Torture has provided the following guidance on the duty to cooperate in the examination of petitions:

> "13.10: Having addressed the merits of the complaint, the Committee must address the failure of the State party to cooperate fully with the Committee in the resolution of the current complaint. The Committee observes that, by making the declaration provided for in article 22 of the Convention against Torture extending to individual complainants the right to complain to the Committee alleging a breach of a State party's obligation under the Convention, a State party assumes an obligation to cooperate fully with the Committee through the procedures set forth in article 22 and in the Committee's rules of procedure. In particular, article 22, paragraph 4, requires a State party to make available to the Committee all information relevant and necessary for the Committee appropriately to resolve the complaint presented to it. The Committee observes that its procedures are sufficiently flexible and its powers sufficiently broad to prevent an abuse of process in a particular case. It follows that the State party committed a breach of its obligations under article 22 of the Convention by neither disclosing to the Committee relevant information, nor presenting its concerns to the Committee for an appropriate procedural decision."[208]

208 Selected Decisions of the Committee Against Torture. Vol. I (2009), p. 200.

II. The Essence of Fact-Finding Procedures

In considering the essence of fact-finding procedures we shall look at the practice of UN human rights special procedures, the ILO fact-finding bodies, the Inter-American Commission on Human Rights, the Committee against Torture, the Sub-Commission on the Prevention of Torture, and the European Committee for the Prevention of Torture. We begin with the UN human rights special procedures.

A. UN Human Rights Special Procedures

As Swiss Ambassador Peter Maurer has noted, the United Nations is in the process of modernizing and updating its human rights machinery in the hope of raising the level of international protection of human rights. That is the fundamental goal, consistent with the General Assembly's affirmation of its commitment to the responsibility to protect. The Human Rights Council, which began functioning in 2006, is meant to spearhead efforts to implement the responsibility to protect and its human rights special procedures – its fact-finding rapporteurs and working groups – are its first-line agents in the quest for international protection.[209]

The Human Rights Council has reaffirmed that special procedures mandate-holders are independent United Nations experts charged with acting in an independent capacity and with exercising their functions in accordance with their mandate, through a professional, impartial assessment of facts based on internationally recognized standards, and free from any kind of extraneous influence, incitement, pressure, threat or interference, either direct or indirect, on the part of any party. The Council has urged all States to cooperate with, and assist, the special procedures in the performance of their tasks and to provide all information in a timely manner, as well as respond to communications transmitted to them by the special procedures without undue delay.

As the system of human rights special procedures goes forward to deal with the continuing and new challenges of human rights protection it is of great value to record and recall the considerable body of practice and precedents they have developed for the protection of human rights since the first special procedure was established in the mid 1960s. The practice of United Nations human rights special procedures brings out the following:

---

209 See P. Maurer, Foreword to B.G. Ramcharan, The Protection Roles of UN Human Rights Special Procedures. Martinus Nijhoff, 2008.

- Special procedures have insisted that it is for the United Nations to determine the means and methods of responding to situations of gross violations of human rights.
- Special procedures have established that no State may opt out of their obligations under the United Nations Charter and international human rights and humanitarian law.
- Special procedures have consistently affirmed that their methods of work must be influenced by the needs for protection in each situation.
- Special procedures have worked on the basis of state, individual, corporate, and international responsibility for gross violations of human rights.
- Special procedures have provided early warning of threatened gross violations of human rights and have called on the international community to contribute to preventive human rights strategies.
- Special procedures have issued public appeals, sent urgent letters to Governments, and acted in various ways to provide preventive and remedial protection for those at risk.
- Special procedures have visited countries and undertaken different measures to help mitigate and stop gross violations of human rights.
- Special procedures have sought to serve as channels of remedies, redress, and compensation for gross violations of human rights.
- Special procedures have examined and investigated the protection challenges thrown up by an evolving international community of new risks and challenges.
- Special procedures have engaged in brilliant advocacy on behalf of human rights protection, especially in dealing with the challenges of poverty and the implementation of basic economic, social and cultural rights.

B. ILO Inquiry Bodies

Some human rights treaties provide for the establishment of fact-finding procedures, obligatory or optional. Commissions of Inquiry established by the International Labour Organization pursuant to Article 26 of the Constitution of the ILO have the longest pedigree in this genre and the essence of human rights fact-finding is to be found in the procedures and practice of these Commissions of Inquiry. An ILO report dealing with Committees of Inquiry captured the essence of human rights fact-finding:

> "The proceedings before a commission of inquiry are essentially of a judicial nature and are designed to enable the commission to prepare a report embodying its findings on questions of fact and containing its recommendations on any steps to be taken to meet the complaint. Commissions of inquiry, in addition to considering documentary material emanating from the parties and other qualified sources, have heard witnesses and, in some cases, have supplemented the information and evidence so obtained by on-the-spot investigations."[210]

The report continued that the procedure followed by such commissions had been designed to ensure that they had at their disposal thorough and objective information concerning the questions at issue. They had not, therefore, confined themselves to examining only such information as might be submitted by the parties. They had invited other governments which might possess factual information relevant to the complaint as well as the international organizations of employers and workers having consultative status with the ILO – and in certain cases national organisations of employers and workers and other non-governmental organizations – to submit any relevant factual information in their possession to the Commission of Inquiry. In particular, they had themselves drawn up lists of the witnesses they wished to hear in addition to those put forward by the parties, and in the cases in which they had visited the country against which the complaint was made they had drawn up their own itineraries and, as well as meeting persons whom the government wished them to see, had themselves selected the persons they wished to interview and the establishment they wished to visit. The witnesses heard in Geneva or interviewed in the country normally included representatives of the trade unions and employers' organizations of the country concerned, who were given every opportunity to put forward their views.[211]

The report added that the procedure followed by commissions of inquiry contained a number of safeguards designed to ensure respect of the principles of due process of law. Thus all written statements, whether received from the other party, or from other governments or organisations invited to submit information, were communicated to the parties, and the government against which the complaint was made was given an opportunity to submit its observations on them. Witnesses were heard in private sittings in the presence of the agents of the parties and, in the

210 ILO document GB.205/21/7: Past practice concerning special inquiries with particular reference to human rights questions, para. 14.

211 Ibid, para. 15.

case of witnesses appearing on behalf of an organisation, or a representative of that organisation. Each witness had to make a solemn declaration identical to that made by witnesses before the International Court of Justice, and was given an opportunity to make a statement, following which questions may be put to him by the representatives of the parties (and, where he or she was being heard on behalf of the organisation, also by its representative). All questions were subject to control by the commission. The members of the commission might put questions to the witness at any stage.[212]

C. *The Inter-American Commission on Human Rights*

Article 55 of the Rules of Procedure of the Inter-American Commission on Human Rights provides that Special Commissions undertaking visits to countries, or any of their members, shall be able to interview any persons, groups, entities or institutions freely and in private. The State shall grant the necessary guarantees to those who provide the Special Commission with information, testimony, or evidence of any kind.

The members of the Special Commission shall be able to travel freely, throughout the territory of the country, for which purpose the State shall extend all the corresponding facilities, including the necessary documentation. The State shall also ensure the availability of local means of transportation.

The members of the Special Commission shall have access to the jails and all other detention and interrogation sites and shall be able to interview in private those persons imprisoned or detained. The State shall provide the Special Commission with any document related to the observance of human rights that the Special Commission may consider necessary for the presentation of its reports. The Special Commission shall be able to use any method appropriate for filming, photographing, collecting, documenting, recording, or reproducing the information it considers useful.

The State shall adopt the security measures necessary to protect the Special Commission. The State shall ensure the availability of appropriate lodging for the members of the Special Commission. The same guarantees and facilities that are provided for the members of the Special Commission shall also be extended to the staff of the Executive Secretariat.

212 Ibid, para. 16.

The expenses incurred by the Special Commission, each of its members and the staff of the Executive Secretariat shall be borne by OAS.[213]

D. *The Sub-Commission on the Prevention of Torture*

As we saw in an earlier chapter, States Parties to the Optional Protocol to the Convention Against Torture, in order to enable the Sub Committee on Prevention to fulfil its mandate, undertake to grant it: (a) Unrestricted access to all information concerning the number of persons deprived of their liberty in places of detention as defined in article 4, as well as the number of places and their location; (b) Unrestricted access to all information referring to the treatment of those persons as well as their conditions of detention; (c) Unrestricted access to all places of detention and their installations and facilities; (d) The opportunity to have private interviews with the persons deprived of their liberty without witnesses, either personally or with a translator if deemed necessary, as well as with any other person who the Subcommittee on Prevention believes may supply relevant information; (e) The liberty to choose the places it wants to visit and the persons it wants to interview.

Objection to a visit to a particular place of detention may be made only on urgent and compelling grounds of national defence, public safety, natural disaster or serious disorder in the place to be visited that temporarily prevent the carrying out of such a visit. The existence of a declared state of emergency as such shall not be invoked by a State Party as a reason to object to a visit. As provided for in Article 15, no authority or official shall order, apply, permit or tolerate any sanction against any person or organization for having communicated to the Sub-Committee on Prevention or to its delegates any information, whether true or false, and no such person or organization shall be otherwise prejudiced in any way.

E. *The European Committee for the Prevention of Torture*

As we saw in an earlier chapter, a Party to the European Convention against Torture shall provide the Committee with the following facilities to carry out its task: a. access to its territory and the right to travel without restriction; b. full information on the places where persons deprived of their liberty are being held; c. unlimited access to any place where persons are deprived of their liberty, including the right to move

213 See, Basic Documents Pertaining to Human Rights in the Inter-American System; Washington, OAS, 2007, p. 190.

inside such places without restriction; d. other information available to the Party which is necessary for the Committee to carry out its task. In seeking such information, the Committee shall have regard to applicable rules of national law and professional ethics.

The Committee may interview in private persons deprived of their liberty. The Committee may communicate freely with any person whom it believes can supply relevant information. If necessary, the Committee may immediately communicate observations to the competent authorities of the Party concerned.

Conclusion

In this chapter on the essence of petitions and fact-finding procedures we revisited the practice of human rights treaty bodies on the concept of international protection as it has been approached in petitions procedures such as that under the Optional Protocol to the International Covenant on Civil and Political Rights. We then looked at the issues of equality of arms and the duty of States parties to cooperate in the examination of petitions. We continued by looking at General Comment No. 33 of the Human Rights Committee.

We looked next at the essence of fact-finding procedures, paying particular attention to the practice of ILO supervisory bodies, the Inter-American Commission on Human Rights, the Committee against Torture, the Sub-Committee on the Prevention of Torture, the European Committee for the Prevention of Torture. We have seen the outstanding record of the ILO organs and the Inter-American Commission. We would underline the standard set by the ILO bodies in this area. It is a wise fact-finding body that would follow the doctrine of the ILO that the proceedings before a commission of inquiry are essentially of a judicial nature and are designed to enable the commission to prepare a report embodying its findings on questions of fact and containing its recommendations on any steps to be taken to meet the complaint. Commissions of inquiry, in addition to considering documentary material emanating from the parties and other qualified sources, have heard witnesses and, in some cases, have supplemented the information and evidence so obtained by on-the-spot investigations. In the next, and final, chapter we look at three great principles of international human rights treaty law: universality, equality, justice.

Chapter Ten

Universality, Equality and Justice

Introduction

In this concluding chapter we look at the jurisprudence and practice of international and regional human rights treaty bodies dealing with three great principles of international human rights law: universality, equality, and justice. These principles undergird the implementation of international and regional human rights treaties and provide the foundations for the emplacement and enhancement of a universal culture of human rights, an enterprise of capital importance for the future of humankind. We begin with the principle of universality.

I. Universality

International and regional human rights commissions, courts, or committees are mandated to apply the instrument from which they derive their competence. The laws they apply and interpret are therefore those that States parties to their particular instruments have voluntarily acceded to. Having said this, it needs to be recalled that all of these instruments and institutions take their moral inspiration from the human rights provisions of the United Nations Charter and of the Universal Declaration of Human Rights. Indeed, this is specifically alluded to in the preambles of all of the regional instruments.

The European Convention for the Protection of Human Rights and Fundamental Freedoms 1950 opens by recalling the Universal Declaration of Human Rights and noted that the Declaration aimed at securing the universal and effective recognition and observance of the Rights therein declared. States had reaffirmed their profound belief in those fundamental freedoms which are the foundation of justice and peace in the world and resolved to take the first steps for the collective enforcement of certain of the rights stated in the Universal Declaration.

The American Convention on Human Rights (1969) reiterated that, in accordance with the Universal Declaration of Human Rights, the ideal of free men enjoying freedom from fear and freedom from want can be achieved only if conditions are created whereby everyone may enjoy his or her economic, social and cultural rights, as well as his civil and political rights.

The African Charter on Human and Peoples' Rights (1981) invoked the Charter of the United Nations and the Universal Declaration of Human Rights and reaffirmed African states' adherence to the principles of human and peoples' rights and freedoms contained in the declarations, conventions and other instruments adopted by the former Organization of African Unity (now the African Union), the Movement of Non-Aligned Countries and the United Nations.

The human rights covenants and treaties promulgated within the United Nations system and within the regional organizations are thus part of a grand enterprise to take forward the vision and the law of the United Nations Charter and the Universal Declaration of Human Rights. It is important that those concerned with, or interested in, international human rights treaty law be cognizant of this dimension of universality.

Universality has practical significance in the following senses: first, as we saw in an earlier chapter, some provisions of international human rights treaty law correspond to norms of *jus cogens* in international law. These norms will call for special care and attention on the part of States parties, supervisory organs, and the wider international community. The prohibition of torture is an example of a norm of *jus cogens*. In its General comment No. 2 (2007), the Committee against Torture explicitly invoked the peremptory character of the prohibition of torture:

> "1. This general comment addresses the three parts of article 2, each of which identifies distinct interrelated and essential principles that undergird the Convention's absolute prohibition against torture. Since the adoption of the Convention against Torture, the absolute and non-derogable character of this prohibition has become accepted as a matter of customary international law. The provisions of article 2 reinforce this peremptory *jus cogens* norm against torture and constitute the foundation of the Committee's authority to implement effective means of prevention, including but not limited to those measures contained in the subsequent articles 3 to 16, in response to evolving threats, issues and practice.
>
> ...
>
> 5. Article 2, paragraph 2, provides that the prohibition against torture is absolute and non-derogable. It emphasizes that *no exceptional circumstances whatsoever* may be invoked by a State Party to justify acts of torture in any territory under its jurisdiction. The Convention identifies as among such circumstances a state of war or threat thereof, internal political instability

> or any other public emergency. This includes any threat of terrorist acts or violent crime as well as armed conflict, international or non-international. The Committee is deeply concerned at and rejects absolutely any efforts by States to justify torture and ill treatment as a means to protect public safety or avert emergencies in these and all other situations. Similarly, it rejects any religious or traditional justification that would violate this absolute prohibition. The Committee considers that amnesties or other impediments which preclude or indicate unwillingness to provide prompt and fair prosecution and punishment of perpetrators of torture or ill-treatment violate the principle of non-derogability."[214]

General comment No. 2 attracted some observations on the part of individual States parties who thought that the Committee might have gone too far in some instances. It does not mean that they are right and that the Committee is in error. In the long run it is the collective expression of the views of the Committee that will hold sway. Probably the most authoritative organ of the international community to pronounce on what is or is not a norm of *jus cogens* is the International Court of Justice and it has on different occasions lent its authority to the concept of human rights norms of *jus cogens*.

Second, some norms of human rights treaties, deriving their origins from the United Nations Charter and from the Universal Declaration of Human Rights, represent norms of international customary law. The Human Rights Committee of the International Law Association has devoted attention to this issue for a number of years.

Third, human rights treaties may contribute to the identification of general principles of law shared by the principal legal systems.

Norms of *jus cogens*, of international customary law, or contained in general principles of law common to the major legal systems, are norms of universal application binding on governments worldwide.

II. Equality

Equality is a principle and a normative provision in every human rights instrument, international or regional. In this section we look at the elucidation of this great principle in the jurisprudence and practice of the leading supervisory bodies, beginning with the Human Rights Committee.

---

214 HRI/GEN/1Rev.9, pp. 376-377.

A. *General Comment 18/37 of the Human Rights Committee (Equality and Non-Discrimination)*

In General Comment 18/37 of 9 November 1989, the Human Rights Committee provided useful guidance on the provisions of the International Covenant on Civil and Political Rights dealing with equality and non-discrimination. The Committee noted that the Covenant neither defined the term 'discrimination' nor indicated what constituted discrimination. It noted, however, that article 1 of the International Convention on the Elimination of All Forms of Racial Discrimination provided that the term 'racial discrimination' shall mean any distinction, exclusion, restriction or preference based on race, colour, descent or national or ethnic origin which has the purpose or effect of nullifying or impairing the recognition, enjoyment or exercise, on an equal footing, of human rights and fundamental freedoms in the political, economic, social, cultural or any other field of public life. Similarly, article 1 of the Convention on the Elimination of All Forms of Discrimination against Women provides that 'discrimination against women' shall mean any distinction, exclusion or restriction made on the basis of sex which has the effect or purpose of impairing or nullifying the recognition, enjoyment or exercise by women, irrespective of their marital status, on a basis of equality of men and women, of human rights and fundamental freedoms in the political, economic, social, cultural, civil or any other field.

While the conventions referred to dealt only with cases of discrimination on specific grounds, the Human Rights Committee believed that the term 'discrimination' as used in the Covenant should be understood to imply any distinction, exclusion, restriction or preference which is based on any ground such as race, colour, sex, language, religion, political or other opinion, national or social origin, property, birth or other status, and which has the purpose or effect of nullifying or impairing the recognition, enjoyment or exercise by all persons, on an equal footing, of all rights and freedoms. However, the enjoyment of rights and freedoms on an equal footing does not mean identical treatment in every instance. The Committee also pointed out that the principle of equality sometimes requires States Parties to take affirmative action in order to diminish or eliminate conditions which cause or help to perpetuate discrimination prohibited by the Covenant.

In an important clarification, the Human Rights Committee expressed the view that Article 26 of the Covenant does not merely duplicate the guarantee already provided in article 2 but provides in itself an autonomous right. It prohibits discrimination in law or in fact in any field regulated and protected by public authorities. Article 26 is therefore concerned with the obligations imposed on States Parties in regard to their legislation and the application thereof. Thus, when legislation is adopted by a State Party, it must comply with the requirement of article 26 that its content should not be discriminatory. In other words, the application of the principle of non-discrimination contained in article 26 is not limited to those rights which are provided for in the Covenant.[215]

Finally, the Human Rights Committee observed that not every differentiation of treatment will constitute discrimination, if the criteria for such differentiation are reasonable and objective and if the aim is to achieve a purpose which is legitimate under the Covenant.[216]

B. *General Comment 4/13 of the Human Rights Committee (Gender Equality)*

The Human Rights Committee, in General Comment 4/13, of 28 July 1991, provided important guidance on the international law of human rights regarding gender equality, and specifically under Article 2(1), 3, and 26

215 In the case of S.W.M. Broeks (Communication No. 172/1984, the Human Rights Committee considered the provisions of articles 84 and 85 of the Netherlands Civil Code which imposed equal rights and obligations on spouses with regard to their joint income. However, under section 13, subsection 1(1) of the Unemployment Benefits Act (WWV), a married woman, in order to receive WWV benefits, had to prove tht she was a "breadwinner" – a condition that did not apply to married men. The Human Rights Committee held that this was a differentiation which appeared on one level to be one of status but was in fact one of sex, placing married women at a disadvantage compared with married men. Such a differentiation, in the Committee's view, was not reasonable. The circumstances in which Mrs Broeks found herself at the material time and the application of the then valid Netherlands law made her a victim of a violation, based on sex, of article 26 of the International Covenant on Civil and Political Rights, because she was denied a social security benefit on an equal footing with men. The Committee was of the view that the State party should offer Mrs Broeks an appropriate remedy.(The Netherlands had changed the law by then). See International Covenant on Civil and Political Rights. Selected Decisions of the Human Rights Committee under the Optional Protocol. Vol. 2. Seventeenth to thirty-second sessions (October 1982 – April 1988. UN publication, Sales No. E.89.XIV.1, pp. 196-201. See similarly the case of F.H. Zwaande Fries, Ibid, pp. 209-214.

216 See M. Novak, *U.N. Convention on Civil on Political Rights. CCPR Commentary* (Kehl, Germany: N.P. Engel Publisher, 2005), 1109-1111.

of the International Covenant on Civil and Political Rights. Importantly, the Committee began with the observation that these articles require not only measures of protection but also affirmative action designed to ensure the positive enjoyment of rights. This cannot be done simply by enacting laws. Hence more information has generally been required regarding the role of women in practice with a view to ascertaining what measures in addition to purely legislative measures of protection have been or are being taken to give effect to the precise and positive obligations under Article 3 and to ascertain what progress is being made or what factors or difficulties are being met in this regard. However, the positive obligation undertaken by States Parties may itself have an inevitable impact on legislation or administrative measures specifically designed to regulate matters other than those dealt with in the Covenant but which may adversely affect rights recognized in the Covenant. It mentioned as an example that immigration laws which distinguish between a male and a female citizen may not adversely affect the scope of the right of the women to marriage to non-citizens or to hold public office.

The Human Rights Committee advised that that it might assist States Parties if special attention were given to a review by specially appointed bodies or institutions of laws or measures which inherently draw a distinction between men and women in so far as those laws or measures adversely affect the rights provided for in the Covenant. The Committee also considered that it might help the States Parties in implementing this obligation if more use could be made of existing means of international cooperation with a view to exchanging experience and organizing assistance in solving the practical problems connected with ensuring of equal rights for men and women.[217]

C. *General Comment No. 16 of the Committee on Economic, Social and Cultural Rights*

In General Comment No. 16, which dealt with the equal right of men and women to the enjoyment of all economic, social and cultural rights, the Committee on Economic, Social and Cultural Rights affirmed that the enjoyment of human rights on the basis of equality between men and women must be understood comprehensively. Guarantees of non-discrimination and equality in international human rights treaties mandated both *de facto* and *de jure* equality. *De jure* (or formal) equality and *de facto* (or substantive) equality are different but interconnected concepts.

217 *U.N. Convention on Civil on Political Rights. CCPR Commentary,* 1091.

Formal equality is achieved if a law or policy treats men and women in a neutral manner. Substantive equality is concerned, in addition, with the effects of laws, policies and practices and with ensuring that they do not maintain, but rather alleviate, the inherent disadvantage that particular groups experience.[218]

The principle of non-discrimination, the Committee continued, is the corollary of the principle of equality. It prohibits differential treatment of a person or group of persons based on his/her particular status or situation, such as race, colour, sex, language, religion, political and other opinion, national or social origin, property, birth, or other status, such as age, ethnicity, disability, marital, refugee or migrant status. Discrimination against women was 'any distinction, exclusion, or restriction made on the basis of sex which has the effect or purpose of impairing or nullifying the recognition, enjoyment or exercise by women, irrespective of their marital status, on a basis of equality of men and women, of human rights and fundamental freedoms in the political, economic,. Social, cultural, civil or any other field', as defined in Article 1 of the Convention on the Elimination of All Forms of Discrimination against Women.[219]

The Committee discussed the obligation to respect as follows:

> "The obligation to respect requires States parties to refrain from discriminatory actions that directly or indirectly result in the denial of the equal right of men and women to their enjoyment of economic, social and cultural rights. Respecting the right obliges States parties not to adopt, and to repeal laws and rescind policies, administrative measures and programmes that do not conform with the right protected by article 3. In particular, it is incumbent upon States parties to take into account the effect of apparently gender neutral laws, policies and programmes and to consider whether they could result in a negative impact on the ability of men and women to enjoy their human rights on a basis of equality."[220]

Turning to the obligation to protect, the Committee stated the following:

> "The obligation to protect requires States parties to take steps aimed directly at the elimination of prejudices, customary and all other practices that perpetuate the notion of inferiority or superiority of either of the sexes,

218 HRI/GEN/Rev.9, pp. 114-115.

219 Ibid, p. 115.

220 Ibid, p. 117.

and stereotyped roles for men and women. States parties' obligation to protect under article 3 of ICESCR includes, *inter alia* the respect and adoption of constitutional and legislative provisions on the equal right of men and women to enjoy all human rights and the prohibition of discrimination of any kind; the adoption of legislation to eliminate discrimination and to prevent third parties from interfering directly or indirectly with the enjoyment of this right; the adoption of administrative measures and programmes, as well as the establishment of public institutions, agencies and programmes to protect women against discrimination.

States parties have an obligation to monitor and regulate the conduct of non-State actors to ensure that they do not violate the equal right of men and women to enjoy economic, social and cultural rights. This obligation applies, for example, in cases where public services have been partially or fully privatized."[221]

As regards the obligation to fulfil, the Committee commented:

"The obligation to fulfil requires States parties to take steps to ensure that in practice, men and women enjoy their economic, social and cultural rights on a basis of equality. Such steps should include:

- To make available and accessible appropriate remedies, such as compensation, reparation, restitution, rehabilitation, guarantees of non-repitition, declaration, declarations, public apologies, educational programmes and prevention programmes.
- To establish appropriate venues for redress such as courts and tribunals or administrative mechanisms that are accessible to all on the basis of equality, including the poorest and most disadvantaged and marginalized men and women.
- To develop monitoring mechanisms to ensure that the implementation of laws and policies aimed at promoting the equal enjoyment of economic, social and cultural rights by men and women do not have unintended adverse effects on disadvantaged or marginalized individuals or groups, particularly women and girls.
- To design and implement policies and programmes to give long-term effect tothe economic, social and cultural rights of both men and women on the basis of equality. These may include the adoption of temporary special measures to accelerate women's equal enjoyment of their rights, gender audits, and gender-specific allocation of resources.

221 Ibid, p. 117.

- To conduct human rights education and training programmes for judges and public officials.
- To conduct awareness-raising and training programmes on equality for workers involved in the realization of economic, social and cultural rights at the grass-roots level.
- To integrate, in formal and non-formal education, the principle of the equal rights of men and women to the enjoyment of economic, social and cultural rights, and to promote equal participation of men and women, boys and girls, in schools and other education programmes.
- To promote equal representation of men and women in public office and decision-making bodies.
- To promote equal participation of men and women in development planning, decision-making and in the benefits of development and all programmes related to the realization of economic, social and cultural rights."[222]

III. Justice

The philosopher Mortimer Adler, discussing the ideas of justice, liberty and equality, argued for the sovereignty of justice:

> "... we must note the sovereignty of justice. It regulates our thinking about liberty and equality. Without its guidance, certain errors are unavoidable and certain problems insoluble.
>
> ...
>
> (J)ustice is the supreme value, a greater good than either liberty or equality, and one that must be appealed to for the rectification of errors with regard to liberty and equality."[223]

He continued:

> "Only justice is an unlimited good ... One can want too much liberty and too much equality – more than is good for us to have in relation to our fellowmen, and more than we have any right to. Not so with justice. No society

222 Ibid, pp. 117-118.

223 Adler, *Six Great Ideas*, Macmillan Publishing, 1981, pp. 135-136.

> can be too just; no individual can act more justly than is good for him or his fellowmen."[224]

The principle of justice has been at the heart of the work of all of the supervisory human rights treaty bodies. As we saw earlier in this Chapter, the signatories to the European Convention, invoking the spirit of the Universal Declaration, reaffirmed their profound belief in those "fundamental freedoms which are the foundation of justice and peace in the world." In this section we shall elucidate the principle of justice as it emerges from the jurisprudence and practice of the monitoring bodies. As we shall see, international human rights law in general and international human rights treaty law in particular, strive for the achievement of just societies grounded in international human rights norms. Human rights treaty organs strive for equitable balances between the State and the individual in relation to, for example, the balance to be struck between security and freedom. Human rights treaty regimes strive for just satisfaction in instances where it has been established that a violation of human rights has taken place. Article 41 of the European Convention on Human Rights specifically invokes the principle of just satisfaction. Furthermore, human rights treaty organs apply the concept of the living law, namely that the provisions of treaties will be interpreted and applied in light of the circumstances prevailing at the time of decision on an application, not necessarily the time when the treaty provision was drafted or at the time when an earlier decision was handed down. The Judge case before the Human Rights Committee brought this point out.

A. *Striving for Just Societies Grounded in Human Rights Norms*

There are numerous examples in the practice of human rights treaty bodies when they have found the conduct of State organs or officials contrary to the provisions of the applicable treaty and at variance with sentiments of justice. We take as examples, a sample of cases taken from the Selected Decisions of the Human Rights Committee, Vol. 2, covering the period October 1982 to April 1988.[225]

---

224 Ibid, 137.

225 International Covenant on Civil and Political Rights. Selected Decisions of the Human Rights Committee under the Optional Protocol. Vol. 2. Seventeenth to thirty-second sessions (October 1982 – April 1988. UN publication, Sales No. E.89.XIV.1

In a number of cases, the Human Rights Committee held that the victim had not been treated "with humanity and with respect for the inherent dignity of the human person" because, for example, he or she had been kept incommunicado at an unknown place of detention for several months during which time his fate and whereabouts were unknown; because the victim had not been treated in prison with humanity and with respect for the inherent dignity of the human person; because while in detention he was not treated with humanity; because the victim had not been treated in prison with dignity and respect for the inherent dignity of the human person; because the victim had not been treated in prison with humanity and with respect for the inherent dignity of the human person; because the victim had been kept in solitary confinement for several month in conditions which failed to respect the inherent dignity of the human person; because of the inhuman conditions in which the victim had been held at times in prison; because the victim had not been treated with humanity and with respect for the inherent dignity of the human person; because the victim was subjected to torture and not treated in prison with humanity and with respect for the inherent dignity of the human person, in particular because he was held incommunicado for several months.[226]

In the case of Hiber Conteris, for example, Communication No. 139 /1983, the Human Rights Committee found violations of the International Covenant on Civil and Political Rights because of the severe ill-treatment which the petitioner suffered during the first three months of detention and the harsh and, at time degrading conditions of his detention since then; because of the manner in which he was arrested and detained, without a warrant, which constituted an arbitrary arrest and detention; because he was not informed of the charge against him for over two years; because he was not brought before a judge and because he was not tried within a reasonable time; because he had no opportunity to challenge his detention; because he was held incommunicado for over three months; because he had no fair and public hearing; because he had no effective access to legal counsel for the preparation of his defence; because he was not tried without undue delay; because he was not tried in his presence and could not defend himself in person or through legal counsel of his own choosing; and because he was forced by means of torture to confess guilt. The Human Rights Committee held that the respondent State party, Uruguay, was under an obligation to take effective measures to remedy

226 Ibid, pp. 118, 121, 126, 130, 135, 148, 154, 157, 160.

the violations which Mr Hiber Conteris had suffered and to grant him compensation.[227]

In another case, involving Surinam, the Human Rights Committee found that the victims had been arbitrarily deprived of their lives and urged the State party to take effective steps to investigate the killings, to bring to justice any persons found to be responsible for the deaths of the victims, to pay compensation to the surviving families and to ensure that the right to life is duly protected in Surinam.[228]

In the case of Elena Quinteros Almeida, in which Uruguay was the respondent, the Human Rights Committee held that a mother had the right to know what had happened to her daughter, who had disappeared. The Committee understood the anguish and stress caused to the mother by the disappearance of her daughter And by the continuing uncertainty concerning her fate and whereabouts.[229] In the case of Jose Herrera and Emma Rubia de Herrera, the Human Rights Committee held that Colombia had failed to take appropriate measures to prevent the disappearance and subsequent killings of the victims and to investigate effectively the responsibility for their murders. The Committee referred to its General Comment No. 6 which had provided that States parties should take specific and effective measures to prevent the disappearance of individuals and establish effective facilities and procedures to investigate thoroughly, by an appropriate impartial body, cases of missing and disappeared persons in circumstances that may involve a violation ofthe right to life.[230]

In the Case of Monja Jaona, in which Madagascar was the respondent, the Human Rights Committee held that the victim had been detained on account of his political opinions and had suffered persecution on account of his political opinions.[231] In the case of Lucia Arzuaga Gilboa, in which Uruguay was the respondent, the Human Rights Committee held that the victim had been subjected to torture and to cruel and degrading treatment and had been subjected to inhuman prison conditions for 14 months.[232] The Human Rights Committee made similar findings in the case of Raul Cariboni, in which Uruguay was again the respondent.[233]

227 Ibid, p. 171.

228 Ibid, p. 176.

229 Ibid, p. 142.

230 Ibid, p. 195.

231 Ibid, p. 164.

232 Ibid, p. 178.

233 Ibid, p. 189.

One can find cases similar to these in the practice of all of the human rights treaty bodies that examine petitions. The point we seek to make in this sample is that the monitoring organs endeavour to guide the States parties to justice on the basis of the human rights treaty provisions involved. We may also see instances of equitable balances between the State and the individual

B. *Equitable Balances Between the State and the Individual*

In the case of David Alberto Campora Schweizer, the Human Rights Committee was faced with a regime of 'prompt security measures' in Uruguay. While indicating that it did not feel that it was in a position to pronounce itself on the general compatibility of the regime of prompt security measures under Uruguayan law with the Covenant, the Committee held that the modalities under which the prompt security measures were ordered, maintained and enforced did not comply with the requirements of article 9 of the Covenant. It held that there had been violations of article 9(3) and (4) of the Covenant because, during the time spent in detention under the regime of prompt security measures the victim had not been brought before a judge and could not take proceedings to challenge his arrest and detention.[234]

In the case of Eric Hammel, the Human Rights Committee held that the victim had not been addorded an effective remedy to challenge his expulsion from Madagascar "and that the State party has not shown that there were compelling reasons of national security to deprive him of that remedy."[235]

In a series of cases, the Human Rights Committee has held that as a matter of justice, the burden of proof of allegations of violations rested not only on the petitioner but passed to the State party as well. As the Committee has stated:

> "With regard to the burden of proof ... the said burden cannot rest on the author of the communication alone, especially considering that the author and the State party do not always have equal access to the evidence, and that frequently the State party alone has access to relevant information. It is implicit in article 4(2) of the Optional Protocol that the State party has the duty to investigate in good faith all allegations of violation of the Covenant

234 Ibid, p. 93.

235 Ibid, p. 182.

made against it and its authorities, and to furnish to the Committee the information available to it."[236]

C. *The Living Law*

In the quest for just societies based on international human rights norms, treaty organs base themselves on what may be termed the living law which is, essentially, what the supervisory body considers the treaty provision to mean in the light of the prevailing circumstances in the society and in the world at large. The canons of interpretation remain, at base, what they are under international treaty law, namely that a treaty is to be interpreted by giving effect to the plain meaning of its provisions and , subsidiarily, in light of the drafting history of the provision if there be need to have recourse to the record of the proceedings when the treaty was drafted. But legal concepts must be given meaning so that they help advance the objectives of a just society in the light of evolving circumstances.

The decisions of supervisory bodies under petitions procedures and their general comments help us discern the content of the living law. As the European Court of Human Rights has put it, the Convention is a living instrument which must be interpreted in light of present-day conditions[237]

D. *Just Satisfaction*

In an earlier chapter we looked at the range of remedies and redress decided upon by human rights treaty organs. The European Convention on Human Rights captures the essence of remedies and redress in the concept of just satisfaction.

Conclusion

This chapter has sought to enrobe the presentation in this book of the fundamentals of international human rights treaty law in the great principles of universality, equality, and justice. From a practical point of view, universality invites international and regional human rights treaty bodies to reflection on the comparative and international jurisprudence that

236 Ibid, p. 86. See, similarly, pp. 86, 108, 116, 120, 187, 188.

237 Tryer v. the United Kingdom, judgment of 25 April, 1978, Series A No. 26, pp. 15-16, para. 31; the Soering judgment, p. 40. para. 102; Lozidou v. Turkey, judgment of 23 March, 1995, Series A. No. 310, pp. 27-27, para. 71.

might help elucidate and give content to treaty provisions that they are called upon to interpret and apply. In essence, the particular treaty provision is in many instances an expression of a universal norm or principle. Universality leads to interpretations and applications that give justice a similar face the world over.

Equality is also a universal principle to be applied in its spirit and mindful of the importance of giving equal life chances to people the world over. The particular facts of a case or situation might be different. Equality may be conditioned by the availability of resources, as the South African Constitutional Court held in the Subramooney case. But there must be clear principles and just criteria for determining the allocation of resources.

Justice is the great principle that beckons us to a just society, equitable balances between the individual and the state, all in the spirit of the living law, and with the aim of achieving just satisfaction in cases or situations where there has been a violation of human rights. Justice is the missing link between what is considered binding and non-binding in the pronouncements of human rights treaty bodies. Even if, formally, their views and general comments were not meant to be binding at the outset, they are morally binding and in time must come to be considered to be legally binding. For how can the law be less than what is morally just? Justice takes the living law further on the road to a just society.

Conclusion

We set out, at the beginning of this book, to offer some guidance to those in national administrations who are called upon to help implement human rights treaties. We suggested that following ratification, a human rights treaty must be incorporated into national law and must take precedence over any conflicting national law or practice. In compliance with the treaty obligations, every country must put into place a national protecting system to ensure compliance with its provisions.

We submitted that human rights treaty obligations are best implemented under democracy and the rule of law. Derogations expressly provided for in the treaty may be brought in but they must be proportionate to the threat, which must have been publicly and constitutionally declared. Governments have an obligation to take preventive measures against violations of human rights treaty obligations.

We discussed the duty to respect, which means that a good faith effort must be made to comply with the provisions of a human rights treaty in law and in practice. The duty to protect means that the State and its agents must act for the prevention of violations of human rights and if violations do take place must act to bring them to a stop speedily and to afford an appropriate remedy to the victim(s). The duty to ensure implies the duty of the States Parties to organize the governmental apparatus and, in general, all structures through which public power is exercised, so that they are capable of juridically ensuring the free and full enjoyment of human rights. We argued that a Government has a duty to provide appropriate and adequate redress for violations of human rights.

In supervising Government reports under a human rights treaty, we noted, the aim of the exercise is to show the degree of actual satisfaction of the rights and freedoms in the convention. In considering petitions under a human rights treaty the aim of the exercise is to render justice to the petitioner. In undertaking fact-finding under a human rights treaty the aim of the exercise is to shed light on the degree of satisfaction of the rights and freedoms in the convention.

We sought to anchor the presentation in this book of the fundamentals of international human rights treaty law in the great principles of universality, equality, and justice. From a practical point of view, universality invites international and regional human rights treaty bodies to reflection on the comparative and international jurisprudence that might help elucidate and give content to treaty provisions that they are called upon to interpret and apply. In essence, the particular treaty provision is in many instances an expression of a universal norm or principle. Universality leads to interpretations and applications that give justice a similar face the world over.

Equality is also a universal principle to be applied in its spirit and mindful of the importance of giving equal life chances to people the world over. Equality means equality in law and in practice.

Justice is the great principle that beckons us to a just society, equitable balances between the individual and the state, all in the spirit of the living law, and with the aim of achieving just satisfaction in cases or situations where there has been a violation of human rights. Justice is the missing link between what is considered binding and non-binding in the pronouncements of human rights treaty bodies. Even if, formally, their views and general comments were not meant to be binding at the outset, they are morally binding and in time must come to be considered to be legally binding. For how can the law be less than what is morally just? Justice takes the living law further on the road to a just society.

We undertook this presentation of the fundamentals of international human rights treaty law because we believe that at this juncture in international relations the human rights treaties can serve a vital anchoring role at a time of great contestation over human rights. While lip service is paid to universality in many quarters, effective universality is far from having been achieved. States violating human rights often challenge the validity of universal norms and the competence of United Nations organs. There is still much contestation over the responsibility to protect. And, in the UN Human Rights Council the countries in the majority argue for approaches of cooperation and dialogue even when dealing with gross and often criminal violations of human rights.

When, however, a State has accepted to be bound by a human rights treaty, there can be no challenge to the validity of the treaty provision or of the competence of the treaty monitoring organ to supervise its compliance through reporting, petitions, or fact-finding procedures. The issue then becomes one of compliance, pure and simple. And here, the longest-existing international supervisory body, the ILO Committee of Experts on the Application of Conventions and Recommendations has set down the standard that must be applicable to every State party. The Committee has consistently insisted that its function is to determine whether the requirements of a given Convention are being met, whatever the economic and social conditions existing in a given country. Subject only to any derogations which are expressly permitted by the Convention itself, these requirements remain constant and uniform for all countries. In carrying out this work, the Committee is guided by the standards laid down in the Convention alone, mindful, however, of the fact that the modes of their implementation may be different in different States. These are international standards, and the manner in which their implementation is evaluated must be uniform and must not be affected by concepts derived from any particular social or economic system.

The human rights treaties provide the normative platforms on which national protection systems must be constructed. An international panel of human rights leaders empanelled by the Swiss government called, in 2008, for a Global Fund to help support national protection and justice systems.[238] The jurisprudence of international human rights treaty bodies represent international standards of justice that must be emulated by national justice systems. Human rights treaty bodies are shaping a global human rights jurisprudence.

Seen from these perspectives, the implementation of human rights treaties should receive more allocation of resources from Governments, and from international and regional organizations. One needs to work systematically at the national level, with cooperation from regional and international bodies, on the implementation of each human rights treaty. An extension of this reasoning would indicate that it is premature to tamper with the existing treaties or their supervisory mechanisms. The decisive criterion must be what the needs are for human rights protection on the ground and how one can best respond to these needs in each country. If governments and international and regional organizations need to deploy resources to the implementation of human rights treaties (resources that are modest compared with, say, resources lost through inefficiency and corruption) then so let it be. The objective is a valid one and the policy must be to persist with efforts to bring the treaty provisions into effect in law and practice in each country.

An institution like the Human Rights Council, which attracts a great deal of controversy, is important because it can serve useful purposes such as standard setting, providing a framework for the special procedures and for NGOs, and reacting rapidly, if it chooses to do so, to urgent human rights situations. But it is, at the end of the day, a political body

---

238 See Agenda for Human Rights, published by the Swiss Foreign Ministry (2008).

made up of representatives of governments with all their characteristics and warts. The equity void that is left by the Human Rights Council should be filled by the treaty bodies. The treaty bodies should be in the forefront on issues of compliance and justice and a fair Human Rights Council should take its cue from them.

The International Criminal Court is a valuable body but it is a reactive one. The goal of international policy should be to work towards societies in which the crimes within the jurisdiction of the Court could be prevented in the first place. Faithful implementation of the international human rights treaties can help precisely in this endeavour. This is another side of the crucial importance of the fundamental principles of international human rights treaty law.

For the reasons just adduced, we would end this book by calling upon governments, international and regional organizations, NGOs and the academic and research community to recognize the centrality of the international human rights treaties and to accord them the priority importance they deserve in future work to embed a culture of human rights in all countries and societies. At stake is the quest for justice world-wide. The call must be to leadership for justice on the basis of the international and regional human rights treaties and the jurisprudence of their supervisory bodies.

Appendix I

General Comment No. 31 of the Human Rights Committee

The Nature of the General Legal Obligation Imposed on States Parties to the Covenant Adopted on 29 March 2004 (2187th meeting)

1. This General Comment replaces General Comment No 3, reflecting and developing its principles. The general non-discrimination provisions of article 2, paragraph 1, have been addressed in General Comment 18 and General Comment 28, and this General Comment should be read together with them.

2. While article 2 is couched in terms of the obligations of State Parties towards individuals as the right-holders under the Covenant, every State Party has a legal interest in the performance by every other State Party of its obligations. This follows from the fact that the 'rules concerning the basic rights of the human person' are *erga omnes* obligations and that, as indicated in the fourth preambular paragraph of the Covenant, there is a United Nations Charter obligation to promote universal respect for, and observance of, human rights and fundamental freedoms. Furthermore, the contractual dimension of the treaty involves any State Party to a treaty being obligated to every other State Party to comply with its undertakings under the treaty. In this connection, the Committee reminds States Parties of the desirability of making the declaration contemplated in article 41. It further reminds those States Parties already having made the declaration of the potential value of availing themselves of the procedure under that article. However, the mere fact that a formal interstate mechanism for complaints to the Human Rights Committee exists in respect of States Parties that have made the declaration under article 41 does not mean that this procedure is the only method by which States Parties can assert their interest in the performance of other States Parties. On the contrary, the article 41 procedure should be seen as supplementary to, not diminishing of, States Parties' interest in each others' discharge of their obligations. Accordingly, the Committee commends to States Parties the view that violations of Covenant rights by any State Party deserve their attention. To draw attention to possible breaches of Covenant obligations

by other States Parties and to call on them to comply with their Covenant obligations should, far from being regarded as an unfriendly act, be considered as a reflection of legitimate community interest.

3. Article 2 defines the scope of the legal obligations undertaken by States Parties to the Covenant. A general obligation is imposed on States Parties to respect the Covenant rights and to ensure them to all individuals in their territory and subject to their jurisdiction (see paragraph 10 below). Pursuant to the principle articulated in article 26 of the Vienna Convention on the Law of Treaties, States Parties are required to give effect to the obligations under the Covenant in good faith.

4. The obligations of the Covenant in general and article 2 in particular are binding on every State Party as a whole. All branches of government (executive, legislative and judicial), and other public or governmental authorities, at whatever level – national, regional or local – are in a position to engage the responsibility of the State Party. The executive branch that usually represents the State Party internationally, including before the Committee, may not point to the fact that an action incompatible with the provisions of the Covenant was carried out by another branch of government as a means of seeking to relieve the State Party from responsibility for the action and consequent incompatibility. This understanding flows directly from the principle contained in article 27 of the Vienna Convention on the Law of Treaties, according to which a State Party 'may not invoke the provisions of its internal law as justification for its failure to perform a treaty'. Although article 2, paragraph 2, allows States Parties to give effect to Covenant rights in accordance with domestic constitutional processes, the same principle operates so as to prevent States parties from invoking provisions of the constitutional law or other aspects of domestic law to justify a failure to perform or give effect to obligations under the treaty. In this respect, the Committee reminds States Parties with a federal structure of the terms of article 50, according to which the Covenant's provisions 'shall extend to all parts of federal states without any limitations or exceptions'.

5. The article 2, paragraph 1, obligation to respect and ensure the rights recognized by in the Covenant has immediate effect for all States parties. Article 2, paragraph 2, provides the overarching framework within which the rights specified in the Covenant are to be promoted and protected. The Committee has as a consequence previously indicated in its General

Comment 24 that reservations to article 2, would be incompatible with the Covenant when considered in the light of its objects and purposes.

6. The legal obligation under article 2, paragraph 1, is both negative and positive in nature. States Parties must refrain from violation of the rights recognized by the Covenant, and any restrictions on any of those rights must be permissible under the relevant provisions of the Covenant. Where such restrictions are made, States must demonstrate their necessity and only take such measures as are proportionate to the pursuance of legitimate aims in order to ensure continuous and effective protection of Covenant rights. In no case may the restrictions be applied or invoked in a manner that would impair the essence of a Covenant right.

7. Article 2 requires that States Parties adopt legislative, judicial, administrative, educative and other appropriate measures in order to fulfil their legal obligations. The Committee believes that it is important to raise levels of awareness about the Covenant not only among public officials and State agents but also among the population at large.

8. The article 2, paragraph 1, obligations are binding on States [Parties] and do not, as such, have direct horizontal effect as a matter of international law. The Covenant cannot be viewed as a substitute for domestic criminal or civil law. However the positive obligations on States Parties to ensure Covenant rights will only be fully discharged if individuals are protected by the State, not just against violations of Covenant rights by its agents, but also against acts committed by private persons or entities that would impair the enjoyment of Covenant rights in so far as they are amenable to application between private persons or entities. There may be circumstances in which a failure to ensure Covenant rights as required by article 2 would give rise to violations by States Parties of those rights, as a result of States Parties' permitting or failing to take appropriate measures or to exercise due diligence to prevent, punish, investigate or redress the harm caused by such acts by private persons or entities. States are reminded of the interrelationship between the positive obligations imposed under article 2 and the need to provide effective remedies in the event of breach under article 2, paragraph 3. The Covenant itself envisages in some articles certain areas where there are positive obligations on States Parties to address the activities of private persons or entities. For example, the privacy-related guarantees of article 17 must be protected by law. It is also implicit in article 7 that States Parties have to take positive measures to ensure that private persons or entities do not inflict tor-

ture or cruel, inhuman or degrading treatment or punishment on others within their power. In fields affecting basic aspects of ordinary life such as work or housing, individuals are to be protected from discrimination within the meaning of article 26.]

9. The beneficiaries of the rights recognized by the Covenant are individuals. Although, with the exception of article 1, the Covenant does not mention he rights of legal persons or similar entities or collectivities, many of the rights recognized by the Covenant, such as the freedom to manifest one's religion or belief (article 18), the freedom of association (article 22) or the rights of members of minorities (article 27), may be enjoyed in community with others. The fact that the competence of the Committee to receive and consider communications is restricted to those submitted by or on behalf of individuals (article 1 of the Optional Protocol) does not prevent such individuals from claiming that actions or omissions that concern legal persons and similar entities amount to a violation of their own rights.

10. States Parties are required by article 2, paragraph 1, to respect and to ensure the Covenant rights to all persons who may be within their territory and to all persons subject to their jurisdiction. This means that a State party must respect and ensure the rights laid down in the Covenant to anyone within the power or effective control of that State Party, even if not situated within the territory of the State Party. As indicated in General Comment 15 adopted at the twenty-seventh session (1986), the enjoyment of Covenant rights is not limited to citizens of States Parties but must also be available to all individuals, regardless of nationality or statelessness, such as asylum seekers, refugees, migrant workers and other persons, who may find themselves in the territory or subject to the jurisdiction of the State Party. This principle also applies to those within the power or effective control of the forces of a State Party acting outside its territory, regardless of the circumstances in which such power or effective control was obtained, such as forces constituting a national contingent of a State Party assigned to an international peace-keeping or peace-enforcement operation.

11. As implied in General Comment 2911 General Comment No.29 on States of Emergencies, adopted on 24 July 2001, reproduced in Annual Report for 2001, A/56/40, Annex VI, paragraph 3. , the Covenant applies also in situations of armed conflict to which the rules of international humanitarian law are applicable. While, in respect of certain Covenant

rights, more specific rules of international humanitarian law may be specially relevant for the purposes of the interpretation of Covenant rights, both spheres of law are complementary, not mutually exclusive.

12. Moreover, the article 2 obligation requiring that States Parties respect and ensure the Covenant rights for all persons in their territory and all persons under their control entails an obligation not to extradite, deport, expel or otherwise remove a person from their territory, where there are substantial grounds for believing that there is a real risk of irreparable harm, such as that contemplated by articles 6 and 7 of the Covenant, either in the country to which removal is to be effected or in any country to which the person may subsequently be removed. The relevant judicial and administrative authorities should be made aware of the need to ensure compliance with the Covenant obligations in such matters.

13. Article 2, paragraph 2, requires that States Parties take the necessary steps to give effect to the Covenant rights in the domestic order. It follows that, unless Covenant rights are already protected by their domestic laws or practices, States Parties are required on ratification to make such changes to domestic laws and practices as are necessary to ensure their conformity with the Covenant. Where there are inconsistencies between domestic law and the Covenant, article 2 requires that the domestic law or practice be changed to meet the standards imposed by the Covenant's substantive guarantees. Article allows a State Party to pursue this in accordance with its own domestic constitutional structure and accordingly does not require that the Covenant be directly applicable in the courts, by incorporation of the Covenant into national law. The Committee takes the view, however, that Covenant guarantees may receive enhanced protection in those States where the Covenant is automatically or through specific incorporation part of the domestic legal order. The Committee invites those States Parties in which the Covenant does not form part of the domestic legal order to consider incorporation of the Covenant to render it part of domestic law to facilitate full realization of Covenant rights as required by article 2.

14. The requirement under article 2, paragraph 2, to take steps to give effect to the Covenant rights is unqualified and of immediate effect. A failure to comply with this obligation cannot be justified by reference to political, social, cultural or economic considerations within the State.

15. Article 2, paragraph 3, requires that in addition to effective protection of Covenant rights States Parties must ensure that individuals also have accessible and effective remedies to vindicate those rights. Such remedies should be appropriately adapted so as to take account of the special vulnerability of certain categories of person, including in particular children. The Committee attaches importance to States Parties' establishing appropriate judicial and administrative mechanisms for addressing claims of rights violations under domestic law. The Committee notes that the enjoyment of the rights recognized under the Covenant can be effectively assured by the judiciary in many different ways, including direct applicability of the Covenant, application of comparable constitutional or other provisions of law, or the interpretive effect of the Covenant in the application of national law. Administrative mechanisms are particularly required to give effect to the general obligation to investigate allegations of violations promptly, thoroughly and effectively through independent and impartial bodies. National human rights institutions, endowed with appropriate powers, can contribute to this end. A failure by a State Party to investigate allegations of violations could in and of itself give rise to a separate breach of the Covenant. Cessation of an ongoing violation is an essential element of the right to an effective remedy.

16. Article 2, paragraph 3, requires that States Parties make reparation to individuals whose Covenant rights have been violated. Without reparation to individuals whose Covenant rights have been violated, the obligation to provide an effective remedy, which is central to the efficacy of article 2, paragraph 3, is not discharged. In addition to the explicit reparation required by articles 9, paragraph 5, and 14, paragraph 6, the Committee considers that the Covenant generally entails appropriate compensation. The Committee notes that, where appropriate, reparation can involve restitution, rehabilitation and measures of satisfaction, such as public apologies, public memorials, guarantees of non-repetition and changes in relevant laws and practices, as well as bringing to justice the perpetrators of human rights violations.

17. In general, the purposes of the Covenant would be defeated without an obligation integral to article 2 to take measures to prevent a recurrence of a violation of the Covenant. Accordingly, it has been a frequent practice of the Committee in cases under the Optional Protocol to include in its Views the need for measures, beyond a victim-specific remedy, to be taken to avoid recurrence of the type of violation in question. Such measures may require changes in the State Party's laws or practices.

18. Where the investigations referred to in paragraph 15 reveal violations of certain Covenant rights, States Parties must ensure that those responsible are brought to justice. As with failure to investigate, failure to bring to justice perpetrators of such violations could in and of itself give rise to a separate breach of the Covenant. These obligations arise notably in respect of those violations recognized as criminal under either domestic or international law, such as torture and similar cruel, inhuman and degrading treatment (article 7), summary and arbitrary killing (article 6) and enforced disappearance (articles 7 and 9 and, frequently, 6). Indeed, the problem of impunity for these violations, a matter of sustained concern by the Committee, may well be an important contributing element in the recurrence of the violations. When committed as part of a widespread or systematic attack on a civilian population, these violations of the Covenant are crimes against humanity (see Rome Statute of the International Criminal Court, article 7). Accordingly, where public officials or State agents have committed violations of the Covenant rights referred to in this paragraph, the States Parties concerned may not relieve perpetrators from personal responsibility, as has occurred with certain amnesties (see General Comment 20 (44)) and prior legal immunities and indemnities. Furthermore, no official status justifies persons who may be accused of responsibility for such violations being held immune from legal responsibility. Other impediments to the establishment of legal responsibility should also be removed, such as the defence of obedience to superior orders or unreasonably short periods of statutory limitation in cases where such limitations are applicable. States parties should also assist each other to bring to justice persons suspected of having committed acts in violation of the Covenant that are punishable under domestic or international law.

19. The Committee further takes the view that the right to an effective remedy may in certain circumstances require States Parties to provide for and implement provisional or interim measures to avoid continuing violations and to endeavour to repair at the earliest possible opportunity any harm that may have been caused by such violations.

20. Even when the legal systems of States parties are formally endowed with the appropriate remedy, violations of Covenant rights still take place. This is presumably attributable to the failure of the remedies to function effectively in practice. Accordingly, States parties are requested to provide information on the obstacles to the effectiveness of existing remedies in their periodic reports.

Appendix II

General Comment No. 33 of the Human Rights Committee

General Comment: 33 [94] Adopted on : 31-10-2008

The Obligations of States Parties under the Optional Protocol to the International Covenant on Civil and Political Rights

1. The Optional Protocol to the International Covenant on Civil and Political Rights was adopted and opened for signature, ratification or accession by the same act of the United Nations General Assembly, resolution 2200 A (XXI) of 16 December 1966, that adopted the Covenant itself. Both the Covenant and the Optional Protocol entered into force on 23 March 1976.

2. Although the Optional Protocol is organically related to the Covenant, it is not automatically in force for all States parties to the Covenant. Article 8 of the Optional Protocol provides that States parties to the Covenant may become parties to the Optional Protocol only by a separate expression of consent to be bound. A majority of States parties to the Covenant has also become party to the Optional Protocol.

3. The preamble to the Optional Protocol states that its purpose is "further to achieve the purposes" of the Covenant by enabling the Human Rights Committee, established in part IV of the Covenant, "to receive and consider, as provided in the present Protocol, communications from individuals claiming to be victims of violations of any of the rights set forth in the Covenant." The Optional Protocol sets out a procedure, and imposes obligations on States parties to the Optional Protocol arising out of that procedure, in addition to their obligations under the Covenant.

4. Article 1 of the Optional Protocol provides that a State party to it recognizes the competence of the Committee to receive and consider communications from individuals subject to its jurisdiction who claim to be victims of a violation by that State party of any of the rights set forth in the Covenant. It follows that States parties are obliged not to hinder ac-

cess to the Committee and to prevent any retaliatory measures against any person who has addressed a communication to the Committee.

5. Article 2 of the Optional Protocol requires that individuals who submit communications to the Committee must have exhausted all available domestic remedies. In its response to a communication, a State party, where it considers that this condition has not been met, should specify the available and effective remedies that the author of the communication has failed to exhaust.

6. Although not a term found in the Optional Protocol or Covenant, the Human Rights Committee uses the description "author" to refer to an individual who has submitted a communication to the Committee under the Optional Protocol. The Committee uses the term "communication" contained in article 1 of the Optional Protocol instead of such terms as "complaint" or "petition", although the latter term is reflected in the current administrative structure of the Office of the High Commissioner for Human Rights, where communications under the Optional Protocol are initially handled by a section known as the Petitions Team.

7. Terminology similarly reflects the nature of the role of the Human Rights Committee in receiving and considering a communication. Subject to the communication being found admissible, after considering the communication in the light of all written information made available to it by the individual author and by the State party concerned, "the Committee shall forward its views to the State party concerned and to the individual."[1]

8. The first obligation of a State Party, against which a claim has been made by an individual under the Optional Protocol, is to respond to it within the time limit of six months set out in article 4 (2). Within that time limit, "the receiving State shall submit to the Committee written explanations or statements clarifying the matter and the remedy, if any, that may have been taken by the State." The Committee's Rules of Procedure amplify these provisions, including the possibility in exceptional cases of treating separately questions of the admissibility and merits of the communication.[2]

9. In responding to a communication that appears to relate to a matter arising before the entry into force of the Optional Protocol for the State party (the *ratione temporis* rule), the State party should invoke that cir-

cumstance explicitly, including any comment on the possible "continuing effect" of a past violation.

10. In the experience of the Committee, States do not always respect their obligation. In failing to respond to a communication, or responding incompletely, a State which is the object of a communication puts itself at a disadvantage, because the Committee is then compelled to consider the communication in the absence of full information relating to the communication. In such circumstances, the Committee may conclude that the allegations contained in the communication are true, if they appear from all the circumstances to be substantiated.

11. While the function of the Human Rights Committee in considering individual communications is not, as such, that of a judicial body, the views issued by the Committee under the Optional Protocol exhibit some important characteristics of a judicial decision. They are arrived at in a judicial spirit, including the impartiality and independence of Committee members, the considered interpretation of the language of the Covenant, and the determinative character of the decisions.

12. The term used in article 5, paragraph 4 of the Optional Protocol to describe the decisions of the Committee is "views".[3] These decisions state the Committee's findings on the violations alleged by the author of a communication and, where a violation has been found, state a remedy for that violation.

13. The views of the Committee under the Optional Protocol represent an authoritative determination by the organ established under the Covenant itself charged with the interpretation of that instrument. These views derive their character, and the importance which attaches to them, from the integral role of the Committee under both the Covenant and the Optional Protocol.

14. Under article 2, paragraph 3 of the Covenant, each State party undertakes "to ensure that any person whose rights or freedoms as herein recognised are violated shall have an effective remedy, notwithstanding that the violation has been committed by a person acting in an official capacity." This is the basis of the wording consistently used by the Committee in issuing its views in cases where a violation has been found:

> "In accordance with article 2, paragraph 3(a) of the Covenant, the State party is required to provide the author with an effective remedy. By becoming a party to the Optional Protocol the State party has recognized the competence of the Committee to determine whether there has been a violation of the Covenant or not and that, pursuant to article 2 of the Covenant, the State party has undertaken to ensure to all individuals within its territory or subject to its jurisdiction the rights recognized in the Covenant and to provide an effective and enforceable remedy in case a violation has been established. In this respect, the Committee wishes to receive from the State party, within 180 days, information about the measures taken to give effect to the Committee's views."

15. The character of the views of the Committee is further determined by the obligation of States parties to act in good faith, both in their anticipation in the procedures under the Optional Protocol and in relation to the Covenant itself. A duty to cooperate with the Committee arises from an application of the principle of good faith to the observance of all treaty obligations.[4]

16. The Committee decided, in 1997, under its rules of procedure, to appoint a member of the Committee as Special Rapporteur for the Follow-Up of Views.[5]

That member, through written representations, and frequently also through personal meetings with diplomatic representatives of the State party concerned, urges compliance with the Committee's views and discusses factors that may be impeding their implementation. In a number of cases this procedure has led to acceptance and implementation of the Committee's views where previously the transmission of those views had met with no response.

17. It is to be noted that failure by a State party to implement the views of the Committee in a given case becomes a matter of public record through the publication of the Committee's decisions inter alia in its annual reports to the General Assembly of the United Nations.

18. Some States parties, to which the views of the Committee have been transmitted in relation to communications concerning them, have failed to accept the Committee's views, in whole or in part, or have attempted to re-open the case. In a number of those cases these responses have been made where the State party took no part in the procedures, having not

carried out its obligation to respond to communications under article 4, paragraph 2 of the Optional Protocol. In other cases, rejection of the Committee's views, in whole or in part, has come after the State party has participated in the procedure and where its arguments have been fully considered by the Committee. In all such cases, the Committee regards dialogue between the Committee and the State party as ongoing with a view to implementation. The Special Rapporteur for the Follow-up of Views conducts this dialogue, and regularly reports on progress to the Committee.

19. Measures may be requested by an author, or decided by the Committee on its own initiative, when an action taken or threatened by the State party would appear likely to cause irreparable harm to the author or the victim unless withdrawn or suspended pending full consideration of the communication by the Committee. Examples include the imposition of the death penalty and violation of the duty of non-refoulement. In order to be in a position to meet these needs under the Optional Protocol, the Committee established, under its rules of procedure, a procedure to request interim or provisional measures of protection in appropriate cases.[6] Failure to implement such interim or provisional measures is incompatible with the obligation to respect in good faith the procedure of individual communication established under the Optional Protocol.

20. Most States do not have specific enabling legislation to receive the views of the Committee into their domestic legal order. The domestic law of some States parties does, however, provide for the payment of compensation to the victims of violations of human rights as found by international organs. In any case, States parties must use whatever means lie within their power in order to give effect to the views issued by the Committee.

Notes

[1] Optional Protocol, article 5(4).
[2] Rules of Procedure of the Human Rights Committee, Rule 97(2). UN Doc. CCPR/C/3/Rev.8, 22 September 2005. CCPR/C/GC/33 page 3
[3] In French the term is "constatations" and in Spanish "observaciones".
[4] Vienna Convention on the Law of Treaties, 1969, article 26.
[5] Rules of Procedure of the Human Rights Committee, Rule 101.
[6] Rules of Procedure of the Human Rights Committee, UN Doc. CCPR/C/3/Rev.8, 22 September 2005, Rule 92 (previously Rule 86): "The Committee

may, prior to forwarding its Views on the communication to the State party concerned, inform the State of its Views as to whether interim measures may be desirable to avoid irreparable damage to the victim of the alleged violation. In doing so, the Committee shall inform the State party concerned that such expression of its Views on interim measures does not imply a determination on the merits of the communication."

Appendix III

The Limburg Principles on the Implementation of the International Covenant on Economic, Social and Cultural Rights

[UN doc. E/CN.4/1987/17, Annex; and *Human Rights Quarterly*, Vol. 9 (1987), pp. 122–135]

Part 1: The Nature and Scope of States Parties' Obligations

A. General Observations

1. Economic, social and cultural rights are an integral part of international human rights law. They are the subject of specific treaty obligations in various international instruments, notably the International Covenant on Economic, Social and Cultural Rights.

2. The International Covenant on Economic, Social and Cultural Rights, together with the International Covenant on Civil and Political Rights and the Optional Protocol, entered into force in 1976. The Covenants serve to elaborate the Universal Declaration of Human Rights: these instruments constitute the International Bill of Human Rights.

3. As human rights and fundamental freedoms are indivisible and interdependent, equal attention and urgent consideration should be given to the implementation, promotion and protection of both civil and political, and economic, social and cultural rights.

4. The International Covenant on Economic, Social and Cultural Rights (hereafter the Covenant) should, in accordance with the Vienna Convention on the Law of Treaties (Vienna, 1969), be interpreted in good faith, taking into account the object and purpose, the ordinary meaning, the preparatory work and the relevant practice.

5. The experience of the relevant specialized agencies as well as of United Nations bodies and intergovernmental organizations, including the United Nations working groups and special rapporteurs in the field of human

rights, should be taken into account in the implementation of the Covenant and in monitoring States parties' achievements.

6. The achievement of economic, social and cultural rights may be realized in a variety of political settings. There is no single road to their full realization. Successes and failures have been registered in both market and non-market economies, in both centralized and decentralized political structures.

7. States parties must at all times act in good faith to fulfill the obligations they have accepted under the Covenant.

8. Although the full realization of the rights recognized in the Covenant is to be attained progressively, the application of some rights can be made justiciable immediately while other rights can become justiciable over time.

9. Non-governmental organizations can play an important role in promoting the implementation of the Covenant. This role should accordingly be facilitated at the national as well as the international level.

10. States parties are accountable both to the international community and to their own people for their compliance with the obligations under the Covenant.

11. A concerted national effort to invoke the full participation of all sectors of society is, therefore, indispensable to achieving progress in realizing economic, social and cultural rights. Popular participation is required at all stages, including the formulation, application and review of national policies.

12. The supervision of compliance with the Covenant should be approached in a spirit of co-operation and dialogue. To this end, in considering the reports of States parties, the Committee on Economic, Social and Cultural Rights, hereinafter called 'the Committee', should analyze the causes and factors impeding the realization of the rights covered under the Covenant and, where possible indicate solutions. This approach should not preclude a finding, where the information available warrants such a conclusion, that a State party has failed to comply with its obligations under the Covenant.

13. All organs monitoring the Covenant should pay special attention to the principles of non-discrimination and equality before the law when assessing States parties' compliance with the Covenant.

14. Given the significance for development of the progressive realization of the rights set forth in the Covenant, particular attention should be given to measures to improve the standard of living of the poor and other disadvantaged groups, taking into account that special measures may be required to protect cultural rights of indigenous peoples and minorities.

15. Trends in international economic relations should be taken into account in assessing the efforts of the international community to achieve the Covenant's objectives.

B. *Interpretative Principles Specifically Relating to Part II of the Covenant*

Article 2(1): 'to take steps ... by all appropriate means, including particularly the adoption of legislation'

16. All States parties have an obligation to begin immediately to take steps towards full realization of the rights contained in the Covenant.

17. At the national level States parties shall use all appropriate means, including legislative, administrative, judicial, economic, social and educational measures, consistent with the nature of the rights in order to fulfill their obligations under the Covenant.

18. Legislative measures alone are not sufficient to fulfill the obligations of the Covenant. It should be noted, however, that article 2(1) would often require legislative action to be taken in cases where existing legislation is in violation of the obligations assumed under the Covenant.

19. States parties shall provide for effective remedies including, where appropriate, judicial remedies.

20. The appropriateness of the means to be applied in a particular state shall be determined by that State party, and shall be subject to review by the United Nations Economic and Social Council, with the assistance of the Committee. Such review shall be without prejudice to the competence of the other organs established pursuant to the Charter of the United Nations.

'to achieve progressively the full realization of the rights'

21. The obligation 'to achieve progressively the full realization of the rights' requires States parties to move as expeditiously as possible towards the realization of the rights. Under no circumstances shall this be interpreted as implying for States the right to defer indefinitely efforts to ensure full realization. On the contrary all States parties have the obligation to begin immediately to take steps to fulfill their obligations under the Covenant.

22. Some obligations under the Covenant require immediate implementation in full by all States parties, such as the prohibition of discrimination in article 2(2) of the Covenant.

23. The obligation of progressive achievement exists independently of the increase in resources; it requires effective use of resources available.

24. Progressive implementation can be affected not only by increasing resources, but also by the development of societal resources necessary for the realization by everyone of the rights recognized in the Covenant.

'to the maximum of its available resources'

25. States parties are obligated, regardless of the level of economic development, to ensure respect for minimum subsistence rights for all.

26. 'Its available resources' refers to both the resources within a State and those available from the international community through international co-operation and assistance.

27. In determining whether adequate measures have been taken for the realization of the rights recognized in the Covenant attention shall be paid to equitable and effective use of and access to the available resources.

28. In the use of the available resources due priority shall be given to the realization of rights recognized in the Covenant, mindful of the need to assure to everyone the satisfaction of subsistence requirements as well as the provision of essential services.

'individually and through international assistance and co-operation, especially economic and technical'

29. International co-operation and assistance pursuant to the Charter of the United Nations (arts. 55 and 56) and the Covenant shall have in view

as a matter of priority the realization of all human rights and fundamental freedoms, economic, social and cultural as well as civil and political.

30. International co-operation and assistance must be directed towards the establishment of a social and international order in which the rights and freedoms set forth in the Covenant can be fully realized (cf. art. 28 Universal Declaration of Human Rights).

31. Irrespective of differences in their political, economic and social systems, States shall co-operate with one another to promote international social, economic and cultural progress, in particular the economic growth of developing countries, free from discrimination based on such differences.

32. States parties shall take steps by international means to assist and co-operate in the realization of the rights recognized by the Covenant.

33. International co-operation and assistance shall be based on the sovereign equality of states and be aimed at the realization of the rights contained in the Covenant.

34. In undertaking international co-operation and assistance pursuant to article 2(1) the role of international organizations and the contribution of non-governmental organizations shall be kept in mind.

Article 2(2): Non-discrimination

35. Article 2(2) calls for immediate application and involves an explicit guarantee on behalf of the States parties. It should, therefore, be made subject to judicial review and other recourse procedures.

36. The grounds of discrimination mentioned in article 2(2) are not exhaustive.

37. Upon becoming a party to the Covenant states shall eliminate *de jure* discrimination by abolishing without delay any discriminatory laws, regulations and practices (including acts of omission as well as commission) affecting the enjoyment of economic, social and cultural rights.

38. *De facto* discrimination occurring as a result of the unequal enjoyment of economic, social and cultural rights, on account of a lack of resources or otherwise, should be brought to an end as speedily as possible.

39. Special measures taken for the sole purpose of securing adequate advancement of certain groups or individuals requiring such protection as may be necessary in order to ensure to such groups or individuals equal enjoyment of economic, social and cultural rights shall not be deemed discrimination, provided, however, that such measures do not, as a consequence, lead to the maintenance of separate rights for different groups and that such measures shall not be continued after their intended objectives have been achieved.

40. Article 2(2) demands from States parties that they prohibit private persons and bodies from practising discrimination in any field of public life.

41. In the application of article 2(2) due regard should be paid to all relevant international instruments including the Declaration and Convention on the Elimination of all Forms of Racial Discrimination as well as to the activities of the supervisory committee (CERD) under the said Convention.

Article 2(3): Non-nationals in developing countries

42. As a general rule the Covenant applies equally to nationals and non-nationals.

43. The purpose of article 2(3) was to end the domination of certain economic groups of non-nationals during colonial times. In the light of this the exception in article 2(3) should be interpreted narrowly.

44. This narrow interpretation of article 2(3) refers in particular to the notion of economic rights and to the notion of developing countries. The latter notion refers to those countries which have gained independence and which fall within the appropriate United Nations classifications of developing countries.

Article 3: Equal rights for men and women

45. In the application of article 3 due regard should be paid to the Declaration and Convention on the Elimination of All Forms of Discrimination

against Women and other relevant instruments and the activities of the supervisory committee (CEDAW) under the said Convention.

Article 4: Limitations

46. Article 4 was primarily intended to be protective of the rights of individuals rather than permissive of the imposition of limitations by the state.

47. The article was not meant to introduce limitations on rights affecting the subsistence or survival of the individual or integrity of the person.

'determined by law'[239]

48. No limitation on the exercise of economic, social and cultural rights shall be made unless provided for by national law of general application which is consistent with the Covenant and is in force at the time the limitation is applied.

49. Laws imposing limitations on the exercise of economic, social and cultural rights shall not be arbitrary or unreasonable or discriminatory.

50. Legal rules limiting the exercise of economic, social and cultural rights shall be clear and accessible to everyone.

51. Adequate safeguards and effective remedies shall be provided by law against illegal or abusive imposition or application of limitations on economic, social and cultural rights.

'promoting the general welfare'

52. This term shall be construed to mean furthering the wellbeing of the people as a whole.

'in a democratic society'[240]

53. The expression 'in a democratic society' shall be interpreted as imposing a further restriction on the application of limitations.

239 The Limburg Principles 48–51 are derived from the Siracusa Principles 15–18, UN Doc. E/CN.4/1984/4, 28 September 1984 and 7 *Human Rights Quarterly* 3, 5 (1985).

240 Compare Siracusa Principles 19–21, *id.* at 5.

54. The burden is upon a state imposing limitations to demonstrate that the limitations do not impair the democratic functioning of the society.

55. While there is no single model of a democratic society, a society which recognizes and respects the human rights set forth in the United Nations Charter and the Universal Declaration of Human Rights may be viewed as meeting this definition.

'compatible with the nature of these rights'

56. The restriction 'compatible with the nature of these rights' requires that a limitation shall not be interpreted or applied so as to jeopardize the essence of the right concerned.

Article 5

57. Article 5(1) underlines the fact that there is no general, implied or residual right for a state to impose limitations beyond those which are specifically provided for in the law. None of the provisions in the law may be interpreted in such a way as to destroy 'any of the rights or freedoms recognized'. In addition article 5 is intended to ensure that nothing in the Covenant shall be interpreted as impairing the inherent right of all peoples to enjoy and utilize fully and freely their natural wealth and resources.

58. The purpose of article 5(2) is to ensure that no provision in the Covenant shall be interpreted to prejudice the provisions of domestic law or any bilateral or multilateral treaties, conventions or agreements which are already in force, or may come into force, under which more favourable treatment would be accorded to the persons protected. Neither shall article 5(2) be interpreted to restrict the exercise of any human right protected to a greater extent by national or international obligations accepted by the State party.

C. *Interpretative Principles Specifically Relating to Part III of the Covenant*

Article 8: 'prescribed bylaw'[241]

59. See the interpretative principles under the synonymous term 'determined by law' in article 4.

241 The Limburg Principles 59–69 are derived from the Siracusa Principles 10, 15–26, 29–32 and 35–37, *id.* at 4–7.

'necessary in a democratic society'

60. In addition to the interpretative principles listed under article 4 concerning the phrase 'in a democratic society', article 8 imposes a greater restraint upon a State party which is exercising limitations on trade union rights. It requires that such a limitation is indeed necessary. The term 'necessary' implies that the limitation:

a) responds to a pressing public or social need,
b) pursues a legitimate aim, and
c) is proportional to that aim.

61. Any assessment as to the necessity of a limitation shall be based upon objective considerations.

'national security'

62. National security may be invoked to justify measures limiting certain rights only when they are taken to protect the existence of the nation or its territorial integrity or political independence against force or threat of force.

63. National security cannot be invoked as a reason for imposing limitations to prevent merely local or relatively isolated threats to law and order.

64. National security cannot be used as a pretext for imposing vague or arbitrary limitations and may be invoked only when there exist adequate safeguards and effective remedies against abuse.

65. The systematic violation of economic, social and cultural rights undermines true national security and may jeopardize international peace and security. A state responsible for such violation shall not invoke national security as a justification for measures aimed at suppressing opposition to such violation or at perpetrating repressive practices against its population.

'public order (ordre public)'

66. The expression 'public order (*ordre public*)' as used in the Covenant may be defined as the sum of rules which ensures the functioning of society or the set of fundamental principles on which a society is founded. Respect for economic, social and cultural rights is part of public order (ordre public).

67. Public order (*ordre public*) shall be interpreted in the context of the purpose of the particular economic, social and cultural rights which are limited on this ground.

68. State organs or agents responsible for the maintenance of public order (*ordre public*) shall be subject to controls in the exercise of their power through the parliament, courts, or other competent independent bodies.

'rights and freedoms of others'

69. The scope of the rights and freedoms of others that may act as a limitation upon rights in the Covenant extends beyond the rights and freedoms recognized in the Covenant.

D. Violation of Economic, Social and Cultural Rights

70. A failure by a State party to comply with an obligation contained in the Covenant is, under international law, a violation of the Covenant.

71. In determining what amounts to a failure to comply, it must be borne in mind that the Covenant affords to a State party a margin of discretion in selecting the means for carrying out its objects, and that factors beyond its reasonable control may adversely affect its capacity to implement particular rights.

72. A State party will be in violation of the Covenant, inter alia, if:

- it fails to take a step which it is required to take by the Covenant;
- it fails to remove promptly obstacles which it is under a duty to remove to permit the immediate fulfilment of a right;
- it fails to implement without delay a right which it is required by the Covenant to provide immediately;
- it wilfully fails to meet a generally accepted international minimum standard of achievement, which is within its powers to meet;
- it applies a limitation to a right recognized in the Covenant other than in accordance with the Covenant;
- it deliberately retards or halts the progressive realization of a right, unless it is acting within a limitation permitted by the Covenant or it does so due to a lack of available resources or *force majeur*;
- it fails to submit reports as required under the Covenant.

73. In accordance with international law each State party to the Covenant has the right to express the view that another State party is not complying

with its obligations under the Covenant and to bring this to the attention of that State party. Any dispute that may thus arise shall be settled in accordance with the relevant rules of international law relating to the peaceful settlement of disputes.

Part II. Consideration of States Parties' Reports and International Co-Operation under Part IV of the Covenant

A. *Preparation and Submission of Reports by States Parties*

74. The effectiveness of the supervisory machinery provided in Part IV of the Covenant depends largely upon the quality and timeliness of reports by States parties. Governments are therefore urged to make their reports as meaningful as possible. For this purpose they should develop adequate internal procedures for consultations with the competent government departments and agencies, compilation of relevant data, training of staff, acquisition of background documentation, and consultation with relevant non-governmental and international institutions.

75. The preparation of reports under article 16 of the Covenant could be facilitated by the implementation of elements of the programme of advisory services and technical assistance as proposed by the chairmen of the main human rights supervisory organs in their 1984 report to the General Assembly (UN Doc. A 39/484).

76. States parties should view their reporting obligations as an opportunity for broad public discussion on goals and policies designed to realize economic, social and cultural rights. For this purpose wide publicity should be given to the reports, if possible in draft. The preparation of reports should also be an occasion to review the extent to which relevant national policies adequately reflect the scope and content of each right, and to specify the means by which it is to be realized.

77. States parties are encouraged to examine the possibility of involving non-governmental organizations in the preparation of their reports.

78. In reporting on legal steps taken to give effect to the Covenant, States parties should not merely describe any relevant legislative provisions. They should specify, as appropriate, the judicial remedies, administrative procedures and other measures they have adopted for enforcing those rights and the practice under those remedies and procedures.

79. Quantitative information should be included in the reports of States parties in order to indicate the extent to which the rights are protected in fact. Statistical information and information on budgetary allocations and expenditures should be presented in such a way as to facilitate the assessment of the compliance with Covenant obligations. States parties should, where possible, adopt clearly defined targets and indicators in implementing the Covenant. Such targets and indicators should, as appropriate, be based on criteria established through international co-operation in order to increase the relevance and comparability of data submitted by States parties in their reports.

80. Where necessary, governments should conduct or commission studies to enable them to fill gaps in information regarding progress made and difficulties encountered in achieving the observance of the Covenant rights.

81. Reports by States parties should indicate the areas where more progress could be achieved through international co-operation and suggest economic and technical co-operation programmes that might be helpful toward that end.

82. In order to ensure a meaningful dialogue between the States parties and the organs assessing their compliance with the provisions of the Covenant, States parties should designate representatives who are fully familiar with the issues raised in the report.

B. Role of the Committee on Economic, Social and Cultural Rights

83. The Committee has been entrusted with assisting the Economic and Social Council in the substantive tasks assigned to it by the Covenant. In particular, its role is to consider States parties' reports and to make suggestions and recommendations of a general nature, including suggestions and recommendations as to fuller compliance with the Covenant by States parties. The decision of the Economic and Social Council to replace its sessional Working Group by a Committee of independent experts should lead to a more effective supervision of the implementation by States parties.

84. In order to enable it to discharge fully its responsibilities the Economic and Social Council should ensure that sufficient sessions are provided to the Committee. It is imperative that the necessary staff and facilities

for the effective performance of the Committee's functions be provided, in accordance with ECOSOC Resolution 1985/17.

85. In order to address the complexity of the substantive issues covered by the Covenant, the Committee might consider delegating certain tasks to its members. For example, drafting groups could be established to prepare preliminary formulations or recommendations of a general nature or summaries of the information received. Rapporteurs could be appointed to assist the work of the Committee in particular to prepare reports on specific topics and for that purpose consult States parties, specialized agencies and relevant experts and to draw up proposals regarding economic and technical assistance projects that could help overcome difficulties States parties have encountered in fulfilling their Covenant obligations.

86. The Committee should, pursuant to articles 22 and 23 of the Covenant, explore with other organs of the United Nations, specialized agencies and other concerned organizations, the possibilities of taking additional international measures likely to contribute to the progressive implementation of the Covenant.

87. The Committee should reconsider the current six-year cycle of reporting in view of the delays which have led to simultaneous consideration of reports submitted under different phases of the cycle. The Committee should also review the guidelines for States parties to assist them in preparing reports and propose any necessary modifications.

88. The Committee should consider inviting States parties to comment on selected topics leading to a direct and sustained dialogue with the Committee.

89. The Committee should devote adequate attention to the methodological issues involved in assessing compliance with the obligations contained in the Covenant. Reference to indicators, in so far as they may help measure progress made in the achievement of certain rights, may be useful in evaluating reports submitted under the Covenant. The Committee should take due account of the indicators selected by or in the framework of the specialized agencies and draw upon or promote additional research, in consultation with the specialized agencies concerned, where gaps have been identified.

90. Whenever the Committee is not satisfied that the information provided by a State party is adequate for a meaningful assessment of progress achieved and difficulties encountered it should request supplementary information, specifying as necessary the precise issues or questions it would like the State party to address.

91. In preparing its reports under ECOSOC Resolution 1985/17, the Committee should consider, in addition to the 'summary of its consideration of the reports', highlighting thematic issues raised during its deliberations.

C. *Relations between the Committee and Specialized Agencies, and other International Organs*

92. The establishment of the Committee should be seen as an opportunity to develop a positive and mutually beneficial relationship between the Committee and the specialized agencies and other international organs.

93. New arrangements under article 18 of the Covenant should be considered where they could enhance the contribution of the specialized agencies to the work of the Committee. Given that the working methods with regard to the implementation of economic, social and cultural rights vary from one specialized agency to another, flexibility is appropriate in making such arrangements under article 18.

94. It is essential for the proper supervision of the implementation of the Covenant under Part IV that a dialogue be developed between the specialized agencies and the Committee with respect to matters of common interest. In particular consultations should address the need for developing indicators for assessing compliance with the Covenant; drafting guidelines for the submission of reports by States parties; making arrangements for submission of reports by the specialized agencies under article 18. Consideration should also be given to any relevant procedures adopted in the agencies. Participation of their representatives in meetings of the Committee would be very valuable.

95. It would be useful if Committee members could visit specialized agencies concerned, learn through personal contact about programmes of the agencies relevant to the realization of the rights contained in the Covenant and discuss the possible areas of collaboration with those agencies.

96. Consultations should be initiated between the Committee and international financial institutions and development agencies to exchange information and share ideas on the distribution of available resources in relation to the realization of the rights recognized in the Covenant. These exchanges should consider the impact of international economic assistance on efforts by States parties to implement the Covenant and possibilities of technical and economic co-operation under article 22 of the Covenant.

97. The Commission on Human Rights, in addition to its responsibilities under article 19 of the Covenant, should take into account the work of the Committee in its consideration of items on its agenda relating to economic, social and cultural rights.

98. The Covenant on Economic, Social and Cultural Rights is related to the Covenant on Civil and Political Rights. Although most rights can clearly be delineated as falling within the framework of one or other Covenant, there are several rights and provisions referred to in both instruments which are not susceptible to clear differentiation. Both Covenants moreover share common provisions and articles. It is important that consultative arrangements be established between the Economic, Social and Cultural Rights Committee and the Human Rights Committee.

99. Given the relevance of other international legal instruments to the Covenant, early consideration should be given by the Economic and Social Council to the need for developing effective consultative arrangements between the various supervisory bodies.

100. International and regional intergovernmental organizations concerned with the realization of economic, social and cultural rights are urged to develop measures, as appropriate, to promote the implementation of the Covenant.

101. As the Committee is a subsidiary organ of the Economic and Social Council, non-governmental organizations enjoying consultative status with the Economic and Social Council are urged to attend and follow the meetings of the Committee and, when appropriate, to submit information in accordance with ECOSOC Resolution 1296 (XLIV).

102. The Committee should develop, in co-operation with intergovernmental organizations and non-governmental organizations as well as

research institutes an agreed system for recording, storing and making accessible case law and other interpretative material relating to international instruments on economic, social and cultural rights.

103. As one of the measures recommended in article 23 it is recommended that seminars be held periodically to review the work of the Committee and the progress made in the realization of economic, social and cultural rights by States parties.

Appendix IV

The Siracusa Principles

UNITED NATIONS
ECONOMIC
AND
SOCIAL COUNCIL

Distr.
GENERAL
E/CN .4/1985/4
28 September 1984
Original: ENGLISH

COMMISSION ON HUMAN RIGHTS
Forty-first session
Item 18 of the provisional agenda

Status of the International Covenants on Human Rights

Note verbale dated 24 August 1984 from the Permanent Representative of the Netherlands to the United Nations Office at Geneva addressed to the Secretary-General

As is well known, the Commission on Human Rights has attached, and is continuing to attach, the highest importance to the implementation of the International Covenant on Civil and Political Rights, particularly to its provisions from which no derogation is permissible. The Commission has, *inter alia*, examined an important study of the implications for human rights of recent developments concerning situations known as states of siege and emergency, prepared by Mrs. Nicole Questiaux (E/CN.4/Sub.2/1982/15) and has requested that the Sub-Commission pursue its consideration of this matter (Commission decision 1984/104).

The interpretation and application of the limitation and restriction clauses of the Covenants have also become matters of great concern and the Human Rights Committee, in its individual views adopted under the Optional Protocol, as well as in its general comments, has sought to ensure that those clauses of the International Covenant on Civil arid Political Rights are interpreted and applied in a manner consistent with the objects and purposes of the Covenant.

The importance of the above-mentioned issue led a number of non-governmental organizations to sponsor a high-level international conference on the limitation and derogation provisions of the International Covenant on Civil and Political Rights. The Conference was held at Siracues (Italy) from 30 April to 4 May 1984. It was sponsored by the following organizations: the International Commission of Jurists, the International Association of Penal Law, the American Association for the International Commission of Jurists, the Urban Morgan Institute of Human Rights and the international Institute of Higher Studies in Criminal Sciences.

The participants at the Conference included professors, practitioners and other experts in human rights from all regions of the world. The Conference resulted in the adoption of a series of pertinent principles entitled "The Siracusa principles on the limitation and derogation provisions in the International Covenant on Civil and Political Rights".

Annex

The Siracusa Principles on the Limitation and Derogation Provisions in the International Covenant on Civil and Political Rights.

Introduction

(i) A group of 31 distinguished experts in international law, convened by the International Commission of Jurists, the International Association of Penal Law,the American Association for the International Commission of Jurists, the Urban Morgan Institute of Human Rights, and the International Institute of Higher Studies in Criminal Sciences, met in Siracusa, Sicily, in April and May 1984 to consider the limitation and derogation provisions of the International Covenant on Civil and Political Rights. The participants came from Brazil, Canada, Chile, Egypt, France, Greece, Hungary, India, Ireland, Kuwait, the Netherlands, Norway, Poland, Switzerland, Turkey, the United Kingdom, the United States of America, the United Nations Centre for Human Rights, the International Labour Organisation (ILO) and the sponsoring organizations.

(ii) The participants were agreed upon the need for a close examination of the conditions and grounds for permissible limitations and derogations enunciated in the Covenant in order to achieve an effective implementation of the rule of law. As frequently emphasized by the General Assembly of the United Nations, a uniform interpretation of limitations on rights in the Covenant is of great importance.

(iii) In examining these limitations and derogations the participants sought to identify:
   - Their legitimate objectives,
   - The general principles of interpretation which govern their imposition and application, and
   - Some of the main features of the grounds for limitation or derogation.

(iv) It was recognized that other criteria determined the scope of rights in the Covenant, e.g. the concept of arbitrariness, but time was not available to examine them. It was hoped that it might be possible to examine these other limits on some future occasion.

(v) The participants were agreed that:
   (a) There is a close relationship between respect for human rights and the maintenance of international peace and security; indeed the systematic violation of human rights undermines na-

tional security and public order and may constitute a threat to international peace;

(b) Notwithstanding the different stages of economic development reached in different States, the implementation of human rights is an essential requirement for development in the broadest sense.

(vi) These principles are considered by the participants to reflect the present state of international law, with the exception of certain recommendations indicated by the use of the verb "should" instead of "shall".

Part I. The Limitation Clauses in the Covenant

A. *General interpretative principles relating to the justification limitations**

1. No limitations or grounds for applying them to rights guaranteed by the Covenant are permitted other than those contained in the terms of the covenant itself.

2. The scope of a limitation referred to in the Covenant shall not be interpreted so as to jeopardize the essence of the right concerned.

3. All limitation clauses shall be interpreted strictly and in favour of the rights at issue.

4. All limitations shall be interpreted in the light and context of the particular right concerned.

5. All limitations on a right recognized by the Covenant shall be provided for by law and be compatible with the objects and purposes of the Covenant.

6. No limitation referred to in the Covenant shall be applied for any purpose other than that for which it has been prescribed.

* The term "limitations" in these principles includes the term "restrictions" as used in the Covenant.

7. No limitation shall be applied in an arbitrary manner.

8. Every limitation imposed shall be subject to the possibility of challenge to and remedy against its abusive application.

9. No limitation on a right recognized by the Covenant shall discriminate contrary to article 2, paragraph I.

10. Whenever a limitation is required in the terms of the Covenant to be "necessary", this term implies that the limitation:
(a) Is based on one of the grounds justifying limitations recognized by the relevant article of the Covenant,
(b) Responds to a pressing public or social need,
(c) Pursues a legitimate aim, and
(d) Is proportionate to that aim.

Any assessment as to the necessity of a limitation shall be made on objective considerations.

11. In applying a limitation, a State shall use no more restrictive means than are required for the achievement of the purpose of the limitation.

12. The burden of justifying a limitation upon a right guaranteed under the Covenant lies with the State.

13. The requirement expressed in article 12 of the Covenant, that any restrictions be consistent with other rights recognized in the Covenant, is implicit in limitations to the other rights recognized in the Covenant.

14. The limitation clauses of' the Covenant shall not be interpreted to restrict the exercise of any human rights protected to a greater extent by other international obligations binding on the State.

B. Interpretative principles relating to specific limitation clauses "Prescribed by law"

15. No limitation on the exercise of human rights shall be made unless provided for by national law of general application which is consistent with the Covenant and is in force at the time the limitation is applied.

16. Laws imposing limitations on the exercise of human rights shall not be arbitrary or unreasonable.

17. Legal rules limiting the exercise of human rights shall be clear and accessible to everyone.

18. Adequate safeguards and effective remedies shall be provided by law against illegal or abusive imposition or application of limitations on human rights.

"In a democratic society"

19. The expression "in a democratic society" shall be interpreted as imposing a further restriction on the limitation clauses it qualifies.

20. The burden is upon a State imposing limitations so qualified to demonstrate that the limitations do not impair the democratic functioning of the society.

21. While there is no single model of a democratic society, a society which recognizes, respects and protects the human rights set forth in the Charter of the United Nations and the Universal Declaration of Human Rights may be viewed as meeting this definition.

"Public order (*ordre public*)"

22. The expression "public order (*ordre public*)" as used in the Covenant may be defined as the sum of rules which ensure the functioning of society or the set of fundamental principles on which society is founded. Respect for human rights is part of public order (*ordre public*).

23. Public order (*ordre public*) shall be interpreted in the context of the purpose of the particular human right which is limited on this ground.

24. State organs or agents responsible for the maintenance of public order (*ordre public*) shall be subject to controls in the exercise of their power through the parliament, courts or other competent independent bodies.

"Public health"

25. Public health may be invoked as a ground for limiting certain rights in order to allow a State to take measures dealing with a serious threat to the health of the population or individual members of the population. These

measures must be specifically aimed at preventing disease or injury or providing care for the sick and injured.

26. Due regard shall be had to the International Health Regulations of the World Health Organization.

"Public morals"

27. Since public morality varies over time and from one culture to another, a State which invokes public morality as a ground for restricting human rights, while enjoying a certain margin of discretion, shall demonstrate that the limitation in question is essential to the maintenance of respect for fundamental values of the community.

28. The margin of discretion left to States does not apply to the rule of non-discrimination as defined in the Covenant.

"National security"

29. National security may be invoked to justify measures limiting certain rights only when they are taken to protect the existence of the nation, its territorial integrity or political independence against force or threat of force.

30. National security cannot be invoked as a reason for imposing limitations to prevent merely local or relatively isolated threats to law and order.

31. National security cannot be used as a pretext for imposing vague or arbitrary limitations and may only be invoked when there exist adequate safeguards and effective remedies against abuse.

32. The systematic violation of human rights undermines national security and may jeopardize international peace and security. A State responsible for such violation shall not invoke national security as a justification for measures aimed at suppressing opposition to such violation or at perpetrating repressive practices against its population.

"Public safety"

33. Public safety means protection against danger to the safety of persons, to their life or physical integrity or serious damage to their property.

34. The need to protect public safety can justify limitations provided by law. It cannot be used for imposing vague or arbitrary limitations and

may only be invoked when there exist adequate safeguards and effective remedies against abuse.

"Rights and freedoms of others" or the "Rights and reputations of others"

35. The scope of the rights and freedoms of others that may act as a limitation upon rights in the Covenant extends beyond the rights and freedoms recognized in the Covenant.

36. When a conflict exists between a right protected in the Covenant and one which is not, recognition and consideration should be given to the fact that the Covenant seeks to protect the most fundamental rights and freedoms. In this context especial weight should be afforded to the rights from which no derogation may be made under article 4 of the Covenant.

37. A limitation to a human right based upon the reputation of others shall not be used to protect the State and its officials from public opinion or criticism.

Restrictions on public trial

38. All trials shall be public unless the Court determines in accordance with law that:

- The press or the public should be excluded from all or part of a trial on the basis of specific findings announced in open court showing that the interest of the private lives of the parties or their families or of juveniles so requires; or
- The exclusion is strictly necessary to avoid publicity (a) prejudicial to the fairness of the trial or (b) endangering public morals, public order (*ordre public*) or national security in a democratic society.

Part II. Derogations in a Public Emergency

A. *"Public emergency which threatens the life of the nation"*

39. A State party may take measures derogating from its obligations under the International Covenant on Civil and Political Rights pursuant to article 4 (hereinafter called "derogation measures") only when faced with a situation of exceptional and actual or imminent danger which threatens the life of the nation.

A threat to the life of the nation is one that:

(a) Affects the whole of the population and either the whole or part of the territory of the State, and
(b) Threatens the physical integrity of the population, the political independence or the territorial integrity of the State or the existence or basic functioning of institutions indispensable to ensure and protect the rights recognized in the Covenant.

40. Internal conflict and unrest that do not constitute a grave and imminent threat to the life of the nation cannot justify derogations under article 4.

41. Economic difficulties per se cannot justify derogation measures.

B. *Proclamation, notification and termination of a public emergency*

42. A State party derogating from its obligations under the Covenant shall make an official proclamation of the existence of a public emergency threatening the life of the nation.

43. Procedures under national law for the proclamation of a state of emergency shall be prescribed in advance of the- emergency.

44. A State party derogating from its obligations under the Covenant shall immediately notify the other States parties to the Covenant, through the intermediary of the Secretary-General of the United Nations, of the provisions from which it has derogated and the reasons by which it was actuated.

45. The notification shall contain sufficient information to permit the States parties to exercise their rights and discharge their obligations under the Covenant. In particular it shall contain:
(a) The provisions of the Covenant from which it has derogated;
(b) A copy of the proclamation of emergency,together with the constitutional provisions, legislation, or decrees governing the state of emergency in order to assist the States parties to appreciate the scope of the derogation;
(c) The effective date of the imposition of the state of emergency and the period for which it has been proclaimed;
(d) An explanation of the reasons which actuated the Government's decision to derogate, including a brief description of the factual

circumstances leading up to the proclamation of the state of emergency;

(e) A brief description of the anticipated effect of the derogation measures on the rights recognized by the Covenant, including copies of decrees derogating from these rights issued prior to the notification.

46. States parties may require that further information necessary to enable them to carry out their role under the Covenant be provided through the intermediary of the Secretary-General.

47. A State party which falls to make an immediate notification in due form of its derogation is in breach of its obligations to other States parties and may be deprived of the defences otherwise available to it in procedures under the Covenant.

48. A State party availing itself of the right of derogation pursuant to article 4 shall terminate such derogation in the shortest time required to bring to an end the public emergency which threatens the life of the nation.

49. The State party shall, on the date on which it terminates such derogation, inform the other States parties, through the intermediary of the Secretary-General of the United Nations, of the fact of the termination.

50. On the termination of a derogation pursuant to article 4, all rights and freedoms protected by the Covenant shall be restored in full. A review of the continuing consequences of derogation measures shall be made as soon as possible. Steps shall be taken to correct injustices and to compensate those who have suffered injustice during or in consequence of the derogation measures.

C. *"Strictly required by the exigencies of the situation"*

51. The severity, duration and geographic scope of any derogation measure shall be such only as are strictly necessary to deal with the threat to the life of the nation and are proportionate to its nature and extent.

52. The competent national authorities shall have a duty to assess individually the necessity of any derogation measure taken or proposed to deal with the specific dangers posed by the emergency.

53. A measure is not strictly required by the exigencies of the situation where ordinary measures permissible under the specific limitation clauses of the Covenant would be adequate to deal with the threat to the life of the nation.

54. The principle of strict necessity shall be applied in an objective manner. Each measure shall be directed to an actual, clear, present or imminent danger and may not be imposed merely because of an apprehension of potential danger.

55. The national constitution and laws governing states of emergency shall provide for prompt and periodic independent review by the legislature of the necessity for derogation measures.

56. Effective remedies shall be available to persons claiming that derogation measures affecting them are not strictly required by the exigencies of the situation.

57. In determining whether derogation measures are strictly required by the exigencies of the situation, the judgement of the national authorities cannot be accepted as conclusive.

D. Non-derogable rights

58. No State party shall, even in time of emergency threatening the life of' the nation, derogate from the Covenant'$ guarantees of the right to life; freedom from torture, cruel, inhuman or degrading treatment or punishment, and from medical or scientific experimentation without free consent; freedom from slavery or involuntary servitude; the right not to be imprisoned for contractual debt; the right not to be convicted or sentenced to a heavier penalty by virtue of retroactive criminal legislation; the right to recognition as a person before the law; and freedom of thought, conscience and religion. These rights are notderogable under any conditions even for the asserted purpose of preserving the life of the nation.

59. States parties to the Covenant, as part of their obligation to ensure the enjoyment of these rights to all persons within their jurisdiction (article 3, paragraph I), and to adopt measures to secure an effective remedy for violations (article 2, paragraph 3), shall take special precautions in time of public emergency to ensure that neither official nor semi-official groups

engage in a practice of' arbitrary and extrajudicial killings or involuntary disappearances, that persons in detention are protected against torture and other forms of cruel, inhuman or degrading treatment or punishment, and that no persons are convicted or punished under laws or decrees with retroactive effect.

60. The ordinary courts should maintain their jurisdiction, even in a time of public emergency, to adjudicate any complaint that a non-derogable right has been violated.

E. *Some general principles on the introduction and application of a public emergency and consequent derogation measures.*

61. Derogation from rights recognized under international law in order to respond to a threat to the life of the nation is not exercised in a legal vacuum. It is authorized by law and as such it is subject to several legal principles of general application.

62. A proclamation of a public emergency shall be made in good faith based upon an objective assessment of the situation in order to determine to what extent, if any, it poses a threat to the life of the nation. A proclamation of a public emergency, and consequent derogations from Covenant obligations that are not made in good faith, are violations of international law.

63. The provisions of the Covenant allowing for certain derogations in a public emergency are to be interpreted restrictively.

64. In a public emergency the rule of law shall still prevail. Derogation is an authorized and limited prerogative to respond adequately to a threat to the life of the nation. The derogating State shall have the burden of justifying its actions under law.

65. The Covenant subordinates all procedures to the basic objectives of human rights, Article 5, paragraph I, of the Covenant sets definite limits to actions taken under the Covenant:

> "Nothing in the present Covenant may be interpreted as implying for any State, group or person any right to engage in any activity or perform any act aimed at the destruction of any of the rights and freedoms recognized

herein or at their limitation to a greater extent than is provided for in the present Covenant."

Article 29, paragraph 2, of the IJriiver3al Declaration of Human Rights seta out the ultimate purpose of law:

> "In the exercise of his rights and freedoms, everyone shall be subject only to such limitations as are determined by law solely for the purpose of securing due recognition and respect for the rights and freedoms of others and of meeting the just requirements of morality, public order and the general welfare in a democratic society."

These provisions apply with full force to claims that a situation constitutes a threat to the life of a nation and hence enables authorities to derogate.

66. A bona fide proclamation of a public emergency permits derogation from specified obligations in the Covenant, but does not authorize a general departure from international obligations. The Covenant in articles 4, paragraph I and 5, paragraph 2, expressly prohibits derogations which are inconsistent with other obligations under international law. In this regard, particular note should be taken of international obligations which apply in a public emergency under the Geneva and ILO Conventions.

67. In a situation of a non-international armed conflict, a State party to the 1949 Geneva Conventions for the protection of war victims may not under any circumstances suspend the right to a trial by a court offering the essential guarantees of independence and impartiality (article 3 common to the 1949 Conventions). Under the 1977 additional Protocol II the following rights with respect to penal prosecution shall be respected under all circumstances by States parties to the Protocol:

(a) The duty to give notice of charges without delay and to grant the necessary rights and means of defence;
(b) Conviction only on the basis of individual penal responsibility;
(c) The right not to be convicted, or sentenced to a heavier penalty, by virtue of retroactive criminal legislation;
(d) Presumption of innocence;
(e) Trial in the presence of the accused;
(f) No obligation on the accused to testify against himself or to confess guilt;

(g) Duty to advise the convicted person on judicial and other remedies.

68. The ILO basic human rights conventions contain a number of rights dealing with such matters as forced labour, freedom of association, equality in employment and trade-union and workers' rights which are additional to those in the Covenant. Some of these are not subject to derogation during an emergency; others permit derogation, but only to the extent strictly necessary to meet the exigencies of the situation.

69. No State, including those that are not parties to the Covenant, may suspend or violate, even in times of public emergency:
- The right to life;
- Freedom from torture or cruel, inhuman or degrading treatment or punishment and from medical or scientific experimentation;
- The right not to be held in slavery or involuntary servitude; and
- The right not to be subjected to retroactive criminal penalties as defined in the Covenant.

Customary international law prohibits in all circumstances the denial of such fundamental rights.

70. Although protections against arbitrary arrest and detention (article 9) and the right to a fair and public hearing in the determination of a criminal charge (article 14) may be subject to legitimate limitations if strictly required by the exigencies of an emergency situation, the denial of certain rights fundamental to human dignity can never be strictly necessary in any conceivable emergency, and respect for them is essential in order to ensure enjoyment of non-derogable rights and to provide an effective remedy against their violation. In particular:
(a) All arrests and detention and the place of detention shall be recorded, if possible centrally, and made available to the public without delay;
(b) No person shall be detained for an indefinite period of time, whether detained pending judicial investigation or trial or detained without charge;
(a) No person shall be held in isolation without communication with his family, friend or lawyer for longer than a few days, e.g. three to seven days;
(d) Where persons are detained without charge, the need for their continued detention shall be considered periodically by an independent review tribunal;

(e) Any person charged with an offence shall be entitled to a fair trial by a competent, independent and impartial court established by law;

(f) Civilians shall normally be tried by the ordinary courts; where it is found strictly necessary to establish military tribunals or special courts to try civilians, their competence, independence and impartiality shall be ensured and the need for them reviewed periodically by the competent authority;

(g) Any person charged with a criminal offence shall be entitled to the presumption of innocence and to at least the following rights to ensure a fair trial:
   - The right to be informed of the charges promptly, in detail and in a language he understands,
   - The right to have adequate time and facilities to prepare the defence including the right to communicate confidentially with his lawyer,
   - The right to a lawyer of his choice, with free legal assistance if he does not have the means to pay for it and to be informed of this right,
   - The right to be present at the trial,
   - The right not to be compelled to testify against himself or to make a confession,
   - The right to obtain the attendance and examination of defence witnesses,
   - The right to be tried in public save where the court orders otherwise on grounds of security with adequate safeguards to prevent abuse,
   - The right to appeal to a higher court;

(h) An adequate record of the proceedings shall be kept in all cases;

(i) No person shall be tried or punished again for an offence for which he has already been convicted or acquitted.

F. Recommendations concerning the functions and duties of the Human Rights Committee and United Nations bodies

71. In the exercise of its power to study, report and make general comments on States parties' reports under article 40 of the Covenant, the Human Rights Committee may and should examine the compliance of States parties with the provisions of article 4. Likewise it may and should do so when exercising its powers in relevant cases under article 41 and the Optional Protocol relating, respectively, to inter-State and individual communications.

72. In order to determine whether the requirements of article 4, paragraphs I and 2 have been met and for the purpose of supplementing information in States parties' reports, members of the Human Rights Committee, as persons of recognized competence in the field of human rights, may and should have regard to information they consider to be reliable provided by other intergovernmental bodies, non-governmental organizations and communications by individuals.

73. The Human Rights Committee should develop a procedure for requesting additional reports under article 40, paragraph 1 (b), from States parties which have given notification of derogation under article 4, paragraph 3, or which are reasonably believed by the Committee to have imposed emergency measures subject to the constraints of article 4. Such additional reports should relate to questions concerning the emergency in so far as it affects the implementation of the Covenant and should be dealt with by the Committee at the earliest possible date.

74. In order to enable the Human Rights Committee to perform its fact-finding functions more effectively it should develop its procedures for the consideration of communications under the Optional Protocol in order to permit the hearing of oral submissions and evidence and visits to States parties alleged to be in violation of the Covenant. If necessary, the States parties to the Optional Protocol should consider amending it to this effect.

75. The United Nations Commission on Human Rights should request its Sub-Commission on Prevention of Discrimination and Protection of Minorities to prepare an annual list of States, whether parties to the Covenant or not,that proclaim, maintain or terminate a public emergency together with:

- In the case of a State party, the proclamation and notification;and
- In the case of other States, any available and apparently reliable information concerning the proclamation, threat to the life of the nation, derogation measures and their proportionality, non-discrimination and respect for non-derogable rights.

76. The United Nations Commission on Human Rights and its Sub-Commission should continue to utilize the technique of appointment of special rapporteurs and investigatory and fact-finding bodies in relation to prolonged public emergencies.

Appendix V

The Council of Europe and the Rule of Law

Ministers' Deputies / Rapporteur Groups
GR-J
Rapporteur Group on Legal Co-operation
GR-J(2008)11 16 September 2008[242]

The Council of Europe and the Rule of Law
An overview

"Wherever law ends, tyranny begins"

(John Locke)

I. Introduction

1. At its meeting on 1 July 2008, the Rapporteur Group on Legal Co-operation (GR-J) held a first discussion on the item "Examination of how full use can be made of the Council of Europe's potential in enhancing the rule of law". This discussion took place on the basis of a document submitted by the Swedish delegation (DD(2008)393) proposing the development of a Council of Europe strategy to reinforce the promotion of the rule of law.

2. The GR-J requested the Secretariat to prepare a descriptive document seeking to define key components of the concept of rule of law and draw up a typology of activities undertaken by the Council of Europe relevant to the rule of law, notably standard-setting and co-operation activities.

242 This document has been classified restricted at the date of issue. Unless the Committee of Ministers decides otherwise, it will be declassified according to the rules set out in Resolution Res(2001)6 on access to Council of Europe documents.

The document should also contain information about relevant activities of the EU and other international organisations. Delegations were invited to forward any written contributions to the Secretariat.[243]

3. This document was prepared in response to the GR-J's request.

II. The Rule of Law as Part of the Core Mission of the Council of Europe

Basic texts

4. The rule of law is one of the three core principles of the Council of Europe, along with the enjoyment of human rights and fundamental freedoms and the concept of genuine democracy (1949 Statute, recital 3 of the preamble and Article 3). More particularly, the rule of law is, together with individual freedom and political liberty, referred to as "principles which form the basis of all genuine democracy" (recital 3 of the preamble).

5. The preamble to the European Convention on Human Rights (ECHR; 1950) expresses the resolve of governments of European countries which are like-minded and have a common heritage of political traditions, ideals, freedom and rule of law, to take the first steps for the collective enforcement of certain of the rights stated in the Universal Declaration of Human Rights (6th recital).

6. While neither the Statute nor the ECHR elaborate on the concept of the rule of law as such, it should be noted that the rule of law is considered to be a "*principle*" and that its close links with democracy and human rights are already highlighted in these early fundamental texts of the Council of Europe. Furthermore, important guidance on the content of the rule of law principle can be derived from the ECHR, which contains many rule of law-related provisions (see Section III below).

7. The rule of law has been systematically referred to in the major political documents of the Council of Europe, as well as in numerous legal instruments such as Conventions and Recommendations. The three Summits of Heads of State and Government have resulted in Declarations and

243 No such contributions were received to date.

Plans of Action underlining the importance of the rule of law as central part of the Council of Europe's mission.

8. In the *Vienna Declaration* (1993), emphasis was laid on the fact that accession to the Council of Europe presupposes that the applicant country has brought its institutions and legal system into line with the basic principles of democracy, the rule of law and respect for human rights. Observance of the principles of international law was seen as a decisive criterion for membership and acceptance of the ECHR's supervisory machinery within a short period as fundamental. The Declaration also states that the setting up of appropriate legal structures and the training of administrative personnel are essential conditions for the success of economic and political transition in Central and Eastern Europe.

9. In the *Strasbourg Final Declaration and Action Plan* (1997) the Heads of State and Government solemnly reaffirmed their attachment to the fundamental principles of the Council of Europe – pluralist democracy, respect for human rights, and the rule of law. They underlined the contribution of the Council of Europe's essential standard-setting role to the development of international law through European conventions. The Action Plan sets out an agenda for action in five fields, including democracy and human rights. The rule of law is not included as a distinct field but there is a section entitled "Security of citizens" covering actions to combat terrorism, corruption and organised crime, to prevent drug abuse, and to protect children.

10. The *Warsaw Declaration (2005)* states that the Council of Europe shall pursue its core objective of preserving and promoting human rights, democracy and the rule of law. All its activities must contribute to this fundamental objective. The Heads of State and Government committed themselves to "developing those principles, with a view to ensuring their effective implementation by all member states. In propagating these values, we shall enhance the role of the Council of Europe as an effective mechanism of pan-European co-operation in all relevant fields." (paragraph 1).

11. This is elaborated further in paragraph 4: "We are committed to strengthening the rule of law throughout the continent, building on the standard-setting potential of the Council of Europe and on its contribution to the development of international law. We stress the importance of an independent and efficient judiciary in the member states in this re-

spect. We will further develop legal co-operation within the Council of Europe with a view to better protecting our citizens and to realising on a continental scale the aims enshrined in the Statute."

12. A separate paragraph of the Declaration dealing with security of citizens states that the Council of Europe will continue to play an active role in combating terrorism, corruption, organised crime, trafficking in human beings, cybercrime and the challenges attendant on scientific and technical progress. Measures shall be promoted "consistent with our values to counter those threats." (paragraph 8).

13. The *Warsaw Action Plan* likewise places rule of law – related action in a different section (Chapter I, section 3: Strengthening democracy, good governance and the rule of law in member states) from action designed to strengthen the security of European citizens (Chapter II).

14. As regards the rule of law, support is expressed for, and impetus given to, the work of the Venice Commission, the European Commission for the Efficiency of Justice (CEPEJ) and the Consultative Council of Judges of Europe (CCJE). Nationality law and family law are highlighted as focus points for continued Council of Europe action. More generally, the Action Plan states that full use will be made of the Council of Europe's standard-setting potential and that implementation and further development of its legal instruments and mechanisms of legal co-operation will be promoted.

15. Regarding the security of citizens, actions are announced concerning the various security threats mentioned in the Declaration. The rule of law is explicitly mentioned in the section on the information society: "The Council of Europe shall further elaborate principles and guidelines to ensure respect for human rights and the rule of law in the information society." (Chapter II, section 5).

16. Finally, the rule of law is referred to in the Action Plan sections dealing with co-operation with the EU and the OSCE, including in the Guidelines and Declaration appended to it. As regards the EU, the rule of law occupies a prominent place in the Memorandum of Understanding between the Council of Europe and the EU which was elaborated on the basis of the Guidelines of the Warsaw Action Plan and adopted on 10 May 2007.

2008 Programme of activities: a snapshot

17. The 2008 POA structure comprises five main thematic chapters: Human Rights, Rule of Law, Democracy and good governance, Social cohesion and Culture and intercultural dialogue.

18. The rule of law chapter contains three lines of action (LoA): Functioning and efficiency of justice, Strengthening rule of law standards, and Strengthening the security of European citizens.

19. The first LoA "Functioning and efficiency of justice" covers the work of CEPEJ (evaluating and improving the efficiency of Justice) as well as capacity-building concerning the organisation of independent judicial systems and the strengthening of the status, role and functions of judges and prosecutors. This LoA is linked to several Joint Programmes (CoE-EC) and VC projects which are country or region-specific.

20. The second LoA "Strengthening rule of law standards" focuses, first of all, on CM monitoring and support to states in implementing their commitments, strengthening national legal frameworks and raising awareness about European standards, and developing Council of Europe standards in public and private law[244] and ensuring their implementation (CDCJ). A second focus is given to the implementation of specific co-operation activities in post-conflict situations, in particular in the Chechen Republic of the Russian Federation and in Kosovo[245] and the coordination of Council of Europe activities in these areas. Finally, the LoA also covers the strengthening of the role and development of international law in order to promote international co-operation (CAHDI).

21. The third LoA "Strengthening the security of European citizens" comprises two programmes: Democratic responses to terrorism and European standards for crime control. The first covers the promotion of sig-

244 In the POA "public law" is seen as the area of law concerning the relations between the state and the individual, whereas "private law" is seen as governing the relations between individuals (p. 73). For these two areas, the following priority fields are mentioned for the years to come: justice, family law, nationality, civil and administrative law (*ibidem*).

245 All reference to Kosovo, whether the territory, institutions or population, in this text shall be understood in full compliance with United Nation's Security Council Resolution 1244 and without prejudice to the status of Kosovo.

natures, ratifications and implementation of relevant Council of Europe conventions, and the identification of gaps in international law applicable to the fight against terrorism as well as means to fill them (CODEXTER). The second covers a wide range of intergovernmental activities to help criminal justice systems to fight crime effectively and humanely, including through standard-setting and international co-operation (CDPC). It also comprises monitoring in specific fields (GRECO, MONEYVAL) and a host of technical and targeted co-operation activities in fields such as fighting (organised) economic crime and cybercrime, implementation of European standards regarding law enforcement officials, criminal sanctions policies, imprisonment and prison systems, rehabilitation, alternative sanctions, etc. Several Joint Programmes and VC projects are linked to this LoA.

Some interim conclusions

22. The foregoing overviews are not sufficient to allow the drawing up of a list of key rule of law requirements accepted by the Council of Europe, let alone a definition. At best, they give some indirect impressions of the meaning of rule of law, by identifying (only) some areas of activity of the Council of Europe which are deemed relevant and important in rule of law terms. It would be wrong to assume, for example, that all rule of law-related activities of the Council of Europe are covered under the above-mentioned headings in the Programme of Activities.

23. However, some first conclusions can be noted concerning the Council of Europe's understanding of the rule of law concept:

- rule of law is a principle, not a distinct area of activity for the Council of Europe (although some of its areas of activity are seen to be more closely associated with the rule of law than others); this explains why it is impossible to place *all* relevant activities together in a single chapter of the Programme of Activities;
- the rule of law principle is one of the three fundamental principles of the Council of Europe, together with pluralist democracy and respect for human rights;
- these three principles are closely interconnected: preserving and promoting human rights, democracy and the rule of law is nowadays even seen as a single objective – the core objective – of the Council of Europe.

24. Like democracy and respect for human rights, the rule of law is a principle pertaining to the organisation and functioning of the state. In accordance with Article 3 of the Statute, Council of Europe member states must accept this principle; they are therefore expected to be states based on the rule of law.

Relationship between rule of law, democracy and human rights

25. The interrelationship between these three notions can be illustrated by the following figure:

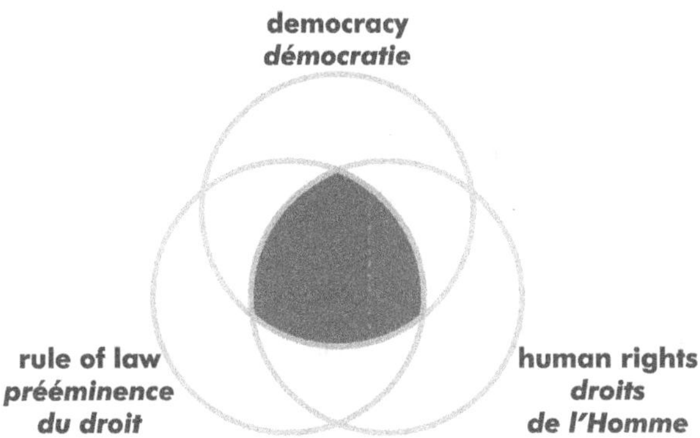

26. Democracy, rule of law and human rights can be seen as three partly overlapping circles. Some principles, such as equality and non-discrimination, belong to all three notions (the grey area in the figure). Others are more directly associated with two of the three notions, such as the fair trial principle (rule of law and human rights) or the principles of freedom of expression, assembly and association (democracy and human rights). Still other principles operate principally in relation to one of the three notions (e.g. the human rights principle of freedom of movement).

27. However, this simplified representation does not show the *interdependence* between the three notions. There can be no democracy without

the rule of law and respect for human rights; there can be no rule of law without democracy and respect for human rights, and no respect for human rights without democracy and the rule of law.

28. The fact that the three concepts, taken together, form a single fundamental objective for the Council of Europe makes it less necessary for it to adopt a particular definition of the rule of law. Such an exercise of disentangling notions that are so closely intertwined and mutually supportive might even be risky in terms of overlooking essential human rights and democratic requirements and aspects.

III. The Key Components of the Rule of Law as Understood by the Council of Europe

29. It is somewhat paradoxical that, although no authoritative definition of the rule of law exists within the Council of Europe,[246] the Organisation works pragmatically on a daily basis to promote and strengthen the rule of law in and among its member states. In fact, there is a strong consensus within the Council of Europe as to the basic requirements that flow from the rule of law principle.

30. A recent illustration is the White Paper on Intercultural Dialogue which was officially launched by Ministers at the 118th Session of the Committee of Ministers in May 2008, section 3.4.1 of which deals with the rule of law in the following terms: "The fundamental standards of the rule of law in democratic societies are necessary elements of the framework within which intercultural dialogue can flourish. They ensure a clear separation of powers, legal certainty and equality of all before the law. They stop public authorities taking arbitrary and discriminatory decisions, and ensure that individuals whose rights are violated can seek redress from the courts." Contrary to other sections of the White Paper,

246 The Parliamentary Assembly Resolution 1594 (2007) "The principle of the rule of law" does not contain such a definition either, although it points out that "rule of law" (*prééminence du droit*) must not be conceived of or translated as "supremacy of statute law" (*prééminence de la loi*), as is the case in some recent democracies in eastern Europe. The Assembly considers that such a formalistic interpretation of "rule of law" runs counter to the essence of the concept.

approval of this particular paragraph required little or no debate among the member states.

31. This high degree of consensus in the Council of Europe about the basic requirements of the rule of law is all the more significant in view of the conceptual and philosophical differences between the main legal traditions in Europe on this score. The German concept of *Rechtsstaat* which began to develop in the 19th century and which French scholars adapted into the *Etat de droit* in the early 20th century, differs from the concept of the rule of law which became part of constitutional theory in the UK in the late 19th century. Although there are certainly common features and objectives (put very simply, the rule of law is about restraining the exercise of public and political power by subjecting it to certain principles such as the principle of legality), there are important conceptual differences. The British rule of law concept traditionally tends to emphasise formal/procedural requirements, whereas the German concept, in its original form and even more so today, adds an important substantive dimension by stressing the protection of fundamental rights as a *Rechtstaat* principle.[247]

32. There is an ongoing discussion in legal theory about different conceptions of the rule of law: more formal (or "thinner") conceptions vs. more substantive (or "thicker") conceptions.[248] Simply put, this distinction mostly concerns the question of whether the rule of law principle consists only of process and form – related requirements or whether, in addition, it contains requirements regarding the *content* of the laws that rule. Human rights and human dignity are the key example of value requirements inherent in a substantive conception.

33. In practice, however, rule of law (*Rechtsstaat; Etat de droit*) conceptions are not static but evolving. Especially since WW II, there has been a significant and steady process, not necessarily of convergence of traditionally different rule of law conceptions in national legal systems in Europe (these conceptions remain quite strongly impregnated by national

247 For a helpful comparative overview, see Erik O. Wennerström, *The Rule of Law and the European Union*, Uppsala 2007, pp. 61–76.

248 See Wennerström 2007, p. 76-84, and the report by the Hague Institute for the Internationalisation of Law on its second High level expert meeting on the rule of law (pp. 2–3): http://hiil.tritac.com/uploads/File/Second%20High%20Level%20Expert%20RoL%2020%2004%202007%20Report.pdf

traditions and contexts), but of recognition of a common core of rule of law requirements that apply in Europe across different national traditions and contexts.[249] Notions of *Rechtsstaat, Etat de droit* and rule of law tend to amalgamate in the European legal order.[250] The process of European integration and co-operation both in the EC/EU and in the Council of Europe has indeed been (and continues to be) an important factor, as has the development of European human rights law as part of that process. The adherence of all Council of Europe member states to the ECHR and their being subject to the jurisdiction of the European Court of Human Rights was highly instrumental in creating a common European core of rule of law requirements which is still developing further.

The relevance of the ECHR

34. As was stated in Section II above, the ECHR contains many rule of law-related provisions. But the relevance of the ECHR for the rule of law and vice versa does not stop here. In its landmark judgment in the *Golder* case (21.2.1975, § 34), the Court underlined the relevance of the rule of law for the interpretation of the ECHR. Referring to the preamble, the Court stated that "one of the reasons why the signatory Governments decided to take the first steps for the collective enforcement of certain of the rights stated in the Universal Declaration of Human Rights was their profound belief in the rule of law." Many subsequent judgments have confirmed that the rule of law clearly is a fundamental guiding principle to the application and interpretation of the ECHR.

The case-law has clarified that the principle inspires the whole Convention and is inherent in all the Articles of the Convention (see, e.g., *Engel and Others*, 8.6.1976, § 69; *Amuur*, 25.6.1996, § 50). Today, there exists

249 These common requirements have thus become "decontextualised" so as to become either principles of general application in very different national legal systems (the Council of Europe method) or principles that apply in the distinct EC/EU legal system and are "recontextualised" when and by becoming part of that system's legal tradition (the Community method). See, as far as the EU is concerned, Wennerström 2007, p. 89.

250 Guy Canivet, L'incidence de la *rule of law* sur le système juridique français, in S. Breitenmoser et al. (eds), *Human Rights, democracy and the rule of law – Menschenrechte, Demokratie under Rechtsstaat – Droits de l'homme, démocratie et Etat de droit* (Liber amicorum Luzius Wildhaber), Zürich/Baden-Baden 2007, pp. 1169-1184.

such an impressive body of case-law on rule of law-related requirements that it is not exaggerated to state that the ECHR and the Court are not only instruments for the protection of human rights but also tools for the protection of the rule of law and the collective enforcement of its requirements.[251]

35. On the basis of that case-law, it is possible to list a number of rule of law-related requirements (components, constitutive elements or sub-principles) that form part of the law of the ECHR.[252]

36. These can be grouped under three main headings.

A. *The institutional framework and organisation of the state*

37. It is in this context that the Court tends to refer to *Etat de droit* ("State based on the rule of law")[253] rather than *prééminence du droit* ("rule of law"), the expression used in the preamble to the ECHR.

38. The notion of **separation of powers**, notably between the political organs of the state (executive, legislature) and the judiciary has assumed a growing importance in the Court's case-law. While the Court has refrained from elaborating a general theory on separation of powers or on checks and balances between the legislature, the executive and the judiciary, it is careful to protect the judicial process from interferences by the legislature or the executive (e.g. *Stafford*, 28.5.2002 § 78; *Beaumartin*, 24.11.1994, § 38; *Öcalan*, 12.5.2005, §§112 and 114; *Kleyn and Others*, 6.3.2003, §§ 193 and 200; *Zielinski and Pradal & Gonzales*, 28.10.1999, § 57; *Stran Greek Refineries and Stratis Andreadis*, 9.12.1994, § 49). Furthermore, it is not compatible with the rule of law if the legislature gives excessive discretion to the executive (*Malone*, 2.8.1984, § 68) or the judiciary (*Kruslin and Huvig*, 24.4.1990, § 36) to take measures which negatively affect human rights.

39. The **role of the judiciary** is essential in a state based on the rule of law. It is the guarantor of justice, a fundamental value in a law-governed

251 Much the same could be said about the requirements of a democratic society.

252 The Court's Registry (Research Division) provided very valuable assistance for this section. References to the Court's judgments are non-exhaustive.

253 Sometimes: "law-governed State" or "State subject to the rule of law".

state (*De Haes and Gijsels*, 27.1.1997, § 37). In criminal matters its role in the prevention and repression of crime, in particular when committed by State agents, is linked to the notion of the rule of law notably when **procedural obligations under Articles 2 (right to life) and 3 (prohibition of torture) ECHR** are at stake. **Impunity**, de jure or de facto, for violations of these Articles, is incompatible with the principle of the rule of law. In this context, the Court has repeatedly stressed the importance of maintaining public confidence in the (authorities' adherence to) the rule of law and preventing any appearance of the authorities' tolerance of or collusion in unlawful acts (*Hugh Jordan*, 4.5.2001, § 108; *Okkali*, 17.10.2006, § 65). A state based on the rule of law has the duty to employ the necessary measures **to uphold the law on its territory and to ensure the security of all** as well as the enjoyment of human rights (*Lelièvre*, 8.11.2007, § 104). As one element of a state subject to the rule of law, prosecuting authorities must show the necessary diligence in the implementation of criminal law in order to prevent and repress crime and protect the citizens (*Saygili*, 8.1.2008, § 35).

40. Article 6 § 1 ECHR requires that **a tribunal must always be established by law**. This reflects the principle of the rule of law inherent in the whole ECHR system. Legislation on the establishment and competence of judicial organs must be enacted by parliament, failing which a tribunal would lack the necessary legitimacy in a democratic society to hear the cases of individuals (*Lavents*, 28.11.2002, § 81; *Jorgic*, 12.7.2007, § 65).

41. More generally as regards the legislature, the Court has systematically described the right to vote and stand for election as a right "central to democracy and the rule of law", thus illustrating the interdependence between these notions (*Hirst*, 6.10.2005, § 58; *Albanese*, 23.3.2006, § 44).

42. The **duty of the state, notably the executive, to respect and apply the law**, including the duty to enforce final domestic judgments, will be further addressed under the principle of legality below. Here, reference should be made to the importance of **administrative courts** which the Court has highlighted as one of the most conspicuous achievements of a state based on the rule of law, in particular because the jurisdiction of those courts to adjudicate on acts of the administrative authorities was not accepted without a struggle (*Kress*, 7.1. 2001, § 69).

B. *The principle of legality: principles of lawfulness, legal certainty and equality before the law*

43. The principle of legality (sometimes referred to as supremacy of the law) forms a traditional core part of the rule of law concept. The rule of law requires that the state acts on the basis of, and in accordance with, the law. This offers essential legal protection of the individual vis-à-vis the state and its organs and agents. Many ECHR provisions reflect this principle through references to the notion of "law", in most cases in the form of a requirement that interference with human rights must be lawful.[254]

• Principle of lawfulness

44. The notion of law systematically used by the Court is a material or substantive one.[255] It covers not only statute law but also unwritten law (case-law) and regulations. The Court assesses whether domestic law as a whole has been complied with in the context of interferences with ECHR rights. In the context of deprivation of liberty (Article 5), the Court stresses the importance of the lawfulness of the detention, both procedurally and substantively, requiring scrupulous adherence to the rule of law (*Winterwerp*, 24.10.1979, § 39). Non-compliance with domestic law leads to a violation of Article 5 (*Bozano*, 18.12.1986, § 58; *Wassink*, 27.9.1990, § 27). In some cases, even where the law may have been formally respected, the Court has found a breach of the requirements of lawfulness on the ground that the authorities have attempted to circumvent the applicable legislation (*Karagöz*, 8.11.2005, § 59; *John*, 10.5.2007, § 33).

45. The state is not only obliged to respect and apply, in a foreseeable and consistent manner, the laws it has enacted, but also, as a corollary of this duty, to ensure the legal and practical conditions for their implementation (*Broniowski*, 22.6.2004, § 184).

46. The notion of "law" in the ECHR does not merely refer back to domestic law but also relates to the quality of the law, requiring it to be compatible with the rule of law. In particular, the **law must be sufficiently accessible and foreseeable** (*Sunday Times (No. 1)*, 26.4.1979, § 49). These requirements have been developed in a rich case-law. Foreseeability

254 Articles 2, 5, 6, 7, 8, 9, 10, 11, 1 of Protocol No. 1, 2 of Protocol No. 4, Protocol No. 7.

255 With the exception of the right to a tribunal "established by law" (Article 6 § 1) dealt with under A above.

means that the law must be foreseeable as to its effects, that is formulated with **sufficient precision** to enable the individual to regulate his conduct. In this context, a law which confers a discretion to a state authority must indicate the scope of that discretion. **It would be contrary to the rule of law for the legal discretion granted to the executive to be expressed in terms of an unfettered power. Consequently, the law must indicate the scope of any such discretion and the manner of its exercise with sufficient clarity, to give the individual adequate protection against arbitrariness.** (*Malone*, 2.8.1984, § 68).

47. The **principle of legality takes on a special importance in criminal matters.** Article 7, ECHR enshrines two principles essential to the rule of law: a criminal conviction must be based on a norm which existed at the time of the act or omission (***nullum crimen sine lege***), and no heavier penalty may be imposed than the one applicable at the time the offence was committed (***nulla poena sine lege***). Neither is it permissible to apply new, more severe legislation to an ongoing situation that arose before the legislation came into force (*Achour*, 10.11.2004, § 37). In addition, the authority applying the criminal law may not interpret it extensively, for example by analogy, to the accused's detriment. The offence must be clearly defined in law (here, too, requirements of accessibility and foreseeability apply) (*Coëme*, 22.6.2000, § 145). This is also true in respect of the penalty imposed (*Kafkaris*, 12.2.2008, § 145). These principles all serve to offer essential safeguards against arbitrary prosecution, conviction and punishment (*Kokkinakis*, 25.5.1993, § 52).

- **Principle of legal certainty**

48. This principle is one of the basic elements of the rule of law (*Beian*, 6.12.2007, § 39). It can be linked to some of the principles and requirements set out above (such as lawfulness and foreseeability). The state has a duty to respect and apply, **in a foreseeable and consistent manner**, the laws it has enacted (*Broniowski*, 22.6.2004, § 184).

Legal certainty requires respect for the **principle of *res judicata*.** Final judgments by domestic courts should not be called into question; systems which allow for the quashing of final judgments for an indefinite period of time are incompatible with the principle of legal certainty (*Brumarescu*, 28.10.1999, § 61; *Riabykh*, 24.7.2003, §§ 54 and 57).

49. The rule of law, in particular the principles of legality and legal certainty, also requires that **final court judgments be enforced**. In private

disputes, enforcement of final judgments may require the assistance of the police in order to avoid any risk of "private justice" contrary to the rule of law (*Matheus*, 31.3.2005, § 70). The **administration of the state's obligation to execute final domestic judgments** is an essential feature of a state founded on the rule of law and the principle of legal certainty (*Taskin and Others*, 30.3.2005, § 136). Violations of this obligation are sanctioned under different ECHR provisions.

50. Likewise, authorities are obliged to **respect final decisions ordering the release of a person from detention.** A practice of detaining a person without the basis of a concrete legal provision or judicial decision is itself contrary to the principle of legal certainty (*Baranowski*, 28.3.2000, § 56; *Svipsta*, 9.3.2006, § 86).

51. The existence of **conflicting decisions within a supreme court** is contrary to the principle of legal certainty. It is therefore required that the courts, especially the highest courts, establish **mechanisms to avoid conflicts and ensure the coherence** of their case-law. The principle of legal certainty is essential to the public's confidence in the judicial system and the rule of law (*Beian*, 6.12.2007, § 39).

52. The principle of legal certainty may also justify certain limitations of rights, notably in the form of **time-limits for lodging appeals or the use of statutory limitations.** However, the ECHR may still be violated in case of particularly strict interpretations or rigid application of time-limits regardless of individual circumstances (*Miragall Escolano*, 25.1.2000, § 33; *Phinikaridou*, 20.12.2007, § 51).

- **Principle of equality before the law**

53. The principle that all are equal before the law is reflected in various ways in the ECHR. Article 1 requires states to secure ECHR rights to "everyone" within their jurisdiction, and most ECHR rights are similarly framed: "Everyone has the right ...". In addition, Article 14 prohibits any discrimination in the enjoyment of ECHR rights, and Article 1 of Protocol No. 12 prohibits discrimination generally, including as regards the enjoyment of any right set forth by law and any other discrimination by a public authority. Equality before the law and non-discrimination are human rights principles as much as they are rule of law principles, and the Court's case-law tends to apply the prohibition of discrimination without there being a special need to refer to it as a rule of law principle, although

there is some recognition that equality in rights and duties of all human beings before the law is an aspect of the rule of law.[256]

C. *Due process: judicial review, access to courts and remedies, fair trial*

54. The principle of the rule of law implies that an interference by the executive authorities with an individual's rights should be subject to an effective control which should normally be assured by the judiciary, at least in the last resort, judicial control offering the best guarantees of independence, impartiality and a proper procedure (*Klass and Others*, 6.9.1978, § 55); This **principle of judicial control of the executive** was reaffirmed in more recent cases (*Dumitru Popescu (No. 2)*, 26.4.2007, § 76; *Sissanis*, 25.1.2007, § 71). As regards deprivation of liberty, the requirements of Article 5 §§ 3 and 4 ECHR, with their emphasis on promptitude and judicial control, assume a particular importance in the context of secret detentions and disappearances. What is at stake is both the protection of the physical liberty of individuals as well as their personal security in a context which, in the absence of safeguards, could result in a subversion of the rule of law and place detainees beyond the reach of the most rudimentary forms of legal protection (*Kurt*, 25.5.1998, § 123).

55. The due process aspect of the rule of law entails certain **positive obligations of the state in the form of procedural requirements and safeguards** (such as the right to be heard and have one's views considered, e.g. for a pregnant woman concerning the therapeutic termination of her pregnancy: *Tysiac*, 20.3.2007, §§ 112 and 117).

56. **The right of access to a court** was established on the basis of the rule of law principle. In the *Golder judgment* (21.2.1975, § 35), the Court rejected an interpretation of Article 6 § 1 which would allow states to abolish their courts, take away their jurisdiction to decide certain classes of civil actions and entrust it to organs dependent of the government. Individuals must have a clear, practical opportunity to challenge an act that interferes with their rights (*Bellet*, 4.12.1995, § 36). This right may imply

256 *Refah Partisi and Others*, Chamber judgment of 31.7.2001. The *GC judgment* of 13.2.2003 did not refer to equality but to the principle of secularism. The principle of equality before the law is also expressed through specific ECHR requirements concerning judicial proceedings such as equality of arms and impartiality of the judge (Article 6 ECHR).

an obligation to provide for legal aid in civil disputes (*Airey*, 9.10.1979, § 26) or to exempt actions for damages from high and inflexible court fees (*Stankov*, 12.7.2007, § 59). The right of access to court may be subject to certain limitations, but these, in turn, are themselves subject to certain requirements.

57. The **right to an effective remedy** (Article 13 ECHR) for any arguable claim about violation of ECHR rights is also closely linked to the rule of law. Referring to that principle, the Court has established that, in expulsion cases, Article 13 may require a remedy with an automatic suspensive effect especially where there is a serious risk of torture or ill-treatment in case of deportation (*Conka*, 5.2.2002, § 83; *Gebremedhin*, 26.4.2007, § 66).

58. The **right to a fair trial** enshrined in Article 6 ECHR reflects the fundamental principle of the rule of law (*Sunday Times (No. 1)*, 26.4.1979, § 55) and occupies a prominent place in a democratic society (*Kostovski*, 20.11.1989, § 44). Unsurprisingly, the notion of the rule of law is used in the interpretation and application of the different guarantees of Article 6, such as the presumption of innocence (*Salabiaku*, 7.10.1988, § 28), the rights of the defence (*Leempoel*, 9.11.2006, § 75) and the right to a fair trial within a reasonable time (*Sürmeli*, 8.6.2006, § 104).[257] In the latter judgment, attention was drawn to the important danger that exists for the rule of law within national legal orders when **excessive delays in the administration of justice** occur in respect of which litigants have no domestic remedy. **Article 6 also applies to the execution of a judicial decision**: where authorities fail to execute such a decision, the fair trial guarantees enjoyed by a litigant during the proceedings are rendered devoid of purpose (*Hornsby*, 19.3.1997, § 40; *Immobiliare Saffi*, 28.7.1999, § 63). This again illustrates the relevance of enforcement of the law as a rule of law principle (see under legal certainty above).

Conclusion

59. All these rule of law requirements under the ECHR pursue an important objective: to avoid arbitrariness and offer individuals protection from arbitrariness, especially in the relations between the individual and

257 The requirements concerning judicial independence are dealt with under point A. above.

the state.[258] In addition, there are some indications that the rule of law may on occasion take on a broader meaning in the Court's case-law, for example when the Court refers to the state's duty to uphold the law on its territory (see para. 39 above). In this broader sense, the rule of law means that not only the state and its agents but all individuals are subject to the law ("no one is above the law"). This explains why the state's duty to ensure the security of all persons as well as everyone's enjoyment of human rights (see para. 39 above) also extends to countering threats posed by other individuals.[259]

Rule of law at the international level

60. There is also an important *international* dimension to the rule of law. As was reaffirmed in the 2005 UN World Summit Outcome, an international order based on law where rule of law principles are respected is essential for peaceful coexistence and co-operation among states. Itself an example of regional co-operation promoting a European legal order founded on the principle of the rule of law, the Council of Europe is also active in this international dimension. This is true, first of all, as regards the operation of its own instruments (accountability and monitoring of states' compliance with legal obligations; the ECHR system and supervision of execution of Court judgments – to that extent the Council of Europe itself can be seen as a rule of law institution at European level). As regards the rule of law at the global level, the Council of Europe works towards the strengthening of international law and promoting the rule of law in international affairs (see section IV under E below).

IV. The Council of Europe's Work to Promote the Rule of Law and Ensure Its Respect: A Typology

61. The Council of Europe is a mechanism of pan-European co-operation for preserving and promoting the rule of law (see para. 10 above). Its co-operation in the legal and human rights fields, where common Euro-

258 This is borne out by numerous judgments of the Court. See, e.g., *Winterwerp*, 24.10.1979, § 39, and *Malone*, 2.8.1984, § 67.

259 While an individual criminal act , as such, would not normally be considered as being contrary to the rule of law (but simply as being contrary to the law), a lack of adequate measures by the state to uphold the law by investigation, prosecution and punishment of such crime would be a rule of law issue (see para. 39 above).

pean standards are developed and monitored and assistance is provided towards the implementation of these standards and the results of such monitoring, is itself an essential contribution to the rule of law in Europe. The Parliamentary Assembly's recommendations are an important driving force for such activities. Among other things, this co-operation leads to further *rapprochement* between different legal systems and greater coherence between them on essential points, it facilitates co-operation between states in the justice field and it gives rise to common legal standards – which themselves reflect rule of law principles – thus building a common European legal space.

62. The Council of Europe works to preserve and promote the rule of law in different ways. Using the *manner in which its activities further the rule of law* as a criterion, several categories of activities can be distinguished.[260] There are no sharp dividing lines between these categories: some activities may well fall in several of them. The categories proposed below pretend nothing more than to offer an analytical matrix in order to illustrate with examples *how* the Council of Europe's work contributes to strengthening_the rule of law. Their purpose is not to give an exhaustive overview of all rule of law-related activities.[261]

A. Promoting the conditions necessary for the rule of law

63. Many activities promote the conditions necessary for the rule of law. This primarily concerns issues related to the existence, organisation and efficient functioning of institutions necessary for the rule of law: institutions of justice (civil, criminal, administrative), independence of judges, institutions of law enforcement and execution of judgments, non-judicial

260 Several of the examples of activities mentioned under each category below are not "pure" rule of law activities in that they also serve to promote and protect other core values of the Council of Europe. This is true, for example, for activities in the field of prisons, which usually promote both the proper functioning of prisons and the respect for human rights as regards prison conditions. Similarly, anti-corruption activities are important from the rule of law perspective and from the point of view of democratic principles. The interdependence between rule of law, human rights and democracy is thus also borne out in the concrete activities of the Council of Europe.

261 In addition, some important activities that seek to promote the rule of law in indirect ways, such as education for democratic citizenship and human rights, are not categorised here.

institutions such as the Ombudsman and national human rights institutions.

64. These activities take the form of standard-setting instruments, country-specific recommendations and co-operation activities.

65. There are numerous legal instruments in this area, covering a wide range of issues, such as the independence, efficiency and role of judges; appeal systems in civil and commercial matters, the role of public prosecution in the criminal justice system, the freedom of exercise of the profession of lawyer, judicial review of administrative acts, enforcement of judicial decisions, design of court systems and legal information systems, various aspects of management of prison sentences, prison overcrowding, the setting up of Ombudsman and national human rights institutions.

66. Three Steering Committees were responsible for the drafting of these instruments: most of them were prepared by the CDCJ or the CDPC and some by the CDDH. It may be noted that the CDCJ is currently working on a revision of *Recommendation No. R (94)12 on the independence, efficiency and role of judges*, with the purpose of tackling new challenges faced by national judicial systems in this field.[262]

67. In addition, the European Commission for the Efficiency of Justice (CEPEJ) drafts measures and prepares pragmatic tools for policy makers and judicial practitioners to improve the efficiency and quality of the functioning of judicial systems (expl: Time management Checklist; Compendium of best practices on judicial time management; Checklist for the promotion of the quality of justice and courts; Guidelines on mediation; Specific studies on the functioning of court systems) and develops networking between courts of the member states.

262 The Recommendation addresses issues such as the role of independent authorities (for example the High Councils of the Judiciary); the safeguards to the independence of judges with respect to the remuneration, irrevocability, criminal and civil liability of judges and avenues of appeal available to them, balance between freedom of expression and judicial independence; as well as training and ways of reconciling efficiency of justice and judicial independence.

68. The Consultative Council of European Judges (CCJE) and Prosecutors (CCPE) define European standards for the status and activity of judges / prosecutors through their Opinions to the Committee of Ministers.

69. Country-specific recommendations regarding the requirement of an independent judiciary (including separation of prosecutors' powers and functions) and on the enforcement of judicial decisions are made by the Council of Europe Commissioner for Human Rights in the context of his country visits and reports. He also publishes "Viewpoints" on the rule of law and issues closely related to it. The recommendations and standards contained in CPT reports also cover aspects concerning the organisation of institutions such as prisons, psychiatric establishments and police stations (and other places of deprivation of liberty).

70. The Commissioner also promotes the setting-up of national human rights structures (ombudsman and human rights institutions) that are created and function in abidance with the Paris Principles so as to enhance respect of the rule of law by non-judicial means.

71. The Council of Europe also promotes the conditions necessary for the rule of law through its **co-operation activities.**[263] The relevant projects include activities aimed at:

- helping set up or strengthening high judicial councils;
- improving transparency of the judicial systems, for example as regards the public character of hearings, well-drafted reasoned judicial decisions and systematic public access to all laws and regulations;
- putting in place or strengthen effective systems of free legal aid;
- strengthening the formal role and status of the lawyer's profession;
- improving the enforcement of judicial decisions;
- developing well-functioning penitentiary establishments and alternatives thereto such as probation services.

263 The majority of projects are funded fully or partially (50-90%) by the EC. Some are funded by voluntary contributions by member states. The same applies to co-operation activities mentioned below in this Section.

B. *Promoting respect for the rule of law*

72. The Council of Europe's work in this area is again a combination of standard-setting, country-specific recommendations and co-operation activities.

73. While much of the Council of Europe's standard-setting work on specific themes (e.g., in recent years: conventions on trafficking in human beings, adoption of children, sexual exploitation and abuse of children) may be associated more directly with the protection of human rights and human dignity, it also bears a natural relationship with the duty of a state based on the rule of law to ensure the security of all persons as well as everyone's enjoyment of human rights (see § 59 above).

74. In the fields of **public and private law**, many standards have been drawn up through the CDCJ, as a body that promotes law reform and co-operation in these fields. The rule of law is at heart of this work, and in particular in standard setting activities concerning justice, administrative law, civil law, family law, nationality, refugees and asylum seekers and data protection. One example is its work in the area of *administrative law,* where legal instruments have been adopted on key rule of law issues such as the protection of the individual in relation to the acts of the administrative authorities, and the exercise of discretionary powers by administrative authorities. The latest achievements are the Recommendation (2007)7 on Good Administration and the Report of the Project Group on Administrative Law (CJ-DA) on the desirability of preparing a recommendation on administrative appeals which concluded to the importance of preparing such a legal instrument. In its ongoing process of identifying its future priorities in the field of administrative law, the CDCJ is also considering reviewing the handbook "The Administration and you", published in 1996.

75. Another important cluster of standard-setting work (CDCJ; CDDH) concerns issues such as access to justice, legal aid, availability of domestic remedies for ECHR claims, non-criminal remedies for crime victims and alternative dispute resolution systems. Access to justice for vulnerable groups is an important theme, with work under way on the drafting of European Guidelines on Child-Friendly justice. Rule of law principles are also promoted through the drafting of guidelines on human rights protection in the context of accelerated asylum procedures.

76. In the **criminal law** field, the implementation of the set of relevant Council of Europe conventions and recommendations (transfer of sentenced persons, extradition, mutual legal assistance, cybercrime, prison issues) is regularly discussed within the framework of the CDPC and its subordinate bodies PC-OC and PC-CP. Where needed, specific measures to promote their effective implementation are agreed, including through amendments to the existing legal instruments, targeted assistance, discussion of topical issues at Ministerial Conferences and adoption of resolutions thereon.

77. It is especially important to promote respect for the rule of law as regards **new societal or technological developments**, because they may give rise to uncertainty regarding the applicable legal regime and principles. Here, the Council of Europe is often at the forefront of elaborating innovative instruments and approaches. Prime examples of relevant Council of Europe sectors are its work concerning the information society (cf. the CM Declaration of 2005 on human rights and the rule of law in the Information Society, the Cybercrime Convention and many other legal instruments) and the field of bio-ethics (the Convention on Human Rights and Biomedicine and its additional protocols).

78. The *Venice Commission* plays an important role in promoting respect for rule of law principles. Article 1.2 of the Statute of the Venice Commission establishes that its work will focus on the "constitutional, legislative and administrative principles and techniques which serve the efficiency of democratic institutions and their strengthening, as well as the principle of the rule of law". The principle of the rule of law is promoted in different activities of constitutional assistance provided by the Commission to different countries, including the principle of separation of powers. Through its recommendations and opinions prepared for its Member States on draft constitutions and legislation in different fields, the Venice Commission promotes the idea that the definition and assimilation of the idea of the State based on the rule of law is a basic feature of European constitutionalism.[264]

79. The Venice Commission has also elaborated a number of recommendations that contribute to the strengthening of the principle of the rule

264 One of the Venice Commission's conferences focussed on issues related to the principle of the rule of law: http://www.venice.coe.int/docs/1996/CDL-STD(1996)018-e.asp#_Toc90369210.

of law, such as the Guidelines on prohibition and dissolution of political parties and analogous measures, the Report on the Democratic oversight of the Security Services, Report on the Democratic Control of the Armed Forces and others.

80. The CEPEJ supports individual member states in their judicial reforms, on the basis of European standards and other member states' experience. It contributes specific expertise to the debate on the functioning of the justice system in Europe and beyond: it provides the legal and judicial community with a forum for discussion and suggestions and brings justice systems and their users closer (including through its internet web site and its publications in the Series: "CEPEJ Studies").The Council of Europe co-organises (with the European Commission) the European Day of civil Justice, including the European Prize of innovative practice contributing to the quality of justice: "The Crystal Scales of Justice".

81. The CCJE and the CCPE may be called upon to provide practical assistance to help States comply with standards relating to judges and prosecutors.

82. The Lisbon Network (judicial training institutions in Europe) promotes the initial and in-service training of judges and prosecutors from common standards and shared experience and supports individual member states in developing their judicial training systems. The HELP Programme promotes the integration of training on the ECHR in national training schemes for judges and prosecutors.

83. Networking and co-operation also takes place with national human rights structures in the member states. Through intensive and ongoing co-operation with the national human rights structures in the member states and by nurturing an active network of them, the Commissioner for Human Rights increases the ability and readiness of these structures to defend the rule of law at domestic level.

84. The Council of Europe also promotes respect for rule of law principles through its **co-operation activities**. They focus on the manner in which those structures and institutions operate, seeking to ensure that qualitatively they respect the requirements of rule of law and of course of the specific treaty obligations to which the state is a party. The relevant projects include activities to:

- train:
  - legal professionals (judges, prosecutors, lawyers);
  - members of the high judicial councils so as to strengthen the administration of justice;
  - auxiliary court personnel (clerks, registrars) and bailiffs;
  - civil society groups and their legal representatives on how to contribute to the public debate, how to be a "check" on the administration and the judiciary, and how to advocate specific human rights/judiciary related issues;
- strengthen awareness of the specific requirements related to the appointment, dismissal and salaries for judges and prosecutors;
- provide legislative expertise to ensure that national regulatory frameworks conform to the requirements of the rule of law and that member states are aware of the implications as regards actual implementation;
- improve the management of detention facilities (pre-trial and following sentencing).

85. Where possible, such activities are conducted in co-operation with other international organisations. Co-operation with the OSCE on rule of law issues has included capacity building for non-judicial protection mechanisms, data protection within the civil registry framework, and training for civil society on freedom of assembly. Joint activities with the UNHCR concern ECHR-related issues in the field of immigration and asylum, especially Article 5 and 6 issues.

C. *Addressing threats to the rule of law*

86. Certain phenomena such as terrorism or corruption pose a threat to the rule of law because they directly challenge, or gradually undermine, the state's authority and capacity to uphold the law and the state's respect for rule of law principles.

87. The Council of Europe assists states in **combating economic crime** as a major threat to democracy and the rule law. This is the very aim of the projects run by the Council of Europe. These include projects against economic crime, against corruption, money laundering and terrorist financing, and cybercrime.

88. Activities aimed at improvement of legislation (workshops, legal opinions) or training of professionals (including judges, law enforcement,

prosecutors etc) may, depending on the specific subject, address the conditions necessary for the rule of law (category A above) and/or promote respect for rule of law principles (category B above). In particular, the activities to strengthen capacities of the member states to fight corruption certainly fall in both categories.

89. The Council of Europe is highly active in the area of **fighting terrorism**. It has adopted a number of legal instruments in this field:

- Revised Convention of the Suppression of Terrorism,
- Convention on the Prevention of Terrorism,
- Convention on Laundering, search, seizure and Confiscation of the proceeds from Crime and on the Financing of Terrorism.

90. The Committee of Experts on Terrorism (CODEXTER) monitors the signatures and ratifications of the conventions mentioned above and promotes their effective implementation.

91. In creating a legal framework that allows substantial international co-operation the Council of Europe seeks to **ensure that rule of law principles are fully respected in countering terrorism**. This is borne out by the safeguards contained in the above-mentioned instruments, but also by other instruments such as the two sets of CM Guidelines (on human rights and the fight against terrorism, and on the protection of victims of terrorist acts) prepared by the CDDH and based on the ECHR case-law. Mention should also be made of work of the Parliamentary Assembly, which has adopted several Recommendations in this field. In various reports by the Parliamentary Assembly, the Secretary General (acting under Article 52, ECHR) and the Venice Commission, a strong focus was placed on the need to ensure full respect for the rule of law in inter-state co-operation regarding the detention and transfer of persons suspected of involvement in acts of terrorism, and as regards oversight and accountability of security services.

92. One of the CODEXTER's priorities lies in research on the concepts of "apologie du terrorisme" and "incitement to terrorism". In addition **causes of terrorism** are addressed by exploring ways to reduce the tensions existing in today's society (see the Council of Europe conference on "Why terrorism? – Addressing the reasons conducive to the spread of terrorism").

93. It is clear that conditions conducive to the spread of terrorism must be addressed through promotion of inter-cultural dialogue, activities in the field of education, youth and the media, ensuring the protection of minorities and fighting intolerance, racism and social exclusion, thereby weakening sources of discontent that may fuel terrorism. Much of the Council of Europe's work in these areas therefore contributes to addressing the threat to the rule of law that terrorism poses.

94. In addition, the Council of Europe has set up a number of specific legal co-operation programmes designed to help the beneficiary countries to proceed with their institutional, legislative and administrative reforms in order to strengthen the rule of law in the fight against terrorism. Co-operation projects include workshops and seminars on specific themes related to the fight against terrorism, such as mutual extradition of terrorist suspects or financing of terrorism.

95. The Commissioner for Human Rights raises the issues of impunity, counter-terrorism measures, corruption, the rule of law in exceptional circumstances and the rule of law in dealing with the past in the context of his country visits and makes recommendations to the authorities with a view to addressing shortcomings. He publishes relevant "Viewpoints" on these topics. Specific workshops/seminars have been organised on the themes of anti-terrorism measures and data protection and of complaints mechanisms against police misconduct.

96. The Council of Europe's monitoring mechanisms in the field of combating corruption (GRECO) and countering money laundering and terrorist financing (MONEYVAL) will be addressed in the next section.

D. Ensuring respect for the rule of law

97. Within the Council of Europe, there is no mechanism to ensure respect for the principle of the rule of law as such. However, various mechanisms exist which contribute significantly to ensuring that rule of law requirements are respected. Leaving aside the crucial role of the European Court of Human Rights (see the conclusions in § 34 above), mention should first of all be made of the political monitoring of member states' commitments by the Parliamentary Assembly and by the Committee of Ministers, which covers rule of law-related commitments.

98. Furthermore, there are other mechanisms that help ensure respect for the rule of law. Some do so in the context of their competence in the field of human rights; others in the context of a specific thematic mandate in other fields.

99. The CM supervision of execution of the Court's judgments ensures that the obligations of states under Article 46 ECHR are respected. Apart from this general contribution to upholding the rule of law, such supervision also ensures respect for the rule of law in a more specific manner wherever the violation found by the Court concerns rule of law-related shortcomings in a national legal system (see the overview of case-law in Section III. above). A clear example of such dysfunctioning of national systems which states are obliged to remedy under Article 46, ECHR are the cases concerning non-execution of domestic courts' judgments.

100. Other human rights bodies such as the CPT and ECRI each have a monitoring role that extends to respect of rule of law principles in specific settings and contexts. The monitoring mechanism set up under the Social Charter, especially the collective complaints system, makes an important contribution to the legal protection and justiciability of social rights in Europe. As from 2009, monitoring in the field of states' action against trafficking in human beings will be conducted by GRETA, a body that is being set up under the Convention on Action against Trafficking in Human Beings.

101. In the context of his country visits the Commissioner for Human Rights examines whether due process, legal certainty and lawfulness stemming from the rule of law principle are afforded and makes recommendations for possible improvement. He publishes "Viewpoints" on these topics.

102. A number of Council of Europe conventions in the field of criminal law designate the CDPC as the body in the framework of which disputes are settled regarding the implementation of those conventions and/or as the body through which amendments of the conventions may be proposed.

103. The Group of States against Corruption (GRECO) monitors states' compliance with the Council of Europe's anti-corruption standards. Its objective is to improve the capacity of its members to fight corruption by monitoring their compliance with anti-corruption standards through

a dynamic process of mutual evaluation and peer pressure. It helps to identify deficiencies in national anti-corruption policies, prompting the necessary legislative, institutional and practical reforms. GRECO also provides a platform for the sharing of best practice in the prevention and detection of corruption. GRECO draws up recommendations and assesses compliance with those recommendations.

104. The Committee of Experts on the Evaluation of Anti-Money Laundering Measures and the Financing of Terrorism (MONEYVAL) is a monitoring mechanism set up with the aim of ensuring that its member states have effective systems in place to counter money laundering and terrorist financing and comply with the relevant international standards in these fields. Such compliance is assessed through a peer review process of mutual evaluation, leading to detailed recommendations to improve the effectiveness of domestic regimes. MONEYVAL also conducts typology studies of money laundering and terrorist financing methods, trends and techniques.

105. The CEPEJ evaluates the functioning of the member states' judicial systems through a regular process for collecting and analysing quantitative and qualitative data on the functioning of justice systems. Its SATURN Centre is due to develop towards a European Observatory of timeframes of court proceedings.

106. The Consultative Council of European Judges (CCJE) and Prosecutors (CCPE) may be requested by relevant Council of Europe bodies or relevant authorities in the member states to analyse specific situations regarding judges / prosecutors in specific member states and to draft opinions (which might include recommendations) to improve given situations.

107. The Council of Europe Convention for the **Protection of Individuals with regard to Automatic Processing of Personal Data** lays down essential principles and safeguards for respecting everyone's right to privacy in accordance with rule of law principles. The Consultative Committee of the Convention for the Protection of Individuals (T-PD) interprets the provisions and improves the implementation of the Convention.

E. *Strengthening the international rule of law*

108. Council of Europe activities to strengthen the rule of law at the international (global) level do not fit neatly into one of the above-mentioned categories. Most of them are a mixture of promoting the conditions necessary for the rule of law and promoting respect for rule of law principles.

109. Through the Committee of Legal Advisers on Public International Law (CAHDI), the Council of Europe aims at creating a framework for international co-operation to strengthen the role of public international law and influence its development, and to bring national viewpoints closer together. All of its activities are aimed at promoting the rule of law in international affairs.

110. The item "Advancing the international rule of law" appears regularly on the agenda of the CAHDI and the work of the Committee on this matter is based on the 2005 UN World Summit Outcome, when Heads of State and Government reaffirmed their "commitment to the purposes and principles of the Charter and international law and to an international order based on the rule of law and international law, which is essential for peaceful coexistence and co-operation among States".

111. The CAHDI considers a number of questions to be related to the concept of international rule of law. The following activities may serve as an example:

- law and practice on reservations and interpretative declarations to treaties, including those applicable to the fight against terrorism: CAHDI activity in its capacity of the European Observatory of Reservations to International Treaties (EORIT);
- jurisdiction of the international tribunals: consideration of the jurisdiction of the International Court of Justice (ICJ) under the optional Clause and under selected treaties and in particular the position of the Council of Europe's member and observer States in that regard as well as consideration of the overlapping jurisdiction of international courts and tribunals;
- preparation of the draft recommendations in the field of dispute settlement: CM/Rec(2008)8 on the acceptance of the jurisdiction of the ICJ and CM/Rec(2008)9 on the nomination of international arbitrators and conciliators. As from October 2008 CAHDI will monitor the implementation of the CM/Rec(2008) 9;

- following pending and decided cases of the European Court of Human Rights involving issues of public international law and exchanges of views on the developments concerning the International ad hoc tribunals (Yugoslavia, Rwanda, Lebanon);
- following developments concerning international humanitarian law;
- databases on State Practice regarding State Immunities; the Organisation and Functions of the Office of the Legal Adviser in the Ministry for Foreign Affairs; and the Implementation of UN Sanctions and Respect for Human Rights ;
- Moreover, the Council of Europe actively supports the International Criminal Court and over the past years organised four consultation meetings which fostered exchanges of views on the legal problems encountered in the implementation of the Rome Statute.

112. Finally, it should be noted that on four occasions (in 2004, 2005 and 2007) the Committee of Ministers submitted a "statement of interest" in support of EU amicus curiae briefs in various stages of a case before the US Supreme Court and the Supreme Court of Texas concerning a Mexican (Mr Medellin) sentenced to death. These proceedings took place after the International Court of Justice had ordered that the case of Mr Medellin be reviewed. The CM statements insisted on respect for the Vienna Convention on Consular Relations and stated that "respect for judgments of the International Court of Justice by states that are party to litigation is a basic requirement of the rule of law at the international level, as expressed in Article 94 of the United Nations Charter."[265]

V. Overview of Rule of Law Activities of other Organisations (EU, OSCE, UN)

General

113. Reference should be made to the "Multilateral organisations' rule of law pledge" issued as a joint press release at the close of the 14th High-level Tripartite meeting between the Council of Europe, the OSCE and the United Nations (Strasbourg, 18 February 2005) (CM/Inf(2005)17 of 28 February 2005). The pledge states that the rule of law is a prerequisite for maintaining and building peace, consolidating democracy and promoting sustainable development.

265 See, most recently, CM/Del/Dec(2007)996/13.2 of 23 May 2007.

114. Highlighting the central role of the rule of law in conflict prevention, the protection and promotion of human rights and other issues such as human displacement, participants urged close co-operation between partner organisations and stressed the importance of social cohesion for achieving long-term stability in post-conflict societies.

115. The rule of law pledge points to certain specific areas of action and co-operation, such as the need for a common and effective framework for responding to terrorism in accordance with the rule of law; the need to step up the fight against racism, xenophobia, intolerance, anti-Semitism, Islamophobia and any other forms of discrimination, and co-operation between international organisations in the field on issues related to legislative transparency, the independence of the judiciary, ombudsmen and national human rights institutions as well as reform of legislation, justice and prisons.

European Union

116. The rule of law is referred to in Article 6 § 1 of the Treaty on European Union as a principle, common to the member states, on which the Union is founded. The Copenhagen criteria of 1993 for EU membership include "stability of institutions guaranteeing democracy, the rule of law, human rights and respect for and protection of minorities" as a condition for membership.

117. Within the legal order of the Community, an essential contribution to upholding the rule of law, and developing rule of law principles, is made by the Community courts, notably through the decisions and the case-law of the European Court of Justice.[266]

118. The European Union promotes the rule of law both within the Union and beyond. It co-operates with the Council of Europe in both aspects.

119. Inside its borders, the Union is developing a European area of "Justice, Security and Liberty". To this end, it adopts legal norms and financial instruments. When adopting new norms in this area, it consults the

266 See, e.g., Case 294/83 *Les Verts v. Parliament* [1986] ECR 1339, § 23, and the recent judgment of 3 September 2008 in Joined Cases C-402/05 P and C-415/05 P, *Kadi and Al Barakaat International Foundation*, §§ 281-284 and 316-326.

Council of Europe's acquis in the same field (e.g. in the fields of terrorism, fight against human trafficking).

120. When promoting the rule of law outside its borders, the Commission frequently co-operates with the Council of Europe as far as non-EU member States of the Council of Europe are concerned (i.e. mostly the Western Balkans, the south Caucasus, Russia and Turkey). Through such "joint programmes", assistance is being given to those States in order to adapt their legislation, practice and institutions to the European standards which form part of the "acquis communautaire". These programmes focus notably on the development of the judiciary, on penitentiary reforms, on the fight against various forms of economic and organized crime as well as on international co-operation in criminal matters.

121. The European Commission also attaches great importance to the respect of the rule of law in its relations with acceding countries and with countries of the Neighbourhood policy. When assessing the situation in the countries concerned, the EC is consulting the Council of Europe.

122. A memorandum of understanding between the two organisations (May 2007) formalises their commitment to co-operate in the development of a European area based on law.

123. The EU and the Council of Europe have also put in place various forms of concrete co-operation between its institutions/bodies:

- The European Judicial Network in civil and commercial matters, the European Judicial Network in criminal matters and EUROJUST are key EU bodies to foster judicial assistance between EU member states and ensure the implementation of the EU instruments in the judicial field (directives in civil and commercial matters, European Arrest Warrant, etc...). These three bodies co-operate regularly with the Council of Europe's relevant bodies (CEPEJ, CCPE, CDCJ, CDPC, etc.).
- The European Commission has set up in 2008 a Forum for Justice aimed to develop regular exchanges between judicial practitioners in Europe. The CEPEJ is a privileged partner in this Forum.
- The EC co-organises with the Council of Europe the European Day of Justice (see above under IV.).
- The European Training Network is supported by the EU (EC) to develop co-operation between EU member states for judicial training. It closely co-operates with the Council of Europe's Lisbon Network.

- The European Network of Judicial Councils is supported by the EU to develop co-operation between the Councils for the judiciary in the EU countries and on issues regarding the functioning of judicial systems and the management of the careers of judges (prosecutors). It has observer status with the CEPEJ and CCJE.

124. In addressing particular topics related to the rule of law, through conferences, workshops, or other specific events, the European Union is regularly consulting and co-operating with the Council of Europe.

Organisation for Security and Co-operation in Europe (OSCE)

125. The OSCE's political commitments in the human dimension include commitments concerning the rule of law. According to the 1990 Copenhagen document (§ 2), the rule of law "does not mean merely a formal legality which assures regularity and consistency in the achievement and enforcement of democratic order, but justice based on the recognition and full acceptance of the supreme value of the human personality and guaranteed by institutions providing a framework for its fullest expression." Democracy is seen as "an inherent element of the rule of law"(§3) and free elections are accordingly considered as an element of justice (§ 5.1).

126. This general rule of law commitment also comprises several other commitments to specific rule of law principles ("elements of justice") which have been set out in the Copenhagen and other OSCE documents. Many of these are expressions of the principles of legality, accountability, equality and non-discrimination, accessibility of the law, and of human rights standards concerning detention and fair trial rights.[267]

127. The rule of law is a recurrent theme at the OSCE Human Dimension Implementation meetings. Under that heading discussion takes place on topics such as legislative transparency, independence of the judiciary, right to a fair trial, constitutional justice, the question of the abolition of capital punishment, prevention of torture, and protection of human rights and fighting terrorism.

267 See the rule of law section in the ODIHR document OSCE Commitments relating to Judicial Systems and Human Rights, Warsaw 2002.

128. The main OSCE body active on rule of law issues is the Office for Democratic Institutions and Human Rights (ODIHR). Its mandate, as set out in the 1992 Helsinki Document, resembles the statutory aims of the Council of Europe: to help participating states "ensure full respect for human rights and fundamental freedoms, to abide by the rule of law, to promote principles of democracy and [...] to build, strengthen and protect democratic institutions, as well as promote tolerance throughout society." ODIHR has a rule of law unit within its Democratization Department.

129. The ODIHR implements various technical assistance projects designed to foster the development of the rule of law. Practical assistance and training is provided through programmes in the areas of criminal justice reform and fair trials. A trial monitoring programme provides for monitoring of criminal trials in Central Asia. Legislative support is also provided through reviews of (draft) legislation, in fields such as electoral legislation, gender equality, freedom of religion, freedom of assembly, counter-terrorism, etc.[268]

130. Specific rule of law-related activities are carried out by OSCE missions in several countries. Examples of co-operation with the Council of Europe on rule of law activities are given in section IV above.

United Nations

131. The rule of law-related activities of the different organs, agencies and bodies of the United Nations system are so manifold and extensive that they cannot be adequately summed up in a short overview. Some general information is given below.

132. The rule of law was referred to in the preamble to the Universal Declaration of Human Rights of 1948: "Whereas it is essential, if man is not to be compelled to have recourse, as a last resort, to rebellion against tyranny and oppression, that human rights should be protected by the rule of law". This underlines the function of the rule of law ("régime de droit" in the French version) as an indispensible framework for the protection of human rights.

268 See ODIHR's annual report 2006.

133. The UN's work on the rule of law finds its normative basis in the UN Charter, international law, and the range of treaties, declaration, guidelines and bodies of principles developed within the UN in order to promote national societies and an international order based on the rule of law.

134. Like the Council of Europe, the UN has developed a host of legal instruments in the legal and human rights fields which contain and develop rule of law-related standards and provide for monitoring of these standards. These are often supplemented by specific principles for certain rule of law sectors and institutions.[269]

135. At the national level, rule of law work by the UN takes the form of technical assistance and capacity building for member states. Strengthening the rule of law at the international level is a natural role of the UN. The UN's Millenium Declaration of 2000 calls upon all member states to strengthen respect for the rule of law, notably through complying with the decisions of the International Court of Justice.

136. Following the 2005 World Summit, a Rule of law Coordination and Resource Group was established as an inter-Agency coordination mechanism and a Rule of law Unit was created in the office of the UNSG.[270] These steps were supported by member states in A/RES/62/70, § 4.

137. The Unit's objectives are:

- ensuring coordination among the many United Nations departments, agencies, funds and programmes engaged in rule of law activities;
- developing guidelines, best practices and other tools for guiding the Organization's activities in promoting the rule of law;
- developing partnerships between the United Nations and the many other actors engaged in rule of law activities.

---

269 To give just one example: the so-called Bangalore Principles have been drafted as the UN standards on rights and duties of judges. The Council of Europe's CCJE has been closely involved in this work (namely on the basis of the European Charter on the Statute of Judges) and continues to co-operate with the UN as regards their implementation.

270 This and the following information is based on an Information Note on the Rule of Law Coordination and Resource Group and Rule of Law Unit which was received from the Director of the Rule of Law Unit.

138. The Unit is not a new operational capacity within the United Nations system. Operational roles within the three "baskets" of rule of law activities (rule of law at the international level, the rule of law in the context of conflict and post-conflict situations, and the rule of law in the context of long-term development) remain with the various UN departments, agencies, funds and programmes.

139. These steps were inspired by the fact that the dispersal of rule of law entities across the UN system has made coordinated action difficult. Examples of such entities are the Office of Legal Affairs (rule of law issues at international level), the Office of the High Commissioner for Human Rights (transitional justice, national human rights institutions, national justice sectors), the UN Development Programme (capacity-building in the justice sector in the framework of long-term development) and the Department of Peacekeeping Operations (rule of law assistance in support of peacekeeping operations).

140. An overview of relevant co-operation between the Council of Europe and the UN can be found in document DER/PR/Inf(2008)2 containing an inventory on the status of implementation of the UN General Assembly Resolution 61/13 on Co-operation between the United Nations and the Council of Europe. This includes many rule of law-related activities.

VI. Conclusion

141. The main purpose of this document was to provide insight into how the concept of the rule of law is understood within the Council of Europe and how various activities of the Organisation contribute to strengthening and upholding the rule of law.

142. The Council of Europe *acquis* regarding rule of law principles demonstrates a high degree of consensus among member states which allows the Organisation to work pragmatically for the promotion and protection of those principles. This state of affairs explains why no need was felt so far to develop a Council of Europe definition of the rule of law concept. In particular, the case-law of the Court provides a solid reference for all rule of law-related activities of the Organisation.

143. However, it is probably also true, precisely because the rule of law is "everywhere" in the work of the Council of Europe, that the principle has to some extent suffered from a lack of visibility in that work.

144. To remedy that shortcoming, this paper has sought to do justice to the vital importance of the rule of law as a core principle promoted by the Council of Europe, by articulating more clearly the rule of law dimension of its activities.

Bibliography

P. Alston, James Crawford. (Eds.) The Future of UN Human Rights Treaty Monitoring. Cambridge: Cambridge University Press, 2000.

P. Alston (Ed.), Labour Rights as Human Rights. Oxford, Oxford University Press, 2005.

A. Bayefsky (Ed.), The UN Human Rights Treaty System in the 21st Century. The Hague, Kluwer Law International, 2000.

I. Boivin and A. Odero, The Committee of Experts on the Application of Conventions and Recommendations: Progress achieved in national labour legislation. International Labour Review, vol. 145, 2006, pp. 1 – 14.

T. Buergenthal, and D. Shelton, Protecting Human Rights in the Americas. Cases and Materials, 4th ed. 1995.

C.P. Cohen, Jurisprudence of the Committee on the Rights of the Child. 4 Vols. Transnational Publishers, 2003.

A. Conte and R. Burchill, Defining Civil and Political Rights. The Jurisprudence of the United Nations Human Rights Committee. Second Edition. Ashgate, 2009.

R.R. Churchill and U. Khaliq, The Collective Complaints System of the European Social Charter: An Effective Mechanism for Ensuring Compliance with Economic and Social Rights, 15 European Journal of International Law (2004).

G. Dutere, Key Case Law Extracts: European Court of Human Rights. Council of Europe Publishing, 2003.

M. Evans and R. Murray (Eds.), The African Charter on Human and Peoples' Rights: The System in Practice 1986-2006. Cambridge, Cambridge University Press, 2008.

H. Fernandez-Ledesma, The Inter-American System for the Protection of Human Rights. San Jose, Costa Rica, Inter-American Institute of Human Rights, 2007.

C. Flinterman, E.V.O Dankwa, and M. Hamalengwa, The International Law of Human Rights in Africa: Basic Documents. 1988. Kluwer Law International.

D. Gomien, D. Harris, L. Zwaak, Law and practice of the European Convention on Human Rights and the European Social Charter. Council of Europe, 1998.

E. Gravel, C. Charbonneau-Jobin, The Committee of Experts on the Application of Conventions and Recommendations: Its Dynamic and Impact, ILO, 2003.

International Labour Office, Protecting Labour Rights as Human Rights: Present and Future of International Supervision. Proceedings of the International Colloquium on the 80th Anniversary of the ILO Committee of Experts on the Application of Conventions and Recommendations, Geneva, 24-25 November 2006. Edited by George P. Politakis. (See the Selected Bibliography at pp. 291-292.

Jacobs and White, European Convention on Human Rights. Fourth Edition, by Clare Ovey and Robin C.A.White. Oxford, Oxford University Press, 2006

N. Jayawickrama, The Judicial Application of Human Rights Law. National, Regional and International Jurisprudence. Cambridge, Cambridge University Press, 2002.

B. Kingsbury, The Concept of Compliance as a Function of Competing Conceptions of International Law, 19 Michigan Journal of International Law, 1998, pp. 345-372.

J.M. Pasqualucci, The Practice and Procedure of the Inter-American Court of Human Rights, 2003.

E.Klein (Ed.) The Monitoring System of Human Rights Treaty Obligations. Berlin, 1998.

J Th. Moller and A. de Zayas, Case Law of the United Nations Human Rights Committee 1977-2007, Kehl, Germany, N.P. Engel Publisher, 2009.

M. Nowak., UN Covenant on Civil and Political Rights. CCPR Commentary. 2nd revised edition. Kehl, Germany, N.P. Engel Publisher, 2005

M. Nowak and E. McArthur, The United Nations Convention Against Torture. Oxford, Oxford University Press, 2008.

M. O'Flaherty, Human Rights and the UN: Practice Before the Treaty Bodies. Second Edition. The Hague, Kluwer Law International, 2002.

O.C. Okafor, The African Human Rights System. Activist Forces and International Institutions. Cambridge, Cambridge University Press, 2007.

T.S. Orlin, A. Rosas, and M. Scheinin, The Jurisprudence of Human Rights Law. A Comparative Interprettive Approach. Institute for Human Rights, Abo Akademi University, Turku/Abo, 2000.

L. Swepston, Supervision of ILO Standards, 13 International Journal of Comparative Labour Law, 1997, pp. 327-344.

P.Van Dijk, F. van Hoof, A. van Rijn, and and L. Zwaak, (Eds.), Theory and Practice of the European Convention on Human Rights. Fourth Edition, Intersentia, Antwerp/Oxford, 2006.

Raoul Wallenberg Institute of Human Rights. Concluding Observations of the UN Committee on the Elimination of Racial Discrimination. Forty-third to Fifty-seventh Sessions (1993-2000) Edited by Leif Holmström. Leiden: Martinus Nijhoff, 2000

Raoul Wallenberg Institute of Human Rights, Lund University. Conclusions and Recommendations of the UN Committee against Torture. Eleventh to Twenty-second Sessions (1993-1999) Edited by Leif Holmström. Leiden: Martinus Nijhoffs, 2000.

Raoul Wallenberg Institute of Human Rights, Lund University. Concluding Observations of the UN Committee on Economic, Social and Cultural Rights. Eighth to Twenty-seventh Sessions (1993-2001) Edited by Leif Holmström. Leiden: Martinus Nijhoff, 2003.

N. Rubin (Ed.), Code of International Labour Law: Law, Practice and Jurisprudence. 2 Vols. Cambridge University Press, 2005.

H.S. Schilling and C. Flinterman (Eds.), The Circle of Empowerment: Twenty-five Years of the Committee on the Elimination of Discrimination against Women (2007).

United Nations. Selected decisions of the Human Rights Committee under the optional protocol. Volumes 1-8. 1985 – 2007. United Nations, Office of the High Commissioner for Human Rights.

United Nations. Selected Decisions of the Committee Against Torture. Volume 1 (2009).

Index

D

M

N

O

P

R

95. F. Francioni and M. Scheinin (eds.): *Cultural Human Rights.* 2008 ISBN 90 04 16294 5

96. M. Feria Tinta: *The Landmark Rulings of the Inter-American Court of Human Rights on the Rights of the Child.* Protecting the Most Vulnerable at the Edge. 2008 ISBN 90 04 16513 7

97. K. Bourquain: *Freshwater Access from a Human Rights Perspective.* A Challenge to International Water and Human Rights Law. 2008 ISBN 90 04 16954 8

98. J. Marshall: *Personal Freedom through Human Rights Law?* Autonomy, Identity and Integrity under the European Convention on Human Rights. 2008 ISBN 90 04 17059 9

99. J. Christoffersen: *Fair Balance: Proportionality, Subsidiarity and Primarity in the European Convention on Human Rights.* 2009 ISBN 90 04 17028 5

100. O.M. Arnardóttir and G. Quinn (eds.): *The UN Convention on the Rights of Persons with Disabilities.* European and Scandinavian Perspectives. 2009 ISBN 90 04 16971 5

101. I.E. Koch: *Human Rights as Indivisible Rights.* The Protection of Socio-Economic Demands under the European Convention on Human Rights. 2009 ISBN 90 04 16051 4

102. G. Pentassuglia: *Minority Groups and Judicial Discourse in International Law.* A Comparative Perspective. 2009 ISBN 90 04 17672 0

103. M. Kloth: *Immunities and the Right of Access to Court under Article 6 of the European Convention on Human Rights.* 2010 ISBN 90 04 18184 7

104. M. K. Addo: *The Legal Nature of International Human Rights.* 2010 ISBN 90 04 17390 3

105. E. Lievens: *Protecting Children in the Digital Era.* The Use of Alternative Regulatory Instruments. 2010 ISBN 90 04 18477 0

106. B.G. Ramcharan: *The Fundamentals of International Human Rights Treaty Law.* 2011 ISBN 90 04 17608 9

This series is designed to shed light on current legal and political aspects of process and organization in the field of human rights

MARTINUS NIJHOFF PUBLISHERS – LEIDEN • BOSTON

www.ingramcontent.com/pod-product-compliance
Lightning Source LLC
LaVergne TN
LVHW010631300926
849162LV00001B/128
* 9 7 8 9 0 0 4 1 7 6 0 8 9 *